BEHAVIOR
SOLUTIONS

Teaching Academic and Social Skills
Through RTI at Work™

John **Hannigan**   ◆   Jessica Djabrayan **Hannigan**
Mike **Mattos**   ◆   Austin **Buffum**

Solution Tree | Press

a division of

Solution Tree

555 North Morton Street
Bloomington, IN 47404
800.733.6786 (toll free) / 812.336.7700
FAX: 812.336.7790

email: info@SolutionTree.com
SolutionTree.com

Visit **go.SolutionTree.com/RTIatWork** to download the free reproducibles in this book.

Printed in the United States of America

Library of Congress Cataloging-in-Publication Data

Names: Hannigan, John E., author. | Djabrayan Hannigan, Jessica, author. |
    Mattos, Mike (Mike William) author. | Buffum, Austin G., author.
Title: Behavior solutions : teaching academic and social skills through RTI
    at work / John Hannigan, Jessica Djabrayan Hannigan, Mike Mattos, Austin
    Buffum.
Description: Bloomington, IN : Solution Tree Press, [2020] | Includes
    bibliographical references and index.
Identifiers: LCCN 2019050187 (print) | LCCN 2019050188 (ebook) | ISBN
    9781947604711 (paperback) | ISBN 9781947604728 (ebook)
Subjects: LCSH: Response to intervention (Learning disabled children) |
    Behavior modification. | School improvement programs.
Classification: LCC LC4705 .H363 2020 (print) | LCC LC4705 (ebook) | DDC
    370.15/28--dc23
LC record available at https://lccn.loc.gov/2019050187
LC ebook record available at https://lccn.loc.gov/2019050188

Solution Tree
Jeffrey C. Jones, CEO
Edmund M. Ackerman, President

Solution Tree Press
President and Publisher: Douglas M. Rife
Associate Publisher: Sarah Payne-Mills
Art Director: Rian Anderson
Managing Production Editor: Kendra Slayton
Senior Production Editor: Tonya Maddox Cupp
Content Development Specialist: Amy Rubenstein
Copy Editor: Jessi Finn
Proofreader: Evie Madsen
Text Designer: Kelsey Hergül
Cover Designer: Rian Anderson
Editorial Assistants: Sarah Ludwig and Elijah Oates

We dedicate this book to our immediate household of Riley, Rowan, and John John, as well as the Hannigan, Navo, and Djabrayan families for your love and support. This book is for you!

—John and Jessica Hannigan

I dedicate this book to my grandparents: Felix Mattos, Anne Mattos, Donald Williams, and Zona-Marie Williams. I am forever grateful for their love and guidance.

—Mike Mattos

To my father, Austin G. Buffum, "Buff." I lost you long ago but will never forget you.

—Austin Buffum

ACKNOWLEDGMENTS

We would like to thank the exceptional professionals at Solution Tree Press: Jeff Jones for your vision and leadership of Solution Tree; Douglas Rife for your leadership and attention to detail over publishing; Tonya Cupp for your editing expertise. It is clear through this process that you care as much about this content as we have in writing it. This book would not have been possible without the support and expertise of the Solution Tree family.

There are many educators who have influenced us over our careers in education; none have been more impactful than Richard DuFour, Robert Eaker, and Rebecca DuFour, the founders and pioneers of Professional Learning Communities at Work®. The PLC at Work process continues to inspire and impact education throughout the world, and we hope this book both honors and advances their work.

Finally, we would like to thank the pantheon of educational researchers who originally challenged the traditional practices of using fear and punishment to control students, and instead applied professional research to develop more effective ways to teach and develop positive behaviors. These researchers include George Sugai, Robert H. Horner, Wayne Sailor, Glen Dunlap, Daniel J. Losen, Russell J. Skiba, Jeffrey R. Sprague, and Edward G. Carr.

Solution Tree Press would like to thank the following reviewers:

Kevin Carroll
Principal
Sparks High School
Sparks, Nevada

Christine Johnson
Principal
Sterling Elementary
Warrensburg, Missouri

Cheyana Leiva
Principal
Constitution Elementary School
Phoenix, Arizona

Matt Renwick
Principal
Mineral Point Elementary School
Mineral Point, Wisconsin

Brad A. Rogers
Principal
Lincoln Elementary School
Merrillan, Wisconsin

Sarah Rogers
Fourth-Grade Teacher
Lincoln Elementary School
Merrillan, Wisconsin

Bo Ryan
Principal
Greater Hartford Academy of the Arts
Middle School
Hartford, Connecticut

Scott Schiller
Principal
Southside Elementary School
Powell, Wyoming

Casey Slama
Principal
Gordon Elementary School
Gordon, Nebraska

Visit **go.SolutionTree.com/RTIatWork** to download the free reproducibles in this book.

TABLE OF CONTENTS

Reproducible pages are in italics.

CHAPTER 3

CHAPTER 4

CHAPTER 5

Implementing Behavior Solutions at Tier 3—Remediation **175**

ABOUT THE AUTHORS

John Hannigan, EdD, is an executive leadership coach for Fresno County Superintendent of Schools in California. He has served in education for more than sixteen years as a principal, assistant principal, instructional coach, and teacher.

In his nine years as principal of Reagan Elementary in California's Sanger Unified School District, John led a highly effective professional learning community (PLC). Reagan Elementary was recognized as a National Model PLC School, a California Distinguished School, a California Gold Ribbon School, and an exemplary response to intervention (RTI) school for both academics and behavior. The school received a Title I Academic Achievement Award, was awarded platinum-level status for positive behavior interventions and supports (PBIS), and was selected as a knowledge-development site for the statewide scale-up of a multitiered system of supports (MTSS). John serves on the California Department of Education design team for the implementation of MTSS.

John has coauthored *The PBIS Tier Two Handbook*, *The PBIS Tier Three Handbook*, *Don't Suspend Me!*, and *Building Behavior*.

John earned a master's degree and doctoral degree in educational leadership from California State University, Fresno.

To learn more about John's work, follow @JohnHannigan75 on Twitter.

Jessica Djabrayan Hannigan, EdD, is an assistant professor in the Educational Leadership Department at California State University, Fresno. She works with schools and districts throughout the United States on designing and implementing effective social-emotional and behavior systems. Her expertise includes RTI, PLCs, MTSS, PBIS, restorative practices, social-emotional learning, and more. The combination of her special education and student support services background, school- and district-level administration, and graduate-level teaching and research experiences has allowed her to develop inclusive research-based best practices for systemically implementing equitable behavior initiatives.

Jessica has coauthored *The PBIS Tier One Handbook*, *The PBIS Tier Two Handbook*, *The PBIS Tier Three Handbook*, *Don't Suspend Me!*, and *Building Behavior*. She serves on the California Department of Education design team for the implementation of MTSS to help advocate and change the trending discipline inequity throughout the state's schools and create positive school climates for all students. Some of her recognitions include the California Outstanding School Psychologist of the Year, Administrator of the Year, and Outstanding Faculty Publications and Service awards. Also, the California Legislature Assembly has recognized her work in social justice and equity, and she received the inaugural Association of California School Administrators Exemplary Woman in Education Award in 2017 for her relentless work around equity in schools.

Jessica received a bachelor's degree in psychology, a master's degree in school psychology, an administrative credential, and a doctorate in educational leadership.

To learn more about Jessica's work, visit www.pbischampionmodelsystem.com or follow @Jess_hannigan on Twitter.

Mike Mattos is an internationally recognized author, presenter, and practitioner who specializes in uniting teachers, administrators, and support staff to transform schools by implementing response to intervention and professional learning communities. Mike cocreated the RTI at Work™ model, which builds on the foundation of the PLC at Work® process by using team structures and a focus on learning, collaboration, and results to drive successful outcomes.

He is former principal of Marjorie Veeh Elementary School and Pioneer Middle School in California. At both schools, Mike helped create powerful PLCs, improving learning for all students. In 2004, Marjorie Veeh, an elementary school with a large population of youth at risk, won the California Distinguished School and National Title I Achieving School awards.

A National Blue Ribbon School, Pioneer is among only thirteen schools in the United States that the GE Foundation selected as a Best-Practice Partner and is one of eight schools that Richard DuFour chose to feature in the video series *The Power of Professional Learning Communities at Work: Bringing the Big Ideas to Life*. Based on standardized test scores, Pioneer ranks among the top 1 percent of California secondary schools and, in 2009 and 2011, was named Orange County's top middle school. For his leadership, Mike was named the Orange County Middle School Administrator of the Year by the Association of California School Administrators.

Mike has coauthored many other books focused on RTI and PLCs, including *Learning by Doing: A Handbook for Professional Learning Communities at Work* (3rd edition); *Concise Answers to Frequently Asked Questions About Professional Learning Communities at Work*; *Simplifying Response to Intervention: Four Essential Guiding Principles*; *Pyramid Response to Intervention: RTI, Professional Learning Communities*, and *How to Respond When Kids Don't Learn*; *Uniting Academic and Behavior Interventions: Solving the Skill or Will Dilemma*; *It's About Time: Planning Interventions and Extensions in Secondary School*; *It's About Time: Planning Interventions and Extensions in Elementary School*; *Best*

Practices at Tier 1: Daily Differentiation for Effective Instruction, Secondary; Best Practices at Tier 1: Daily Differentiation for Effective Instruction, Elementary; The Collaborative Administrator: Working Together as a Professional Learning Community; and *Taking Action: A Handbook for RTI at Work.*

To learn more about Mike's work, visit AllThingsPLC (www.allthingsplc.info) and http://mattos.info, or follow @mikemattos65 on Twitter.

 **Austin Buffum, EdD,** has more than forty-seven years of experience in public schools. His many roles include serving as former senior deputy superintendent of Capistrano Unified School District in California. He has presented in over five hundred school districts throughout the United States and around the world. He delivers trainings and presentations on the RTI at Work model. This tiered approach to RTI centers on PLC at Work concepts and strategies to ensure every student receives the time and support necessary to succeed. Austin also delivers workshops and presentations that provide the tools educators need to build and sustain PLCs.

Austin was named 2006 Curriculum and Instruction Administrator of the Year by the Association of California School Administrators. He attended the Principals' Center at the Harvard Graduate School of Education and was greatly inspired by its founder, Roland Barth, an early advocate of the collaborative culture that defines PLCs today. Austin later led Capistrano's K–12 instructional program on an increasingly collaborative path toward operating as a PLC. During this process, thirty-seven of the district's schools were designated California Distinguished Schools, and eleven received National Blue Ribbon recognition.

Austin is coauthor with Suzette Lovely of *Generations at School: Building an Age-Friendly Learning Community.* He has also coauthored *Uniting Academic and Behavior Interventions: Solving the Skill or Will Dilemma; It's About Time: Planning Interventions and Extensions in Elementary School; It's About Time: Planning Interventions and Extensions in Secondary School; Simplifying Response to Intervention: Four Essential Guiding Principles; Pyramid Response to Intervention: RTI, Professional Learning Communities, and How to Respond When Kids Don't Learn;* and *Taking Action: A Handbook for RTI at Work.*

A graduate of the University of Southern California, Austin earned a bachelor of music and received a master of education with honors. He also holds a doctor of education from Nova Southeastern University.

To learn more about Austin's work, follow him @agbuffum on Twitter.

To book John Hannigan, Jessica Djabrayan Hannigan, Mike Mattos, or Austin Buffum for professional development, contact pd@SolutionTree.com.

Introduction

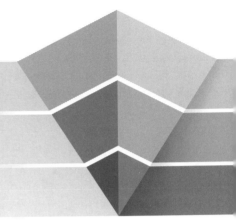

> If the only tool you have is a hammer, you tend to see every problem as a nail.
>
> **—Abraham Maslow**

When working with educators, we often hear them voice the same kinds of concerns.

"We weren't taught how to respond to behavior challenges that go beyond common disruptions."

"We don't use behavior data to make decisions about students."

"We have neither the time nor the resources to address students' academic and social behavior needs during our grade-level team meetings."

"We don't know how to respond to Tier 2 and Tier 3 behaviors."

"We don't know what to do if students don't meet their academic and social behavior goals."

"What about the other students in my class who don't get to learn because of the disruptions from a few?"

"Are you expecting teacher teams to discuss behavior?"

"We don't have time to teach behavior; their parents need to teach them that."

"Our job is to teach our content, not behavior."

"We don't know how to write specific, measurable goals for behavior."

"What are behavior data, and how do we use it?"

1

Do any of these comments resonate with you? These concerns make sense. Most educator preparation programs teach potential educators classroom management skills—how to plan behavior expectations within their individual classroom and how to manage minor misbehaviors in class. Rarely are educators taught how to collaboratively teach essential behaviors across the entire school and then systematically and collectively respond when some students require additional time and support mastering these behaviors. Comments like these demonstrate the need to build the capacity of an entire staff—collaborative teacher teams, administrators, and support staff—to collectively address every student's academic and social behavior needs. Furthermore, they need a mechanism that connects the communication and implementation of tiered levels of behavior supports—for all students—in a coordinated and collaborative fashion.

Behavior Solutions: Teaching Academic and Social Skills Through RTI at Work™ helps educators meet these needs in their schools and districts. This book details how ensuring that all students master the academic and social behaviors required for their success becomes possible when schools function as professional learning communities (PLCs) and effectively apply response to intervention (RTI) practices. The PLC at Work® process (DuFour & Eaker, 1998) provides the collaborative foundation, and the RTI at Work™ process (Buffum, Mattos, & Malone, 2018) provides a three-tiered system of student support. With guidance from *Behavior Solutions*, different teams—of district and school leaders, site interventionists, and teachers—work together to address students' behavior needs. To do this effectively requires schoolwide structures and processes that are collaborative, research based, practical, intentional, and grounded in targeted behavior data.

To this end, this book is designed to do the following.

- Serve as a companion to *Taking Action: A Handbook for RTI at Work* (Buffum et al., 2018), delving much deeper into the specific actions necessary to successfully identify, teach, and intervene on essential academic and social behaviors.

- Show that successful learning for all requires a school to function as a PLC and simultaneously apply RTI.

- Help schools implement the provided essential academic and social behavior standards, processes, tools, and resources to function as a PLC for each tier of support—prevention, intervention, and remediation.

- Provide a process that is inclusive to any behavior initiatives schools are already implementing and help schools systemically align PLC at Work and RTI at Work to any pre-existing behavior initiative (or combination of behavior initiatives) they are currently implementing in their school or district, whether it is positive behavior interventions and supports (PBIS), social-emotional learning (SEL), restorative justice (RJ), culturally responsive teaching (CRT), trauma-informed practices (TIPs), or character education.

- Show how functioning as a PLC and assigning RTI for behavior based on data addresses what we refer to as the *systemic behavior gap* (page 21).

This introduction touches on why and how the RTI at Work approach is necessary and what this approach looks like, functioning as a primer to the rest of the book's full exploration of these subjects and your assessing their current reality in chapter 1.

Why RTI at Work Is Necessary

An increasing number of students need social-emotional support to access their education, and responding to student misbehavior is time consuming, takes away from precious instructional time, and negatively impacts teacher efficacy (Centers for Disease Control and Prevention, 2020; Collie, Shapka, & Perry, 2012; Klassen & Chiu, 2010; Mojtabai, Olfson, & Han, 2016; National Institutes of Mental Health, 2018; Visser et al., 2014). Unmet social-emotional needs often show up as negative behavior. All students must learn about academic and social behaviors as a matter of course; they are the only way to best access an education. If a student's behaviors prevent learning—he or she disrupts class with angry outbursts, cannot keep track of materials, or overwhelmingly interacts poorly with peers—responding with supplemental or intensive behavioral support becomes necessary.

Many schools and educators struggle to effectively meet academic and social behavior needs. These behaviors are actions students take in the academic and social parts of their lives, and both skill sets contribute to school success. Specifically, educators struggle to effectively identify, align, teach, reinforce, use data to monitor, and intervene on academic and social behavior standards. Traditional disciplinary responses have been highly ineffective and inequitably applied. The difficulty of implementing a tiered system of research- and evidence-based behavioral best practices grows with the increasing demands from federal and state or provincial accountability measures, district-level initiatives, mandates, missions, and goals. You can use any research-based behavior initiative you currently implement to teach the academic and social behavior standards identified in this book. More importantly, the process we will introduce can be applied universally across any behavior initiatives.

How RTI at Work Applies to Academic and Social Behaviors

How can educators ensure students learn, master, and *generalize* (apply across multiple settings and situations) a set of academic and social behavior standards that will allow them to access their education and become productive citizens? How do educators design a system that intentionally teaches essential academic and social behavior standards the way it teaches academic content standards? To begin, educators need the tools and practical resources to build, teach, assess, and sustain a foundation for schoolwide behavior expectations at Tier 1 of RTI. This is obviously easier said than done.

On the academic content side, educators receive a set of academic standards for each grade level that students are expected to learn and master. In fact, students, teachers, and administrators are held accountable for these identified academic standards at the federal, state or provincial, and district levels, which requires the alignment of a strong instructional system.

Are schools and districts held accountable for behavior outcomes to the same degree? Do they have as strong a reason to align behavior systems with specific desired outcomes? Do educators teach and reinforce required behaviors with the same emphasis as academic outcomes? Sometimes the answer to these proposed questions is yes, and sometimes it is no. Districts and schools can answer *yes* to these questions when they have committed to providing all students access, both academically and social-emotionally, to accountability structures and goals aligned to these beliefs. Districts and schools must answer *no* if they inconsistently provide components of a behavior initiative and they provide those only to comply or to address discipline, rather than to make behavior skills a priority for *all* students. Making sure they can answer *yes* is how all schools can ensure students master crucial academic and social behavior skills.

Also, when using the term *accountability* with regard to behavior, we do not mean holding students accountable for their behavior in the form of discipline. We are not referring to exclusionary practices such as detention, suspension, and expulsion due to education code violations; we mean holding schools—the *adults*—accountable for designing a system that will teach students the academic and social behavior standards they need to access their education. This doesn't mean there aren't consequences for misbehavior. Educators must hold students accountable for demonstrating essential behaviors.

Educators should view misbehavior as the absence of an academic or social behavior skill; misbehavior or organizational struggles are an educator's cue to fill that gap by teaching the expected skills. A non-fluent reader won't become fluent through more fluency practice. A teacher must first identify where that student is struggling and then target those skills with instruction to put proficient reading in reach. Educators need to respond in the same way for behavior—the adults must explicitly teach the skills needed to demonstrate a specific behavior. Unfortunately, teachers commonly see negative or lackadaisical student behavior through the lens of an adult feeling frustrated or disrespected by the behavior. But a student needs to learn the required skills before changing his or her behavior. This includes students who are not necessarily getting into trouble due to their behaviors but who need behavior supports to access their education and excel.

What RTI at Work Looks Like

This resource is not an educational theory text—it is an application workbook. While the procedures and tools provided are based on powerful research, these proven practices will not help a single student unless you put them into action. With this resource, we ultimately aim to provide more than a toolbox of random behavior resources, but a targeted set of complementary processes that will collectively create an effective system of supports. The RTI at Work pyramid in figure I.1 captures the entire system.

A school or district can use this pyramid as a graphic organizer for guiding its efforts to create a highly effective system of supports. In the next chapter, we will dig deeper into the essential elements of the RTI at Work process.

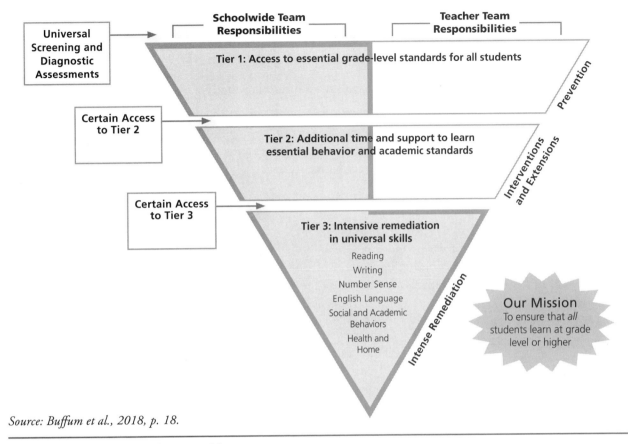

Source: Buffum et al., 2018, p. 18.

FIGURE I.1: RTI at Work pyramid.

What the Chapters of This Book Offer

In the introduction and chapter 1, we focus on why this work is critical in schools for students' long-term success. We would define *long-term success* as mastery toward the next level of grade completion and one step closer to becoming a productive member of the community by establishing healthy relationships and a living-wage job. We will also identify the factors that contribute to what we refer to as the *systemic behavior gap* and we help you audit your school's current state.

The introduction and chapter 1 help you answer the following and more questions.

- ▸ "Why is this work important?"

- ▸ "How do we know if our school has a systemic behavior gap?"

- ▸ "What contributes to the systemic behavior gap?"

- ▸ "How do we continue doing the work as competing initiatives are being pushed on us from the state and district levels?"

- ▸ "How do we know what we have to work on?"

In chapter 2, we explore how to integrate the roles in the PLC at Work and RTI at Work processes to ensure all students master essential behaviors. We also highlight the key differences among integrating the PLC process, RTI, and behavior and describe the roles and responsibilities of a school's different teams—the leadership team, intervention team, and teacher teams—at each tier of RTI.

This chapter helps you answer the following and more questions.

- ▶ "How do we fit behavior into PLC at Work and RTI at Work processes?"

- ▶ "How does PLC and RTI integration differ when it comes to behavior, as opposed to academic structures?"

- ▶ "What is the responsibility of each team member in a PLC and in RTI?"

In chapter 1, you learn about the context and operational definitions required to understand and apply the information in this book, including the systemic behavior gap contributing factors and an audit of your school's current state. In chapter 2, you learn about the roles and responsibilities for the teams involved in this work.

We walk you through each stage and allow you to complete your school's RTI pyramid each step of the way. At the end of this book, you will have a complete picture of your school's RTI pyramid and a plan for continuous improvement for each tier. In addition, you will have the information you need to prevent the systemic behavior gap. Implementation guides for Tiers 1, 2, and 3 help you plan PLC and RTI next steps.

In chapters 3, 4, and 5, we focus on identifying and avoiding the behavior-related challenges of PLC and RTI implementation by demonstrating how to function as a PLC and use RTI for each tier of behavior supports. We highlight what we call the *essential academic and social behavior standards* and provide a Plan–Do–Study–Act framework for implementing behavior solutions at each of the three RTI tiers.

The three reproducibles at the end of chapters 3–5 help you begin to apply or enhance your implementation of PLC and RTI while preventing the systemic behavior gap from stalling your progress. Specifically, in these reproducibles, you will be asked to do the following.

1. Learn the four integration criteria for integrating PLC and RTI in each tier. The four criteria are available at the end of chapters 3–5 and ultimately make up what we refer to as the *behavior integration assessment* (BIA). The "Behavior Integration Assessment" reproducible appears in full at **go.SolutionTree.com/RTIatWork**. This tool helps schools assess mastery of the integration criteria necessary for preventing and avoiding the systemic behavior gap.

2. Complete the designated sections of the RTI at Work pyramid with a focus on behavior for Tier 1 (chapter 3), Tier 2 (chapter 4), and Tier 3 (chapter 5), with a focus on essential academic and social behaviors while learning how to apply the roles and responsibilities of each of the teams (chapter 2) and develop certain access points within and between each tier.

Why to Use the Plan–Do–Study–Act Framework

W. Edwards Deming's (1993) Plan–Do–Study–Act framework is a longstanding learning and improvement model applicable across a wide body of structures, organizations, and fields interested in ongoing improvement. Chapters 3, 4, and 5 follow those stages to help your school's continuous improvement in each tier—specifically, helping you identify what you are trying to accomplish, how you will know that it's working, and what changes you can make that will result in improvement. In addition to the cycle in each tier, each tier's chapter ends with critical actions to consider and evidence indicators for successful implementation.

Understand it is the *process* we emphasize here. Once your leadership team understands the process, it can include any of the essential academic and social behavior standards within any behavior initiative. The point is that your leadership team knows to identify the behavior standards to teach, and it understands your school's RTI needs. Our examples of this process utilize the essential academic and social behavior standards because our findings have indicated that they capture both the academic and social behavior needs of students and they are inclusive of other initiatives and programs.

We provide doable processes and user-friendly tools and forms to answer commonly asked questions about and prevent schoolwide and classroom-level challenges. These tools help the leadership team use data to determine what will best work for its school, students, and staff, no matter what the school has identified as its essential behavior standards.

These sections help you answer the following questions for each tier using the Plan–Do–Study–Act (Deming, 1993) framework.

▶ "How do we identify essential academic and social behavior standards?"

▶ "What does *function as a PLC with a focus on behavior* mean?"

▶ "What are everyone's roles and responsibilities when implementing Tiers 1, 2, and 3 academic and social behavior prevention, intervention, and remediation?"

▶ "What is the behavior connection between PLCs and RTI?"

▶ "What does implementation look like in each RTI tier?"

▶ "How will implementation help address the systemic behavior gap?"

▶ "Where do we start with implementation?"

In appendices A–C, we focus on how to take all the information provided in the previous chapters and create a sustainable, continuous system of supports for this work. We help you identify how to move your teams forward during implementation. We also provide action plans and additional tools and resources to help move your teams from buy-in to ownership.

These chapters add up to a book that helps you build a comprehensive RTI system in each tier that can improve academic and social behavior outcomes for all students.

This book serves two purposes: (1) help as you audit your current RTI pyramid in each tier for behavior and (2) help as you learn how to function as a PLC with the focus on behavior to assign RTI in each tier (Tier 1 prevention, Tier 2 intervention, and Tier 3 remediation). Too often we hear from educators the comments stated in the beginning of this introduction, so we want to provide a toolkit to implement effective systems in schools that are as intentional for behavior as they are for academics.

We highly recommend initially reading this book in its entirety to develop a comprehensive RTI at Work structure for behavior. Then, utilize its design as a workbook to revisit any part of the Plan–Do–Study–Act cycles within each tier to continuously improve your system.

This book will give you the tools to find solutions to any behavior problems you are seeing on your campus and identify methods to address them in each tier; hence our title—*Behavior Solutions*!

CHAPTER 1

Assessing Your Current Reality

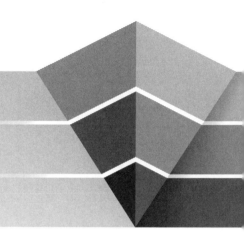

Undoubtedly, every school system has existing practices and policies aimed to improve student achievement. But while many schools organize teams, set goals, utilize data, and develop interventions for this purpose, often there is a communication gap and misalignment between the initiatives that the district or site leadership team directs and the faculty's ownership. This is especially true when it comes to behavior because of two reasons we have observed regularly: (1) behavior tends to elicit a more significant emotional response from all stakeholders, and (2) behavior content expertise and resources are limited when compared to academic content expertise in schools.

We will answer the following questions and others in this chapter.

- ▶ What common language will we utilize throughout this book?

- ▶ What are the behavior challenges in schools?

- ▶ What contributes to a systemic behavior gap?

- ▶ How can you use the content in this book to address a systemic behavior gap in your school?

Before outlining collaborative communication, aligned initiatives, and collective ownership, we present common language for clarity, bring attention to behavior challenges in education, and explain how those challenges lead to a systemic behavior gap.

Common Language for Clarity

To begin, it is critical we calibrate ourselves with the common language in which this work is grounded.

Response to Intervention (RTI)

Also known as a *multitiered system of supports* (MTSS), RTI is a systematic process that ensures all students receive the time and support they need to learn at high levels. Overall:

> RTI's underlying premise is that schools should not delay providing help for struggling students until they fall far enough behind to qualify for special education, but instead should provide timely, targeted, systematic interventions to all students who demonstrate the need. (Buffum, Mattos, & Weber, 2012, p. xiii)

Famed educational researcher John Hattie (2017) finds that, among over 250 factors that influence student learning, RTI has one of the highest impact rates on accelerating student achievement. He gives RTI an effect size of 1.29 standard-deviation growth per year (Hattie, 2017). To put this in context, a 1.0 standard deviation increase is typically associated with advancing student achievement by two to three years (Hattie, 2009). For students struggling below grade level, such growth can rapidly and effectively close achievement gaps and ensure student success.

Response to Intervention *at Work* (RTI at Work)

As mentioned in the introduction, the RTI at Work pyramid (figure 1.1) will serve as this book's primary graphic organizer, uniting process, and culminating activity.

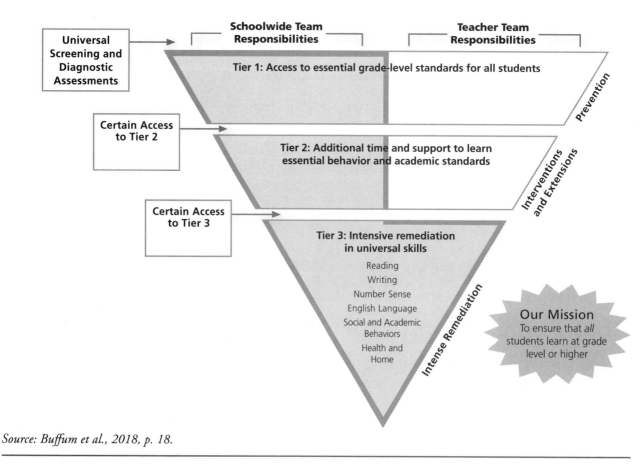

Source: Buffum et al., 2018, p. 18.

FIGURE 1.1: RTI at Work pyramid.

The RTI at Work model, developed by Mike Mattos and Austin Buffum (2015), is built on the PLC at Work process, and is designed to clearly delineate the essential outcomes and team responsibilities needed to create a highly effective multitiered system of supports.

Like any graphic organizer, it is important to correctly understand the thinking behind the design. One might first notice that the RTI at Work pyramid is inverted. We have found that many states, districts, and schools have mistakenly viewed RTI as merely a new pathway to special education identification. This misinterpretation is visually reinforced when special education was placed at the apex of the process, like you see in figure 1.2.

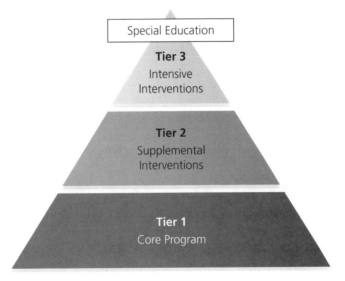

Source: Buffum et al., 2018, p. 19.

FIGURE 1.2: RTI pyramid with special education at the top.

When viewed this way, the tiers of the pyramid become the mandatory steps a school must take to justify special education testing. While a secondary benefit of effective RTI implementation is that educators can use it to identify students with learning disabilities, the tiers must be viewed as the targeted levels of support a school must provide to ensure all students learn at high levels. The inverted pyramid in figure 1.3 (page 12) represents a school's focus on each student's individual needs.

The three tiers of the RTI at Work pyramid represent essential targeted learning outcomes (figure 1.4, page 12). At the top of the pyramid is Tier 1. It is the widest part of the pyramid because it represents what *all* students receive as part of their core instructional program—access to grade-level essential curriculum. As stated in the PLC at Work handbook *Learning by Doing*:

> If the ultimate goal of a learning-focused school is to ensure that every
> student ends each year having acquired the essential skills, knowledge,
> and behaviors required for success at the next grade level, then all stu-
> dents must have access to grade-level essential curriculum as part of their
> core instruction. (DuFour, DuFour, Eaker, Many, & Mattos, 2016, p. 166)

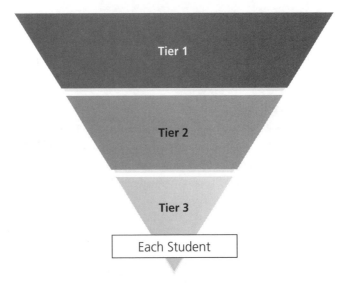

Source: Buffum et al., 2018, p. 19.

FIGURE 1.3: Inverted RTI at Work pyramid.

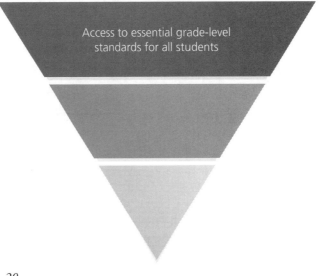

Source: Buffum et al., 2018, p. 20.

FIGURE 1.4: Core instruction program.

The key term is *essential* grade-level standards. Essential standards are a *carefully selected subset* of the total list of the grade-specific and course-specific academic skills and behaviors that students must know and be able to do by the end of each school year in order to be prepared for the next grade-level or course (Ainsworth, 2014). While it is possible that some students might miss portions of Tier 1 core instruction to receive interventions, students cannot be denied access to essential curriculum.

Undoubtedly, some students will not master the essential curriculum by the end of a unit of study. Because these learning outcomes are essential for every student's future success, the school must dedicate time to providing additional support for each student to master this essential grade-level curriculum without missing critical new core instruction. This supplemental help to master grade-level curriculum is the purpose of Tier 2 in the RTI at Work pyramid (figure 1.5).

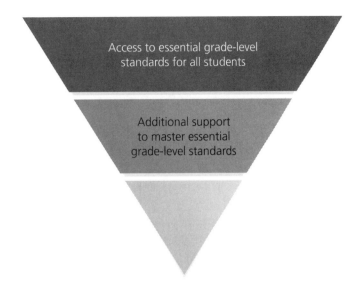

Source: Buffum et al., 2018, p. 21.

FIGURE 1.5: Supplemental help to master grade-level curriculum.

Tier 2 supports should focus on providing targeted students with the additional time and support they need to master the specific skills, knowledge, *and* behaviors identified at Tier 1 to be essential for a student's future success.

If a school provides students access to essential grade-level curriculum and effective initial teaching during Tier 1 core instruction, and targeted supplemental academic and behavioral help in meeting these standards at Tier 2, then most students will succeed. However, some students inevitably enter each school year lacking the foundational skills needed to learn at high levels. These universal skills and behaviors include the following abilities.

▸ Decode and comprehend grade-level text.

▸ Write effectively.

▸ Apply number sense.

▸ Comprehend the English language (or the school's primary language).

▸ Consistently demonstrate essential social and academic behaviors.

▸ Overcome complications due to health or home.

If a student is significantly behind in just one of these universal skills, he or she will struggle in virtually every grade level, course, and subject. And usually, the students most at risk in a school are behind in more than one area. For students who need intensive remediation in foundational skills, the school must have a plan to provide this level of assistance without denying these students access to essential grade-level curriculum (figure 1.6, page 14). This is the purpose of Tier 3.

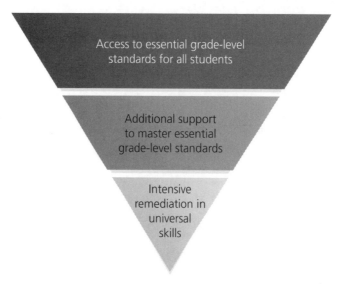

Source: Buffum et al., 2018, p. 22.

FIGURE 1.6: Intensive remediation in foundational skills.

Last and most important, some students will need all three tiers to learn at high levels—this is why it is called a *multitiered* system of supports. Schools do not move students from tier to tier—instead, they are value added! All students need effective initial teaching on essential grade-level standards at Tier 1. In addition to Tier 1, some students will need supplemental time and support in meeting essential grade-level standards at Tier 2. And in addition to Tier 1 and Tier 2, some students will need intensive help in learning essential outcomes from previous years. Students in need of Tier 3 intensive help in remedial skills often struggle with new essential grade-level curriculum the first time their teacher teaches it. This means these students need Tier 2 and Tier 3, all without missing new essential instruction at Tier 1.

Individual teachers cannot effectively provide all three levels of support in their own classrooms. Such support requires a schoolwide, collective, collaborative, coordinated, all-hands-on-deck mentality. This is why structuring a school to function as a professional learning community is the key to effectively implementing RTI.

Professional Learning Community *at Work* (PLC at Work)

A successful intervention system is built on a highly effective core instructional program. Fortunately, our profession has near-unanimous agreement on how to best structure a school to ensure student and adult learning. Comprehensive study of the world's best-performing school systems finds that these systems function as professional learning communities (Barber & Mourshed, 2007; Mourshed, Chijioke, & Barber, 2010).

We specifically advocate for the Professional Learning Community at Work process, originally created by Richard DuFour and Robert Eaker (1998). DuFour and coauthors (2016) define a PLC as a "never-ending process in which educators commit to *working together* to *ensure* higher levels of learning for every student" (p. 11).

To achieve this goal—an unrelenting focus on learning—educators work collaboratively to *learn together* about the practices proven to increase student learning, apply what they have learned, and gather evidence of student learning to validate their efforts and guide their next steps. This collective learning focuses on the factors that support and hinder student success, including teaching essential behaviors and dispositions. (In fact, we hope this book helps PLC schools and districts build shared knowledge in this critical area.)

Because ensuring high levels of learning for every student cannot be achieved by individual teachers working in isolation, the PLC at Work process requires a collaborative culture, in which educators work in teams and take collectively responsibility for student success. Specifically in this book, we recommend three types of teams to guide the school's RTI process (Buffum, Mattos, Weber, & Hierck, 2015).

1. **Teacher teams** are composed of teachers who share essential academic learning outcomes. At the elementary level, they are usually grade-level teams, and at the secondary level, they are usually course-specific teams. Teacher teams take lead responsibility for identifying, teaching, and reteaching essential academic standards, directing supplemental (Tier 2) academic interventions and assisting with academic and social behavior supports.

2. The **leadership team—also called a guiding coalition—**has lead responsibility for efforts that must be coordinated across the school. These include leading schoolwide behavior efforts, allocating resources to support collaboration and student learning, creating a shared school mission, and designing the school master schedule.

3. The **intervention team** solves problems related to the school's most at-risk students. Most often, these students have multiple needs in both academics and behavior. Made up of the school staff best trained in the areas where students most often struggle (such as behavior, literacy, and numeracy), this team meets frequently to diagnose, target, coordinate, and monitor the interventions for students who need Tier 3 intensive remediation.

Visually, we capture the lead responsibilities for these three teams in the RTI at Work pyramid the following ways. Teacher team lead responsibilities at Tier 1 and Tier 2 are listed in the top right-hand portion of the pyramid in figure 1.7 (page 16).

Collaboration alone will not improve student learning unless these efforts focus on the *right work*. To this end, collaboration in the PLC at Work process is guided by four critical questions:

1. What knowledge, skills, and dispositions should every student acquire as a result of this unit, this course, or this grade level?

2. How will we know when each student has acquired the essential knowledge and skills?

3. How will we respond when some students do not learn?

4. How will we extend the learning for students who are already proficient? (DuFour et al., 2016, p. 36)

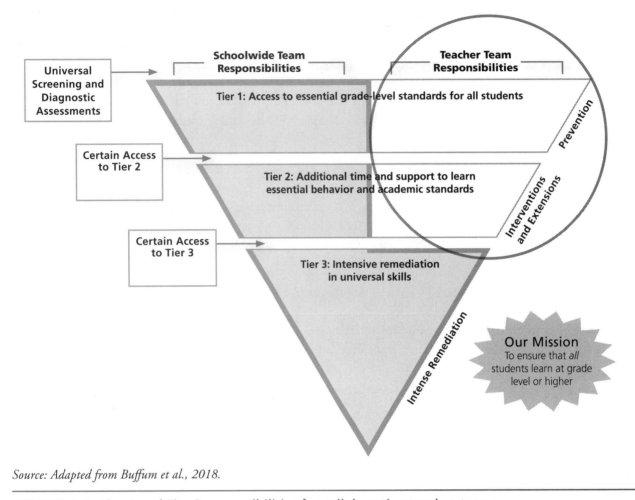

Source: Adapted from Buffum et al., 2018.

FIGURE 1.7: Tier 1 and Tier 2 responsibilities for collaborative teacher teams.

Traditionally, teacher teams have focused on answering these questions for essential academic curriculum. We are advocating that a school staff collectively answer these same questions for essential behavior standards. Likewise, the lead responsibilities of the two schoolwide teams—the leadership and intervention teams—are listed in the left-hand side of the pyramid in figure 1.8.

Finally, educators in a PLC purposefully and relentlessly collect evidence that students are learning. Actual proof of practice—instead of merely past practices, preferences, or intentions—drives decisions (DuFour et al., 2016).

Most schools regularly collect information on student learning of academic curriculum and use these data to assess teaching effectiveness and guide interventions for struggling students. Unfortunately, not many schools do the same, or do so systematically, for behavior outcomes. This book will dive deeply into how a PLC can—and should—use targeted data to guide and evaluate a school's systematic behavior supports.

To learn more about the PLC at Work process, we highly recommend the book *Learning by Doing* (DuFour et al., 2016).

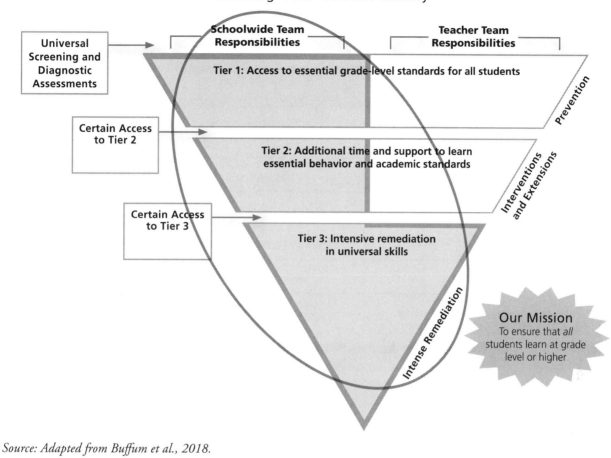

Source: *Adapted from Buffum et al., 2018.*

FIGURE 1.8: Tiers 1, 2, and 3 processes that must be coordinated across the entire school.

Essential Academic and Social Behaviors

Success in school and in a work environment requires the ability to consistently demonstrate appropriate behaviors. In addition to academic skills and knowledge, some academic and social behaviors are critical to developing a successful learner.

We define *essential academic and social behaviors* as actions and concepts that all students must master for interpersonal and career success in and outside school and after formal education (Buffum et al., 2018). Students are required to apply these actions and understand these concepts in all learning environments, throughout all school locations and events, and in the larger community.

Academic and social behavior learning is not limited to one setting, one program or initiative, one student profile, or one teaching or learning style. Some academic and social behaviors run across all grade levels and school settings.

The term *behavior* is interchangeable with *essential academic and social behaviors* in this context, and is also interchangeable with *skill*. Table 1.1 (page 18) provides examples of all the academic and social behavior skills. Chapter 2 (page 33) has more information about roles and responsibilities. Chapter 3 (page 49) provides guidance on how to select standards based on Buffum and colleagues' (2018) essential behaviors.

TABLE 1.1: Academic and Social Behaviors

Academic Behaviors	
Skill	**Requirement**
Metacognition	Having knowledge of and beliefs about one's thinking
Self-concept	Believing in one's abilities
Self-monitoring	Planning, preparing for, and continuing learning
Motivation	Initiating and maintaining interest in tasks
Strategy	Organizing and memorizing knowledge
Volition	Staying motivated and engaged in learning (Many educators refer to this as demonstrating *grit*.)
Social Behaviors	
Skill	**Requirement**
Responsible verbal and physical interactions with peers and adults	Social responsibility, honesty, compassion, respect, self-regulation, and self-control
Appropriate language	Self-awareness, communication, civility, and character
Respect for property and materials	Skills that demonstrate empathy and respect
Independently staying on a required task	Skills that demonstrate on-task behavior and self-monitoring
Regular attendance	Skills that demonstrate punctuality, time management, and accountability

Source: Barber & Mourshed, 2007; Buffum et al., 2012, 2015, 2018; DuFour et al., 2016; Hattie, 2009, 2019; Mourshed et al., 2010.

Behavior Challenges in Education

As educators, practitioners, and researchers, we know that the foundation of a highly effective school is a safe, orderly, and collaborative culture (Lezotte & Snyder, 2011; Marzano, Heflebower, Hoegh, Warrick, & Grift, 2016). And discipline is one of the most time-consuming and energy-draining parts of a school system. Student misbehavior and discipline increase teacher stress and decrease teacher efficacy in managing the classroom, engaging students, and applying effective instructional and behavioral strategies (Collie et al., 2012; Klassen & Chiu, 2010). In order to better address behavior challenges, teachers must abandon a traditional disciplinary approach and recognize that life and career skills are necessary for creating a culture of good behavior.

A Traditional Approach to Misbehavior Equals Inequities

Reacting with rigidity and punishment is not successful (Horner, Sugai, & Vincent, 2005). Discipline research since the 1990s proves that out-of-school suspension and zero-tolerance approaches do not reduce or prevent misbehavior. In fact, they correlate directly with lower achievement (Irvin, Tobin, Sprague, Sugai, & Vincent, 2004; Losen, 2011; Mayer, 1995; Rumberger & Losen, 2016; Skiba & Peterson, 1999; Skiba & Rausch, 2006). Equally important, discipline that removes students from significant class instructional time adds the proverbial *insult to injury*; it does not effectively improve the behavior, *and* these students fall further behind academically, which compounds behavior problems.

Moreover, researchers have found a significant increase in children's mental health needs worldwide.

- ▸ Between 10 and 20 percent of children and adolescents have or have had mental health problems (World Health Organization, n.d.).

- ▸ Almost 6.5 million children are diagnosed with attention deficit hyperactivity disorder (ADHD) in the United States (a 43 percent increase since 2003–2011; Visser et al., 2014). Boys were more likely to have ADHD and behavioral conduct problems (USDHHS, 2011).

- ▸ Adolescents experiencing depression has risen (8.7 percent increase between 2005–2014; Mojtabai et al., 2016).

- ▸ Suicide rates in children ages ten to fourteen worldwide has increased since the 1990s (Kõlves & De Leo, 2014).

- ▸ About 64 percent of children have experienced trauma, including witnessing violence and being direct targets of abuse (Centers for Disease Control and Prevention and Kaiser Permanente, 2016).

- ▸ In 2015, the worldwide prevalence of mental health disorders was 13.4 percent for children between the ages of eleven and fifteen (Polanczyk, Salum, Sugaya, Caye, & Rohde, 2015).

Research also indicates that ineffective disciplinary practices disproportionately impact students of color and special education students. Students of color and students with disabilities receive a disproportionate number of suspensions and expulsions (Office for Civil Rights, 2014). African American students without disabilities are more than three times as likely as their white peers without disabilities to be expelled or suspended. One out of every four African American students with disabilities enrolled in grades K–12 were suspended at least once during the 2009–2010 school year, and they were more likely to be suspended repeatedly in a given year. Researchers have found an increasing number of students are losing important instructional time due to exclusionary discipline (Office for Civil Rights, 2014). Although students who receive special education services represent 12 percent of students in the United States, they make up a substantial portion of students receiving punishments, as the following data show (Office for Civil Rights, 2014).

Those 12 percent of students make up the following.

- 19 percent of students suspended in school

- 20 percent of students receiving a single out-of-school suspension

- 25 percent of students receiving multiple out-of-school suspensions

- 19 percent of students expelled

- 23 percent of students referred to law enforcement

- 23 percent of students experiencing a school-related arrest

Researchers Robert Balfanz and Chris Boccanfuso (2007) find that students who get suspended and expelled are more likely to be retained or drop out of school. The odds grow even higher when the students are repeatedly disciplined (Balfanz & Boccanfuso, 2007). And the most comprehensive meta-analysis on retention finds that being retained one year almost doubles a student's likelihood of dropping out, while being retained twice almost guarantees it (Hattie, 2009). Moreover, students who receive punitive discipline are significantly more likely to enter the juvenile justice system (Leone et al., 2003; Wald & Losen, 2003).

The outcomes for students who struggle academically are similar to the outcomes for students who repeatedly experience stringent discipline. There is a direct connection between low literacy skills and the likelihood of incarceration. In fact, low literacy skills are a key factor in the school-to-prison pipeline:

> The link between academic failure and delinquency, violence, and crime is welded to reading failure . . . when inmates who left school before receiving a high school diploma were asked the main reason they dropped out of school, about one-third reported they lost interest or experienced academic difficulty. (Leone et al., 2003)

While teachers must effectively address student misbehaviors in order to create a safe and orderly school environment, it is equally critical that they teach students essential academic and social behaviors. A student sitting silently for a class period might not pose a behavior problem, but that student is also not engaging in essential academic and social behaviors.

Life and Career Skills Are Necessary for Success

Educators have the charge to academically and socially prepare students for adult life. For example, the Partnership for 21st Century Skills (P21; 2006) provides an overview of the essential skills it says educators need to equip students with if they are to succeed as adults. The P21 (2006) framework divides the essential skills into three sections.

1. Learning and innovation skills (critical thinking, communication, collaboration, and creativity)

2. Life and career skills

3. Information, media, and technology skills

We want to highlight the importance of P21's (2006) life and career skills, which are all directly related to academic and social behavior success in school and beyond. Students need to acquire these skills within the framework of their school's behavior system. As educators begin the work in this book, it is critical that they collaboratively work to *understand and identify* what skills their students need to master in order to access their education and become productive citizens in the community. And it is critical that they *create* a system of supports to ensure every student masters these behaviors.

Table 1.2 (page 22) expands on the life and career skills section of the 21st century framework, which includes the following skills or behaviors deemed essential for student success (P21, 2006).

- ▸ Flexibility and adaptability

- ▸ Initiative and self-direction

- ▸ Social and cross-cultural skills

- ▸ Productivity and accountability

- ▸ Leadership and responsibility

The reproducible "Our School's Preliminary Essential Academic and Social Behaviors" (page 28) allows you to list the essential behaviors that at this point you are thinking about teaching students.

For some students, these behaviors are taught and reinforced at home. Everyone needs practice regardless, and some students come from homes in which not only are these essentials not taught, but counterproductive behaviors are modeled. Unfortunately, many schools fail to systematically teach these essential behaviors and instead merely punish students for not learning them at home.

When we introduce the need for systematic processes to teach these essential academic and social behaviors, educators often voice the justifiable concern, "We already have a lot of work to do. How will we possibly find the time to do this too?" Next, we will think critically about how to design a system that adequately addresses the challenges identified around this learning.

Systemic Behavior Gap

Figure 1.9 (page 23) is a visual representation of what we refer to as the *systemic behavior gap*, which we define as the gap between the implementation of behavior initiatives in each tier and the collective responsibility of all. The patterned arrow signifies a systemic behavior gap at the school-site level of systemic implementation. The patterned arrow demonstrates what the systemic behavior gap *is*. Figure 1.10 (page 24) demonstrates *where* the systemic behavior gap exists within context of the RTI at Work pyramid. Specifically, the gap can appear in the interaction (or lack of) between the two schoolwide teams (leadership and intervention) and teacher teams when they address behavior in a tiered approach.

All teams, from the district office to teacher teams, have a purpose and role within the behavior system; all staff must coherently align themselves in supporting and

TABLE 1.2: P21 Life and Career Skills

Flexibility and Adaptability	Initiative and Self-Direction
Adapt to Change • Adapt to varied roles, job responsibilities, schedules, and contexts. • Work effectively in a climate of ambiguity and changing priorities. **Be Flexible** • Incorporate feedback effectively. • Deal positively with praise, setbacks, and criticism. • Understand, negotiate, and balance diverse views and beliefs to reach workable solutions, particularly in multicultural environments.	**Manage Goals and Time** • Set goals with tangible and intangible success criteria. • Balance tactical (short-term) and strategic (long-term) goals. • Utilize time and manage workload efficiently. **Work Independently** • Monitor, define, prioritize, and complete tasks without direct oversight. **Be Self-Directed Learners** • Go beyond basic mastery of skills and curriculum to explore and expand one's own learning and opportunities to gain expertise. • Demonstrate initiative to advance skill levels toward a professional level. • Demonstrate commitment to learning as a lifelong process. • Reflect critically on past experiences in order to inform future progress.
Social and Cross-Cultural Skills	
Interact Effectively With Others • Know when it is appropriate to listen and when to speak. • Conduct oneself in a respectable, professional manner. **Work Effectively in Diverse Teams** • Respect cultural differences and work effectively with people from a range of social and cultural backgrounds. • Respond open-mindedly to different ideas and values. • Leverage social and cultural differences to create new ideas and increase both innovation and quality of work.	
	Productivity and Accountability

Leadership and Responsibility	**Manage Projects**
	
	• Set and meet goals, even in the face of obstacles and competing pressures.
	
	• Prioritize, plan, and manage work to achieve the intended results.
	
	Produce Results
	
	• Demonstrate additional attributes associated with producing high-quality products, including the abilities to:
	
	  » Work positively and ethically
	
	  » Manage time and projects effectively
	
	  » Multitask
	
	  » Participate actively, as well as be reliable and punctual
	
	  » Present oneself professionally and with proper etiquette
	
	  » Collaborate and cooperate effectively with teams
	
	  » Respect and appreciate team diversity
	
	  » Be accountable for results

Guide and Lead Others • Use interpersonal and problem-solving skills to influence and guide others toward a goal. • Leverage strengths of others to accomplish a common goal. • Inspire others to reach their very best via example and selflessness. • Demonstrate integrity and ethical behavior in using influence and power. **Be Responsible to Others** • Act responsibly with the interests of the larger community in mind.	

Source: P21, 2006.

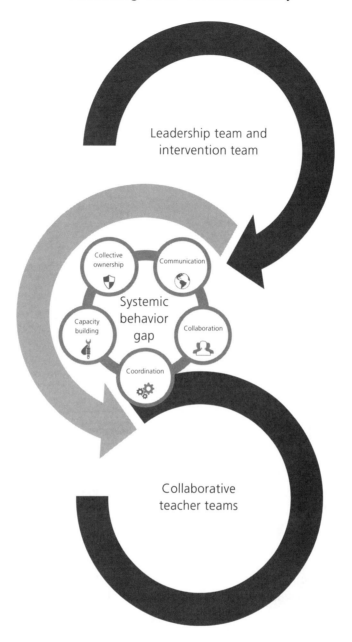

Leadership team and
intervention team

Collective
ownership

Communication

Systemic
behavior
gap

Capacity
building

Collaboration

Coordination

Collaborative
teacher teams

FIGURE 1.9: Systemic behavior gap.

providing access to all students for the behavior initiatives and interventions to successfully function. Often, this gap begins at the district level and widens at the school level when leadership is not clear on how to address the gap. For example, district leadership might give all site principals a district-level directive to implement positive behavioral intervention and supports (such as PBIS) in their schools but not consider adequate training, alignment to the district and school goals, and funding to support the implementation. As a result, poor implementation of PBIS and misconceptions occur.

Why does a systemic gap or disconnect in initiative alignment exist within schools when it comes to behavior supports, as opposed to the more clearly defined and effectively implemented academic supports? To answer this question, we surveyed educators, support staff, behavior specialists, and administrators in over one hundred schools—representing the school leadership team, intervention team, and collaborative teacher teams—regarding their perceptions around implementing a behavior system in their schools.

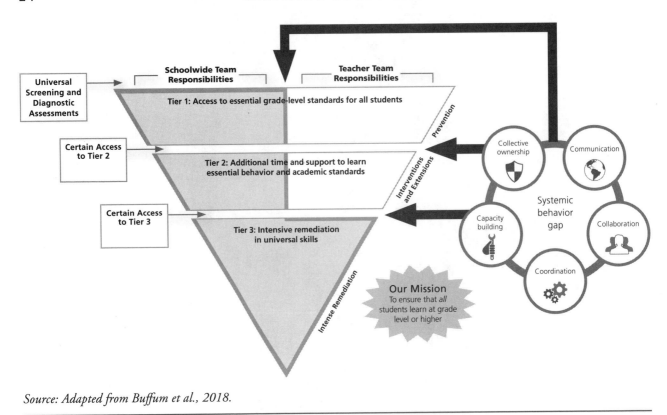

Source: Adapted from Buffum et al., 2018.

FIGURE 1.10: Where the systemic behavior gap exists.

In addition to finding a systemic behavior gap between the school leadership team's initiatives, the intervention team's interventions, and the teacher teams' responsibilities, we found that the following contributing factors (shown in figure 1.11) widen the systemic behavior gap between these teams.

In identifying these contributing factors, we found that teams can strengthen their communication, collaboration, coordination, capacity building, and collective ownership when a school functions as a PLC and successfully applies the RTI at Work process to teaching essential behaviors.

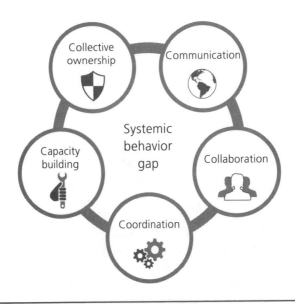

FIGURE 1.11: Systemic behavior gap contributing factors.

Lack of communication: The teams have no process of reciprocal and timely feedback regarding student needs, or the process is unclear. For example, the school leadership team and intervention team decide to put a student into a Tier 2 intervention, but they don't tell the teacher team why or how, or monitor the implementation effectiveness. Transparent dialogue is necessary.

Lack of collaboration: The teams miss opportunities to provide input and work together to identify students' behavior needs. For example, input is not gathered from the teacher teams prior to designing or assigning interventions. Often, interventions are given to the classroom teacher by a behavior specialist without his or her input, therefore feeling like a compliant task rather than a tool of support. Working together is necessary.

Lack of coordination: The teams lack a method for coordinating efforts and an aligned system for implementation and monitoring among the leadership, intervention, and teacher teams. For example, the tiered interventions' purposes and people's implementation responsibilities are unclear among teams—Who takes the lead? What is each member's role and responsibilities? Resource alignment is necessary.

Lack of capacity building: The teams miss opportunities to help stakeholders understand and feel competent in their implementation role. What skills are necessary for the team to fulfill its function within the supports provided? How are those skills developed, and what opportunities exist to build a shared understanding of assigned tiered interventions? For example, a teacher may receive a student participating in a check-in/check-out (CICO) Tier 2 intervention for repeated minor misbehaviors in class but not understand how to implement the intervention within the classroom other than by filling out the student's goal sheet. Learning together is necessary.

Lack of collective ownership: Not all stakeholders own the behavioral development of every student at the school. For example, a teacher may have a student receiving a special education Tier 3 behavior remediation in the classroom but not feel responsible for playing a role in implementing the special education behavior support plan. Another example occurs when stakeholders lack agreement about what behaviors all students must master. It is difficult to intervene on behavior outcomes that are unclear and inconsistently taught across the school. We all take responsibility for the success of every child.

Consider school scenario A—the current state and the future desired outcome—which helps contextualize why this work is so critical for student learning.

Mrs. Darling is a second-grade teacher in a school located in a part of town with a high crime rate, where students regularly face trauma. Four colleagues on her grade-level team are currently in the initiating stage on the PLC continuum. Teachers constantly hijack the team meetings with their venting about repeated behavior challenges in their classrooms. Additionally, the teachers complain about not having administrator support with discipline and not seeing students receive consequences for misbehavior. The teachers feel overwhelmed and resentful of each other and the leadership team.

Although Mrs. Darling is the lead teacher, she also feels resentful and overwhelmed, because whenever she calls for help with her most challenging student, the administrator simply places the student into her colleague's class with a tablet and no expectations for completing work. Her colleague reports to the administrator that the student behaves fine in her class, making Mrs. Darling feel as if she is a bad teacher, her reputation as a good teacher has been tarnished, and she can't handle her students. Due to this current state, students in this grade level do not receive data-based academic or social behavior supports in a timely fashion, and teachers feel like these team meetings are a waste of time.

Consider the following questions.

▶ What is this collaborative teacher team missing?

▶ Why do the teachers feel overwhelmed?

▶ What is the communication and coordination like between the collaborative teacher team and the leadership team?

▶ Why do the teachers resent each other?

▶ As a site leader, what area of capacity building might prevent this scenario in the future?

Scenario B shows the desired state.

Mrs. Darling is the lead second-grade teacher in a PLC school located in a part of town that has a high crime rate and where students regularly face trauma. The second-grade team members consider these factors as they discuss the students "by name, by need" but do not use these factors as excuses for not serving all students academically and social-emotionally. As part of their collaborative teacher team meetings, they discuss the social-emotional behavior and the academic achievement of all second-grade students using the PLC process.

As a result, the teachers clearly know which second-grade students are responding to the Tier 1 behavior supports and which students need additional social-emotional supports. They have identified each student receiving targeted behavior interventions (within or outside the classroom) and individualized interventions (general education or special education). The teachers consider all the second-grade students, not simply the students in their classrooms, to be their students.

The team members request that the school principal and counselor join them during their weekly team meeting to brainstorm potential research-based supports for each identified student. They discuss these interventions by answering the four critical questions that drive the work of their PLC. Also, they work with the leadership team to add additional behavior interventions, refine the time and frequency of existing interventions, or exit the students from interventions based on SMART goal data and the RTI process. The teacher team knows that the principal and counselor will check in on a regular basis to discuss each student's progress and make timely revisions as needed.

This collaborative approach to serving students with social-emotional needs requires both the school leadership team that designs the behavior initiatives and the collaborative teacher teams that implement them to ensure they hear each other's voices, reach consensus, and have collective ownership. This prevents teachers from feeling alone and overwhelmed when faced with behavior challenges in their classrooms. Most importantly, each student in need of social-emotional support will receive targeted interventions designed to meet his or her individual needs, and all the adults who support the student throughout the day will apply these interventions consistently and fairly.

Consider the following questions.

▸ How does this scenario differ from the previous one?

▸ How does the site leader gain support from collaborative teacher teams to collectively own these behavior supports when compared to scenario A?

▸ Why does this meeting format help abbreviate the systemic behavior gap between the school's leadership team and collaborative teacher teams?

▸ How are data obtained for this kind of teacher team meeting format?

▸ How do the teachers implement and discuss levels of academic and social behavior interventions?

The reproducible "Systemic Behavior Gap Audit" (page 29) helps you identify factors that contribute to the systemic behavior gap. The audit is divided into three sections: (1) Current State Contributing Factors, (2) Current State PLC, and (3) Current State RTI. Prior to completing the "Systemic Behavior Gap Audit," please complete the reproducible "Our School's Preliminary Essential Academic and Social Behaviors" (page 28).

Our School's Preliminary Essential Academic and Social Behaviors

List the essential academic and social behaviors you want students to demonstrate at your school. This exercise serves two purposes: (1) it is a precursor to the comprehensive audit coming up next, and (2) it encourages a site leader or site leadership team to think about what is currently in place at the school. Do not worry if your answers are unclear or incomplete. Include what you can based on your background knowledge.

What essential academic and social behavior skills do you want your students to demonstrate?	
Academic Behaviors	**Social Behaviors**

What evidence will show that students are learning these behavior skills?	

How will you ensure students are learning these essential academic and social behavior skills?	

Systemic Behavior Gap Audit

Because your school or district already has behavior policies, it is important to begin by assessing your site's current reality. Consider the relationships among your school's leadership team, intervention team, and teacher teams as you audit the current state of your school's behavior system. The "Systemic Behavior Gap Audit" will provide educators with a look into their current behavior system. The audit items are derived from a combination of the analysis of the contributing factors, PLC at Work, and RTI at Work critical components.

Who is this Systemic Behavior Gap Audit for? Educators such as site leaders, leadership team members, support staff, and district-level administrators who want to create an effective schoolwide behavior system in their schools can benefit from this audit. This can also aid future site and district leaders in reflecting on their practices.

Before completing the audit, know that PLC critical questions 1 through 4 for behavior must be discussed schoolwide, not answered by teacher teams (although, everyone has a role in implementation).

Why does this Systemic Behavior Gap Audit matter? Based on our research and combined experience in this work, we find that the components identified are critical to this work's success. This audit allows a school to address potential contributing factors that impede implementation (page 25).

Review each of the following pages and add the requested information regarding the current state of the contributing factors, PLC process, and RTI model in your school. Please be honest in your responses. Remember, this audit is a reflection and baseline assessment of where you currently are in your implementation.

Systemic Behavior Gap Audit—Continued

Current State: Contributing Factors—Part One	
Question	**Response**
Do you have a school leadership team on your campus? If yes, what is the school leadership team's role with schoolwide academic and social behavior initiatives and their implementation?	
Do you have teacher teams on your campus? If yes, what is their role in schoolwide academic and social behavior initiatives?	
What academic and social behavior programs or initiatives are implemented schoolwide?	
What are the Tier 1 (schoolwide) components of your school's academic and social behavior system?	
What are the Tier 2 (targeted or at-risk) components of your school's academic and social behavior system?	
What are the Tier 3 (individualized) components of your school's academic and social behavior system (for both general education and special education)?	
Do you have SMART goals set based on the student data from your academic and social behavior system? If you have SMART goals set, what are they, how and how often are they monitored, and who monitors them?	
How does your school's academic and social behavior system follow the PLC process? If the behavior system is embedded into your PLC, what are the collaborative teacher teams required to address during their team meetings?	
How does the academic and social behavior system at your school utilize RTI? What process does your school leadership team and teacher teams use to assign, implement, and monitor additional layers of academic and social behavior system supports or interventions?	
How does your school's leadership team assess if the academic and social behavior learning initiatives are being implemented at your school?	

Is this factor a challenge at your school? *(Circle Yes or No.)*		*If yes, how is your school addressing this challenge? If no, what actions will you take to prevent it from becoming a challenge?*
Communication among the school leadership team, the intervention team, and the collaborative teacher teams	Yes or No	
Collaboration among the school leadership team, the intervention team, and the collaborative teacher teams	Yes or No	
Coordination among the school leadership team, the intervention team, and the collaborative teacher teams	Yes or No	
Capacity building among the school leadership team, the intervention team, and the collaborative teacher teams	Yes or No	
Collective ownership among the school leadership team, the intervention team, and the collaborative teacher teams	Yes or No	

Systemic Behavior Gap Audit—Continued

Current State: PLC—Part Two			
PLC Pillar 1: Mission (Clarifies priorities and sharpens focus) *How does your school's mission statement include behavior?*	**PLC Pillar 2: Vision (Gives direction)** *How does your school's vision support behavior?*	**PLC Pillar 3: Values (Guides behavior)** *What are your school's collective commitments regarding behavior?*	**PLC Pillar 4: Goals (Establishes priorities)** *What are your schoolwide goals regarding behavior?*
How do your school's teams utilize the four critical questions of a PLC for academic and social behavior learning?	**Leadership Team**	**Intervention Team**	**Teacher Teams**
Critical Question 1 What do we expect our students to demonstrate in their academic and social behavior? (What are our goals, expectations, or standards?)			
Critical Question 2 How will we know if they are demonstrating the expected academic and social behavior? (What assessments and other data will we use?)			
Critical Question 3 How will we respond if they don't demonstrate the expected academic and social behavior? (What Tier 2 interventions or Tier 3 remediation are we planning on?)			
Critical Question 4 How will we respond if they already demonstrate the expected academic and social behavior? (What innovations and extensions might we use?)			

page 3 of 4

Systemic Behavior Gap Audit—Continued

Current State: RTI—Part Three			
	Leadership Team	**Intervention Team**	**Teacher Teams**
How do your teams use RTI in Tier 1 academic and social behavior: Schoolwide (Prevention)			
How do your teams use RTI in Tier 2 academic and social behavior: Targeted or at risk (Intervention)			
How do your teams use RTI in Tier 3 academic and social behavior: Individualized or intensive (Remediation)			

page 4 of 4

CHAPTER 2

Developing the Structure for Integrating the PLC Process, RTI, and Behavior

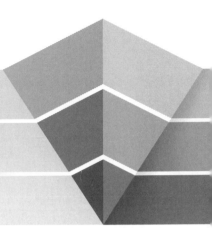

Without a research-based, systematic, tiered approach to both academics and behavior and the PLC process as the foundation to help navigate it effectively, schools cannot address student behavior challenges well. Therefore, it is important that all staff know how the PLC process and RTI academic and social behavior systems compare with strictly academic systems, which includes learning the roles and responsibilities of leadership team, intervention team, and teacher team members.

We will answer the following questions and others in this chapter.

▶ What is the difference between academic and social behaviors and academic achievement?

▶ What are the roles and responsibilities of all stakeholder teams in relation to addressing the systemic behavior gap?

▶ What are the key differences between roles and responsibilities of each team for each tier of the school's system?

▶ What are some effective teacher team communication structures for each tier in the system?

Academic and Social Behavior Systems Compared With Academic Systems

It is very important that we identify the key difference between the academic content and the academic and social behavior sides of functioning as a PLC and utilizing the RTI process. On the academic side, collaborative teacher teams commonly have the collective expertise needed to lead the design and implementation of Tier 1 and 2 interventions for academic skill or academic standard deficits. For example, which staff members in an elementary school are best trained to teach and reteach essential first-grade standards? First-grade teachers, of course! And at a high school, which staff members are most qualified to teach and reteach essential biology curriculum? The biology team members, as they collectively have the greatest level of training and experience in this area. The teacher team's responsibility is to lead the teaching and reteaching of grade-level essential academic standards—what we refer to as *skill interventions*—is visually captured in the top-right section of the RTI at Work pyramid in figure 2.1.

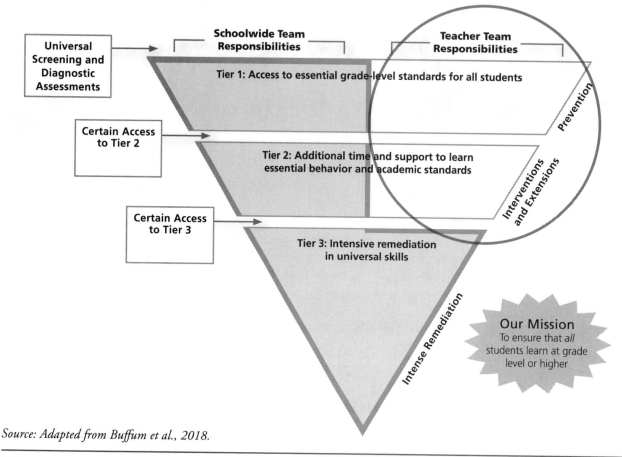

Source: Adapted from Buffum et al., 2018.

FIGURE 2.1: Tier 1 and Tier 2 responsibilities for collaborative teacher teams.

However, teacher teams are usually not as well trained to respond to essential behavior deficits at Tier 2 or Tier 3—what we refer to as *will interventions*. While a majority of classroom teachers take a classroom management course as part of a credentialing program, few hold professional degrees or certificates in behavior sciences. Therefore, when it comes to intervention development and implementation, the leadership team (Tier 2) and intervention team (Tier 3) must work with the teacher teams to ensure students get access to the proper behavioral intervention staff and supports. It also is critical that site and district leadership intentionally include behavior experts such as a school counselor or psychologist on these schoolwide teams. Having the site leadership and intervention teams take lead responsibility for the teaching and reteaching of essential behaviors is captured in the left side of the RTI at Work pyramid in figure 2.2.

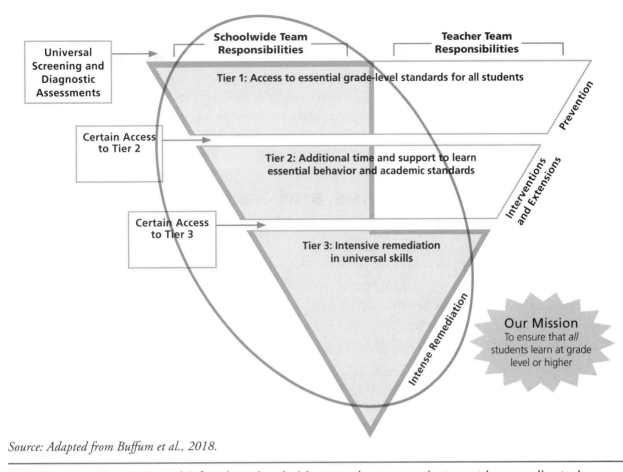

Source: Adapted from Buffum et al., 2018.

FIGURE 2.2: Tiers 1, 2, and 3 for the schoolwide team (processes that must be coordinated across the entire school).

It is important to note our use of the term *lead responsibility*—not *sole responsibility*. Collaborative teacher teams would, of course, be involved in teaching essential behaviors at Tier 1, and in implementing behavior interventions at Tier 2 and Tier 3, but they would not take lead responsibility for Tier 2 and Tier 3 behavior intervention and remediation, since those are not their areas of expertise. For example, we would not advocate for collaborative teacher teams to lead designing and implementing Tier 3 behavior remediation supports—the intervention team should take that role, as the school psychologist or counselor is usually a member of this team.

Often, the intervention team is comprised with the stakeholders mentioned because they are the content experts around behavior and they are not restricted to a classroom setting. This allows them to meet more often and develop the next level of behavior responses and supports. Likewise, teacher teams should collaborate with and follow the leadership team's lead in designing and implementing Tier 2 behavior interventions. The leadership team may include members such as an administrator, a school psychologist, a school counselor, a behavior specialist, or even a classified staff member (in organizing skill support, for example) who can help provide supplemental resources (such as reteaching opportunities).

When behavior needs beyond the Tier 1 prevention level occur in their respective grade level, department, and more, teacher teams can put interventions into place in collaboration with the leadership team, the intervention team, and other identified resources. However, functioning as a PLC with the focus on behavior will require all three team types to continually work together to address the systemic gap identified in chapter 1 (page 9) and ensure all students receive dependable and effective behavior interventions and supports that are based on multiple data points. This is why, in the PLC at Work process, we do not refer to each site team as *a PLC*—the entire school is considered the professional learning community. It will take the collective knowledge and skills of a school staff—including classroom teachers, administrators, and support staff—to ensure every student succeeds.

Team Roles and Responsibilities

The following sections further outline each team's purpose, membership, meeting frequency, and role and responsibilities as the teams do this work. The three stakeholder teams addressed throughout the next chapters include the site leadership team (Tiers 1, 2, 3), intervention team (Tier 3), and teacher teams (Tier 1 and some Tier 2). The designated chapters for Tier 1 prevention (chapter 3, page 49), Tier 2 intervention (chapter 4, page 119), and Tier 3 remediation (chapter 5, page 175) will provide additional how-to information.

We recommend that the school's leadership team serve as the site's guiding coalition— the team responsible for leading and coordinating efforts across the school. Because of this recommendation, we use the terms *leadership team* and *guiding coalition* interchangeably in this book. We advocate for two schoolwide teams: the leadership team (guiding coalition) and the intervention team. While the leadership team is a schoolwide team, it is not *the* schoolwide team.

We recommend that every team—each teacher team and (schoolwide) leadership team and intervention team—identify a team leader. Team leaders are not a group's appointed dictator; they facilitate team meetings to ensure staying focused on vital team responsibilities. To this end, it is best practice that the principal take part on both schoolwide teams (leadership and intervention). Specifics regarding leadership teams, intervention teams, and teacher teams follow.

It is critical to continuously model leading, and to reflect with your leadership team, by using the tools and processes in this book. Table 2.1 lists the kinds of behaviors (actions) team members can show to help close the systemic behavior gap. As you continue learning about each team's role and responsibilities, please look for behaviors that will help your school close the systemic behavior gap.

TABLE 2.1: Behaviors That Help Close the Systemic Behavior Gap

Communication
• Be honest.
• Be transparent.
• Explain the *why* behind actions.
• Provide clear, consistent messages.
• Solve problems by learning.
• Provide multiple streams of communication.

Collaboration

- Get ongoing stakeholder feedback.
- Provide space and time for meaningful collaboration.
- Make sure general education and special education representatives understand they are on one team.
- Alleviate busywork from staff's workload.

 Coordination

- Align resources to ensure implementation happens in a timely manner.
- Advocate and protect school processes and structures that are working.
- Ensure school master schedules support implementation.
- Ensure coverage is available for staff when needed.
- Assign specific roles and responsibilities.
- Have a contingency plan for when staff are off campus.
- Align funding to implementation.

 Capacity Building

- Provide ongoing training and implementation opportunities.
- Highlight best practices.
- Model what you want your staff to model.
- Become competent in the areas you want implemented.
- Build capacity for key implementation areas instead of supplying one-time professional development.

 Collective Ownership

- Help staff understand their roles and responsibilities toward the common goals.
- Hold all teams accountable.
- Hold yourself accountable.
- Use data to guide decisions.
- Roll up your sleeves and help.

Leadership Team (Guiding Coalition)

The leadership team is responsible for the following.

▶ Leading a schoolwide process to identify and teach essential academic and social behavior standards

▶ Ensuring that all students are taught these essential behaviors as part of their Tier 1 core instruction

- ▶ Leading coordination and alignment of tiered behavior supports across the school and in coordination with district goals and processes when the entire system commits to these practices

- ▶ Leading Tier 2 strategic interventions for behavior needs

- ▶ Working with the intervention team to lead Tier 3 resource allocation for intensive behavior remediation

The responsibilities represent essential actions that must be coordinated across the entire school and should not be left for teacher teams or administrators to make in isolation. This is why they are led by the leadership team and should include input from teachers and support staff.

Recommended members of a school leadership team might include the following.

- ▶ It is absolutely essential that the school principal lead this team. Additionally, other site administrators can serve, such as an assistant principal, dean of students, an administrative designee, or the like.

- ▶ A representative from each collaborative teacher team can serve.

- ▶ Behavior specialists, such as the school psychologist and the school counselor, might join the leadership team.

- ▶ Other key stakeholders might also be included, such as teacher union representatives, classified staff leaders, technology experts, and other well-respected staff members that provide credibility and insight to the team's recommendations.

The leadership team takes different actions at different tiers.

Tier 1

At this tier, the leadership team focuses on the schoolwide system of supports and prevention. The team members do the following to look through the lens of school-wide data review and problem solving.

- ▶ Meet as a leadership team at least monthly (potentially more, based on the schoolwide and classroom behavior data).

- ▶ Lead the school faculty in identifying the essential academic and social behaviors that all students must master for future success.

- ▶ Lead a process to systematically teach essential behavior across the school at Tier 1.

- ▶ Identify problem statements based on multiple behavioral data points (including minor and major referrals, suspensions, expulsions, student surveys, universal screeners, collaborative teacher team input, and Tier 1 classroom behavior rounds process). Detailed information on the components (such as Tier 1 classroom behavior rounds process) will be shared later in chapter 3 (page 49).

- ▶ Designate leadership team representatives who *push into* (attend) every collaborative teacher team meeting once a month, for a few minutes at least, to gather the teacher teams' input on schoolwide essential academic and social behavior trends.

- ▶ Use problem statements to develop schoolwide behavior SMART goals and actions that they implement, monitor, and improve on at least monthly.

- ▶ Share schoolwide data, goals, and actions with all stakeholders, and use stakeholder input to continue to design needed Tier 1 behavior preventions in every classroom.

The leadership team members do the following when they look through the lens of prevention and teaching.

- ▶ Lead the organization and implementation of a schoolwide process to identify and teach site-level essential academic and social behaviors.

- ▶ Coordinate resources, training, and personnel to implement schoolwide teaching of the essential academic and social behavior standards throughout the school year.

- ▶ Provide ongoing support and monitoring of the Tier 1 support structures and the collaborative teacher teams' needs.

- ▶ Ensure implementation of Tier 1 in every classroom by intentionally progress-monitoring schoolwide academic and social behavior expectations (for example, by using Tier 1 behavior rounds process, classroom observation process, or a teacher classroom evaluation process).

It is critical to know that while this book specifically focuses on creating schoolwide *behavior* supports, the school's leadership team will also have schoolwide responsibilities for supporting *academic* essential outcomes at all three tiers. These outcomes are described in *Taking Action* (Buffum et al., 2018). Due to limited meeting time, some schools create a site behavior committee, which serves as subgroup of the school's leadership team. This behavior committee, which has some members who also serve on the leadership team, work out the specific details of the outcomes listed earlier, then report their recommendations to the leadership team. Conversely, we have worked with schools that have a very small staff, with potentially one teacher at each grade level or subject. When this is the case, the leadership team responsibilities should be approached together as a faculty, using faculty meeting time to coordinate behavior efforts across the school.

Tier 2

The leadership team ensures additional time, support, structure, and reteaching opportunities at Tier 2 so students can master the essential academic and social behavior standards. Team members do the following to engage in strategic intervention, data parsing, and problem solving.

- Assign a subset of the leadership team—or discipline committee—that meets at least twice a month in addition to the schoolwide team meetings to lead schoolwide supplemental behavior interventions. These Tier 2 interventions are guided by schoolwide data points, input, and recommendations from the collaborative teacher teams.

- Identify Tier 2 problem statements based on multiple behavioral data points (including input from teacher team meetings and schoolwide data that demonstrate the need for Tier 2).

- Designate representatives from the leadership team subset who push into teacher team meetings based on requests from the teacher teams regarding Tier 2 needs. The entire leadership team needs to be in charge of planning and designing Tier 2.

- Establish a Tier 2 data-entry and data-review procedure.

- Establish a data-based process for identifying students who need Tier 2 reteaching of essential academic and social behavior standards.

- Use the behavior data wall process to identify, design, and monitor Tier 2 reteaching interventions based on schoolwide behavior data. (The data wall process is detailed in chapters 4, page 119, and 5, page 175.)

- Develop SMART goals for implementing Tier 2, which they monitor for effectiveness twice a month and update on the behavior data wall. (See detailed behavior data wall information on page 164.)

- Have a process for sharing information regarding the progress of Tier 2.

- Have a process to update and share Tier 2 information with the leadership team.

- Ensure communication among all the teams is coordinated and based on data.

- Provide the resources needed to adjust Tier 2 if the interventions are ineffective.

The team members guide interventions by doing the following.

- Administer and provide coordinated support for implementing Tier 2. (This support includes training, scheduling, resources, and human resources, including additional staff on your campus such as an aide or another staff member to help support implementation.)

- Design a targeted menu of Tier 2 interventions based on data.

- Design, implement, and monitor data-based Tier 2 behavior interventions. (Entry and exit criteria for Tier 2 behavior interventions or reteaching opportunities are discussed in chapter 4.)

▶ Ensure the collaborative teacher teams understand their role and have the supports they need as part of implementing Tier 2.

▶ Develop and deliver Tier 2 reteaching opportunities.

▶ Provide between six and eight weeks, and at least one lesson per week, of the Tier 2 reteaching opportunities.

▶ Establish a process for checking the fidelity of Tier 2 implementation.

▶ Ensure the teachers whose students receive Tier 2 continually help monitor those students in their classrooms and understand the purpose of the Tier 2 intervention and their role in the process.

▶ Have a practical process in place to communicate which students are receiving Tier 2 and to get input on and monitor these students' progress.

▶ Establish training for Tier 2 implementation and maintain a staff commitment to the need for Tier 2.

Tier 3

Leadership team members handle the allocation and coordination of resources for individualized intensive academic and behavioral remediation (developed and provided by the intervention team). Additional responsibilities follow.

▶ Make sure the Tier 3 intervention team is utilizing data to identify students who need an intensive remediation.

▶ Ensure the behavior data wall is updated based on the data from Tier 3 implementation.

▶ Ensure the communication among all the teams is coordinated and timely.

▶ Provide the resources and structures to adjust Tier 3 remediation supports as needed.

▶ Educate staff on the need for Tier 3 remediation opportunities and supports.

The following help leadership team members address intensive remediation opportunities for essential academic and social behavior standards and for students in crisis (based on a behavior's perceived function). A perceived function may include but not be limited to escape, attention seeking, sensory overstimulation, avoidance, or seeking something tangible.

▶ Ensure the intervention team has the resources it needs to develop, schedule, deliver, and monitor Tier 3 behavior interventions based on the behavior's identified function.

▶ Ensure the school has all the permissions and outside services (such as release of information between the school and outside mental health provider or doctor) it needs in order to align with the Tier 3 behavior interventions it has designed to support students.

▶ Ensure the person or persons with the highest expertise in the school or district are represented on the intervention team.

▶ Ensure Tier 3 intervention is taking place with fidelity.

Intervention Team

The intervention team is responsible for diagnosing the need for Tier 3 academic and social behavior remediation opportunities and leading these intensive remediations based on data, stakeholder input, and the school's, grade level's, or department's needs.

The essential members of an intervention team are as follows.

▶ The principal

▶ Special education teachers or representatives

▶ School behavior specialists, such as the school psychologist and the school counselor

▶ Content experts

Since the school's intervention team focuses on remediation for academic achievement and academic and social behaviors, content expertise may include reading, writing, number sense, and English language learning, and behavior interventions and supports.

If the following staff are available in your school or district, they would also participate as members of the intervention team.

▶ A social worker

▶ A speech therapist

▶ A nurse

▶ A board-certified behavior analyst

▶ A district office behavior specialist

▶ Staff with expertise in the areas that impact student success

The intervention team takes different actions at different tiers. The team's primary role is to lead Tier 3 intensive remediation for specific students, including both academic and behavior supports.

Tier 1

The intervention team does not have a specific role in Tier 1, but team members should know the schoolwide system centered around prevention and how it supports students also receiving Tier 3 intensive remediation.

▶ Coordinate with teacher teams to recommend Tier 1 preventions or accommodations for students who also receive Tier 3 intensive supports.

- ▶ Have a process for communicating progress in implementing Tier 3 behavior remediation to the leadership team and teacher teams.

- ▶ Have a structure that allows the leadership team and teacher teams to refer students for Tier 3 remediation supports in a timely way. Suggestions for structuring this will be provided later in the book.

Tier 2

The intervention team does not have a specific role in Tier 2, but team members should address strategic intervention, data collection, and problem solving as follows.

- ▶ Understand the data trends of Tier 2 intervention implementation (including data necessary for Tier 2 intervention referral and progress monitoring of effectiveness of current Tier 2 interventions implemented at the school), and coordinate all behavior interventions in all three tiers for students who need intensive behavior supports.

- ▶ Have a process for communicating progress in implementing Tier 3 behavior interventions to the leadership team and teacher teams.

- ▶ Have a structure that allows the leadership team to refer students for Tier 3 intervention supports in a timely way.

The team addresses interventions and extensions as follows.

Tier 3

Intervention team members handle individualized intensive remediation, data collecting and analyzing, and problem solving at Tier 3 with the following actions and considerations.

- ▶ Meet at least twice a month as an intervention team. (Weekly meetings are recommended, if possible.)

- ▶ Use the behavior data wall process to identify, design, and monitor the school's Tier 3 behavior interventions. (The behavior data wall process is detailed in chapters 4 and 5.)

- ▶ Develop and monitor SMART goals around Tier 3 interventions.

- ▶ Have a simple process for collecting information regarding the progress of Tier 3 behavior interventions and sharing it with the leadership team and collaborative teacher teams. For example, consider designating an intervention team member who gathers that information by pushing into a collaborative teacher team meeting based on a referral from the leadership team or the teacher team.

The intervention team members approach intensive remediation opportunities as follows.

- ▶ Design, implement, deliver, monitor, and communicate Tier 3 behavior interventions for general education and special education students.

▶ Provide daily intensive remediation teaching or social-emotional structures and support opportunities for these students to access their education.

▶ Ensure these interventions are implemented with fidelity.

▶ Work with families to connect them with and educate them on additional wraparound support services.

▶ Have a practical process in place to communicate the progress of students who are receiving Tier 3 interventions in the school.

▶ Develop a process to respond in a timely fashion if students are not responding to the Tier 3 intervention provided or if they are in crisis.

▶ Work with the leadership team to align the additional resources that will stabilize students who need Tier 3 intervention supports.

Teacher Teams

Teacher teams—the team structure advocated for in the PLC at Work process—are groups of educators who share essential learning outcomes for their students. At the elementary level, teacher teams are most likely grade-level teams, while at the secondary level, they are content- and course-specific. While teacher teams will take lead responsibility for identifying, teaching, and intervening on essential *academic* outcomes, they also have a critical role in the school's behavior processes.

Tier 1

To support schoolwide behavior outcomes, teacher teams should use part of their weekly meeting time to do the following.

▶ Work with the school leadership team and fellow faculty members to identify and teach essential academic and social behaviors at Tier 1.

▶ Allocate a portion of each meeting to take a quick inventory of the grade level or department's Tier 1 behavior needs.

▶ Collaborate and communicate with the leadership team on Tier 1 implementation needs at least monthly. For example, plan for an identified leadership team representative to push into one teacher team's meeting each month to gather teacher input on schoolwide, grade-level, or classroom Tier 1 needs.

▶ Identify students in need of Tier 2 or Tier 3 behavior support.

Teacher-team members do the following to look through the lens of prevention and teaching.

▶ Assist with the identification and teaching of essential academic and social behavior standards in their classrooms at Tier 1.

▶ Work together as a grade-level (elementary) team or a department- or course-specific (secondary) team to ensure students have access to first best Tier 1 classroom management systems in every classroom.

▶ Understand what behaviors teachers manage and have an array of Tier 1 responses.

▶ Give the leadership team designee input on Tier 1 needs and implementation at least once a month.

Tier 2

At Tier 2, teacher teams address strategic intervention, data parsing, and problem solving with the following processes and actions.

▶ Allocate a portion of each teacher team meeting to taking the pulse (checking on the student behavior needs and supports) of the grade level or department's behavior needs. See the sample minutes form (page 93), which includes a quick check-in box for Tiers 1, 2, and 3.

▶ Communicate with members of the leadership team subset about data-based Tier 2 implementation needs and supports.

▶ Communicate with the leadership team about Tier 2 effectiveness. It is critical that collaborative teacher teams tell the leadership team if an intervention is not effective, if it needs modification, or if another intervention opportunity is needed.

Teacher teams address Tier 2 interventions and extensions as follows.

▶ Understand and support the role and responsibilities of the teacher in implementing Tier 2 behavior interventions with fidelity.

▶ Understand and support the process of monitoring the progress of students receiving Tier 2 when the intervention requires teacher monitoring (CICO).

▶ Give the leadership team timely feedback on the effectiveness of Tier 2 behavior interventions or needed supports.

▶ Provide input to the designated leadership team person about Tier 2 needs and implementation at least twice a month.

▶ Use other means of timely communication if the intervention need should be addressed before the designated twice-monthly check-ins.

Tier 3

Teacher teams support individualized intensive remediation, data collecting and analyzing, and problem solving with the following actions and considerations during Tier 3 in partnership with the intervention team.

▶ Allocate a portion of each teacher team meeting to taking the pulse of the grade level or department's behavior needs. See the sample minutes form (page 93), which includes a quick check-in box for Tiers 1, 2, and 3.

▶ Communicate with or complete a referral to the intervention team when a student in the grade level or department needs intensive supports.

▶ Communicate with the intervention team if a Tier 3 remediation is not effective or needs modification, especially to prevent escalating behavior or a crisis. Understand teachers' role in implementing Tier 3 behavior remediation for general education and special education students in partnership with the assigned members of the intervention team (special education teacher, school psychologist, school counselor, school nurse, and so on). Understand the process to help implement a Tier 3 intervention and monitor student progress (such as for a student who has an individualized education program [IEP] with a behavior plan and behavior goal in place).

Table 2.2 guides teams on how they can communicate about behavior in order to avoid the systemic behavior gap.

TABLE 2.2: Teacher Team Communication per Tier

Tier 1: How is collaborative teacher teams' input collected?	
Monthly	**Ongoing**
A designated representative (this can be the same leadership team member or a different leadership team member can be assigned to different teacher teams) from the *leadership team* pushes into every teacher team meeting at least once a month to collect teacher input on Tier 1 prevention implementation.	The *leadership team* and *teacher teams* have a shared Google document (such as Tier 1 Teacher Team Minutes) that includes a box for teacher input gathered at every teacher team meeting).

Tier 2: How is collaborative teacher teams' input collected?		
At least monthly	**When requested**	**Ongoing**
The *leadership team* representative who pushes into every teacher team meeting monthly to gather Tiers 1, 2, and 3 input shares the information regarding Tier 2 with the designated representative from the leadership team's Tier 2 subset.	The designated representative from the Tier 2 subset of the *leadership team* pushes into a teacher team meeting when the team makes a request for Tier 2 support, such as "I need a Tier 2 behavior referral."	The *leadership team* and *teacher teams* have a shared Google document (such as Tier 2 Teacher Team Minutes) that includes a behavior box for teacher input and student identification gathered at every teacher team meeting).

Tier 3: How is collaborative teacher teams' input collected?		
At least monthly	**When requested**	**Ongoing**
The *leadership team* representative who pushes into every teacher team meeting monthly to gather Tiers 1, 2, and 3 input shares the information regarding Tier 3 with the designated representative from the *intervention team*.	A designated representative from the *intervention team* pushes into a teacher team meeting when the team makes a request for Tier 3 intervention support, such as "I need a Tier 3 behavior referral."	The *leadership team, intervention team*, and *teacher teams* have a shared Google document (such as Tier 3 Teacher Team Minutes that includes a behavior box for teacher input and student identification gathered at every teacher team meeting).

*Visit **go.SolutionTree.com/RTIatWork** for a free reproducible version of this table.*

Although all the teams must continue to take collective ownership where academic and social behavior skills are concerned, it is essential that the school's or district's behavior experts or specialists work efficiently and effectively at all tiers—especially with designing, implementing, and monitoring Tier 2 and Tier 3 behavior interventions and remediation supports.

Conclusion

This chapter has outlined the core foundation of RTI work in your school: the understanding and purpose, membership, meeting frequency, and roles and responsibilities of each team, and how to use the RTI process to provide behavior supports. With this core foundation in place, schools can delve deeper into the essential actions necessary to successfully implement behavior supports in each tier.

You will find the *how* for functioning as a PLC with the focus on behavior and using RTI for assigning essential academic and social behavior responses in each tier of support. Now it is time to learn how a PLC with the focus on behavior can utilize a Tier 1 prevention cycle. This cycle will assist you with conceptualizing and implementing Tier 1 essential behavior outcomes from both the schoolwide and classroom levels.

CHAPTER 3

Implementing Behavior Solutions at Tier 1—Prevention

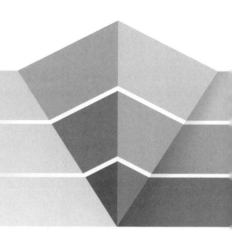

In regard to behavior skills, Tier 1 focuses on providing access to—or teaching—essential academic and social behavior standards for all students schoolwide. The stronger the Tier 1 focus, the fewer students will need Tier 2 and Tier 3 support (Buffum et al., 2018; Lane et al., 2010).

Functioning as a PLC and using RTI practices at Tier 1 helps schools identify and avoid common implementation challenges related to behavior standards. Specifically, in this chapter, we highlight the essential academic and social behavior standards and provide a Tier 1 prevention cycle. We will explore the following questions and others in this chapter.

- ▶ How do we identify Tier 1 essential academic and social behavior standards?

- ▶ How do we align the identified essential academic and social behaviors in a tiered approach?

- ▶ What are everyone's roles and responsibilities in Tier 1 implementation?

- ▶ What is the connection between PLCs and RTI for behavior?

- ▶ What does *function as a PLC* mean?

- ▶ What does Tier 1 mean in regard to behavior skills and standards?

- ▶ What does Tier 1 look like schoolwide and in individual classrooms?

- ▶ Where do we start?

- ▶ How will implementation help address the systemic behavior gap?

Tier 1 implementation challenges will arise. As a result, the questions that we propose in this chapter are intentionally designed to push your thinking deeper and align priorities and accountability with clear targets and best practices for teaching behavior skills. In addition to helping you overcome those challenges, this chapter helps your teams begin addressing the systemic behavior gap. This requires that you build the Tier 1 foundation of prevention schoolwide and in every classroom, which begins with identifying what you universally want students to learn and demonstrate with essential academic and social behaviors.

In this chapter, we will provide an overview of Tier 1 implementation challenges and walk you through how to assign RTI Tier 1 prevention. Specifically, we will provide information on how to apply the Tier 1 prevention cycle schoolwide and in every classroom.

Tier 1 Implementation Challenges

Tier 1 presents some challenges that appear in all tiers, and some that are specific to it. Common Tier 1 implementation challenges include the following, and each is discussed here in turn.

▶ Educators struggle to address the increasing number of students who have social, emotional, and behavioral difficulties (Prothero, 2020).

▶ There is a disproportionate amount of time spent serving a small number of students with social, emotional, and behavior difficulties (Saeki et al., 2011).

▶ Schools commonly address social, emotional, and behavior difficulties with exclusionary practices such as detention, suspension, and expulsion (Skiba & Rauch, 2006).

The PLC and RTI Processes for Behavior in Tier 1

Just as schools function as a PLC and utilize RTI to ensure academic success for all students, schools need to function the same way to ensure behavioral and social-emotional supports for all students. As mentioned previously, four critical questions drive collaboration in the PLC at Work process:

1. What knowledge, skills, and dispositions should every student acquire as a result of this unit, this course, or this grade level?

2. How will we know when each student has acquired the essential knowledge and skills?

3. How will we respond when some students do not learn?

4. How will we extend the learning for students who are already proficient? (DuFour et al., 2016, p. 36)

These same questions should guide collaboration focused on essential behaviors. But unlike academic standards—where each teacher team takes lead responsibility to answer these questions for their shared grade or course—for behavior outcomes, these questions should be answered collectively as a staff. This is because essential core behaviors should be taught and reinforced across the entire school—in every grade, subject, and location on campus.

To specifically apply this structure to behavior, schools must understand the following.

▶ Tier 1's focus is to provide access to (teach) essential academic and social behavior standards for all students schoolwide and in every classroom (prevention).

▶ Tier 2's focus is to provide additional reteaching (intervention) opportunities and supports to help students learn and demonstrate the taught essential academic and social behavior standards.

▶ Tier 3's focus is to provide frequent intensive interventions (remediation) based on the behavior's function and to give structures and supports for the identified essential academic or social behavior standards.

Tier 1 provides access to instruction on essential academic and social behavior standards to all students schoolwide and in every classroom. Because the reproducible "RTI at Work—Culminating Exercise" (page 246) serves as one of this book's culminating activities, let's dig deeper into the essential academic and social behavior components in the design for each tier, beginning with Tier 1—prevention.

By the end of this chapter, you will learn how to complete the circled empty spaces in figure 3.1 (page 52) as part of the culminating activity for Tier 1. Specifically, you will insert into the "RTI at Work Pyramid: Tier 1" (page 117) the Tier 1 behaviors, conditions, and responsibilities of the schoolwide team and teacher teams.

Similar to academics, there are essential standards for behavior. Although the leadership team leads prevention for behavior, the staff will work collaboratively to establish the behaviors and conditions for students to learn and demonstrate these essential academic and social behavior standards schoolwide and in every classroom as part of Tier 1 prevention.

Because students do not traditionally take district benchmark assessments or year-end state or provincial accountability assessments on academic and social behavior, schools need a way—beyond reviewing school discipline data—to gather evidence of how well students are mastering essential behaviors. And the essential behavior standards need to incorporate both skill-based and will-based behaviors.

Consider this: for academic instruction, the first question teacher teams in a PLC ask is "What is it we want our students to know and be able to do?" (DuFour et al., 2016, p. 59). Teacher teams answer this question when they determine essential academic standards and learning targets and decide what mastery for each standard looks like. They design lessons with first best instruction in Tier 1, and the school provides all students access to a guaranteed and viable curriculum aligned to state or provincial standards.

However, when a school faculty considers this same question for behavior, they often meet it with uncertainty and obscurity. If you were to walk into five different schools

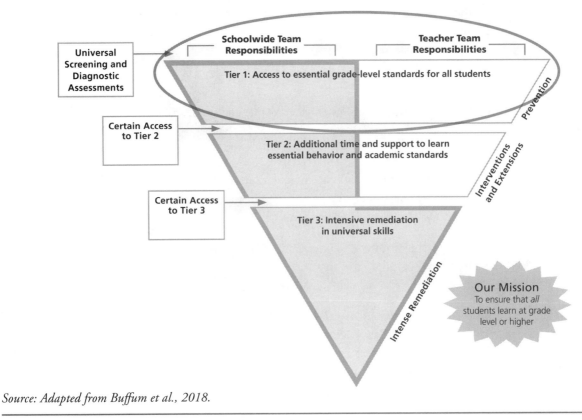

Source: Adapted from Buffum et al., 2018.

FIGURE 3.1: Culminating pyramid reference (Tier 1).

and ask, "What are the essential academic and social behavior standards you want students to learn and demonstrate?" you would probably get five different responses. The following is our unified response based on the RTI at Work process.

Essential Academic and Social Behavior Standards

Essential academic and social behavior standards are as much a part of the schoolwide and classroom foundations as essential academic standards are. Establishing a Tier 1 foundation of prevention for behavior includes creating schoolwide standards (for all settings and events at the school) based on schoolwide data points and in every classroom every day. Tier 1 best practices for teaching essential academic and social behaviors should be based on grade-level and department behavior data trends and needs.

As a note of caution, no matter what essential behavior standards the school decides to teach or what method is decided to teach them schoolwide, it is critical that all staff understand the *why* and the relationship between PLCs and RTI. This way, you can avoid misconceptions and pushback. For example, telling staff it is mandatory to teach social-emotional lessons by just providing the curriculum toolkit and then stating, "Every morning, someone will be walking through classrooms with a clipboard to monitor that social-emotional learning lessons and morning classroom meetings are taking place," is not the best approach because they will not understand the purpose, aim, and relationship to the schoolwide essential academic and social behavior standards for prevention.

As a reminder, we use the term *behavior* interchangeably with *essential academic and social behaviors*, as defined in *Taking Action* (Buffum et al., 2018). Table 3.1 lists the essential academic and social behaviors.

TABLE 3.1: Essential Academic and Social Behaviors

Academic Behaviors	Social Behaviors
In addition to academic skills and knowledge, some academic behaviors are critical to school and career success.	Success in school and career requires the ability to consistently demonstrate socially appropriate behaviors.
Metacognition: Knowledge and beliefs about thinking **Self-concept:** A student's belief in his or her abilities **Self-monitoring:** The ability to plan and prepare for learning **Motivation:** The ability to initiate and maintain interest in tasks **Strategy:** Techniques for organizing and memorizing knowledge **Volition:** The efforts and techniques needed to stay motivated and engaged in learning (Many educators refer to this as demonstrating *grit*.)	**Responsible verbal and physical interactions with peers and adults:** Skills that demonstrate social responsibility, honesty, compassion, respect, self-regulation, and self-control **Appropriate language:** Skills that demonstrate self-awareness, communication, civility, and character **Respect for property and materials:** Skills that demonstrate empathy and respect **Independently staying on a required task:** Skills that demonstrate on-task behavior **Regular attendance:** Skills that demonstrate punctuality, time management, and accountability

Source: Adapted from Buffum et al., 2018.

*Visit **go.SolutionTree.com/RTIatWork** for a free reproducible version of this table.*

The leadership team should use these definitions as a guide when deciding what essential academicand social behaviors students need to learn and demonstrate. In the end, it is critical for each school to create a list of essential behaviors that have the following characteristics.

- ▶ **Research based:** In a PLC at Work process, professionals make decisions by first committing to collective inquiry—learning together. They do not guess when determining which specific behaviors are more important to their students' future success, nor do they average opinions. Instead, they seek relevant research on which to base their decision. The lists provided in this book are an excellent starting point, but they are not definitive.

- ▶ **Site relevant:** The ethnic, regional, religious, and historical uniqueness of the students and community must be considered, helping students bridge the expectations of home and school. For example, we have worked with Native American schools and everyone honored the local tribe's values when selecting essential behaviors. Likewise, we have worked in schools where most of the students came from neighborhoods of deep ethnic diversity. Sometimes, these differences created violent confrontations in the community. These schools determined that respecting cultural diversity was an essential social behavior within the school.

- ▶ **Doable:** When a school selects essential behavior standards, educators are not going to just list or teach them—the staff is making a collective commitment to ensure every student masters every behavior. A school's collective list of essential behaviors—academic and social—must be succinct enough for students to memorize them all, and for the school to be able to intervene on all of them.

Finally, it is unlikely that a faculty will select the "perfect" list of behaviors on their first attempt. Being a PLC is a never-ending cycle of continuous improvement. When a leadership team engages the faculty in essential behavior identifications, it should also acknowledge that this task will be a work in progress and determine how they will purposefully review and revise these outcomes over time.

We are confident this work is essential for building a strong Tier 1 foundation for behavior. We have triangulated these academic and social behavior standards with 21st century skills, federal- and state-level teacher and administrator expectations, best-practice behavior initiative outcomes, teacher and administrator evaluation processes, district and school accountability measures, and our fellow practitioners' and colleagues' collective experiences.

Alignment With Existing Behavior Initiatives

We want to point out how inclusive existing behavior initiatives are to addressing essential academic and social behavior standards before we go through the Tier 1 prevention cycle. Teaching essential academic and social behaviors are not limited to one setting, one method, one behavior program or initiative, one type of behavior challenge or student profile, or one teaching style. In fact, schools can systematically implement and embed academic and social behavior learning opportunities, initiatives, and interventions across a school system and all settings for all levels of student needs (similar to how schools address academic needs—through prevention, intervention, and remediation).

Critically, you must teach the essential academic and social behavior standards to all students and use them as a universal guide to Tier 1 prevention in the school. However, *how* you teach these standards is not limited to one program or initiative. Rest assured, you can utilize existing behavior curriculum, already-developed behavior lessons, or other teaching methods from a variety of behavior initiatives to teach these essential standards schoolwide. Behavior initiatives should not compete with each other. We witness many schools or districts chasing the next best thing to implement in the form of behavior initiatives. What we will demonstrate here is a *process* for responding to students' behavior needs—a process that accommodates any behavior initiative currently implemented on your campus. Your leadership team can decide what meets your school's needs based on data. You can also include other preventive standards, values, and skills that align with your current initiative to help teach, reteach, intervene, or remediate.

For example, the Collaborative for Academic, Social, and Emotional Learning (CASEL; www.casel.org) is a social-emotional learning (SEL) behavior initiative that preidentifies core competencies; Character Counts (www.charactercounts.org) offers character education with a set of preidentified character pillars; and the PBIS (www.pbis.org) framework allows schools to select between three and five behavior expectations. Some behavior initiatives fit nicely into a tiered system for behavior. In fact, we usually find that when behavior initiatives are not delivered in a tiered manner, schools do not deliver them with fidelity for all students. Based on our collective experiences with this work, we find that it does not matter what behavior initiative or combination of initiatives a school is implementing; a tiered approach will improve its delivery.

It does not matter if you are implementing PBIS, SEL, trauma-informed practices, culturally responsive teaching, character education, restorative justice, or a combination of behavior initiatives; you need to implement a tiered system of supports. A tiered system creates the structure in which teachers can use behavior data to decide how they can best support their students for whichever behavior initiative frame your schoolwide team decides is best for prevention on your campus.

If your school has one or more existing behavior initiatives in place, utilize our quick cross-check guide to see how the essential academic and social behavior standards compare with the pre-existing behavior initiative. The guide helps you realize the connection between each initiative and the identified standards. Figure 3.2 is an example of how you may use the guide to cross-check the standards.

Cross-Check: PBIS		
Pre-Existing Behavior Initiative	Essential Academic and Social Behavior Standards (Buffum et al., 2018)	Comparison *Does the behavior initiative align with at least two essential academic behavior standards and two essential social behavior standards?*
PBIS • Self-control • On-task • Achievement • Respect	**Academic Behaviors** • Metacognition • Self-concept • Self-monitoring • Motivation • Strategy • Volition	• Self-control • Achievement
	Social Behaviors • Responsible verbal and physical interactions with peers and adults • Appropriate language • Respect for property and materials • Independently staying on a required task • Regular attendance	• On task • Respect

FIGURE 3.2: Sample guide for cross-checking PBIS with the essential academic and social behavior standards.

As you cross-check how existing behavior initiatives or programs align with the standards, keep in mind we recommend that behavior initiatives align with at least two standards from the essential academic behavior list and at least two standards from the essential social behavior list.

Finally, one very important caution: a school's behavior initiatives should be a vehicle for teaching agreed-on academic and social behaviors across the school and in every classroom, but the behavior initiatives or programs themselves do not replace the need for faculty to determine and define essential academic and social behavior standards (prevention). Using pre-existing behavior programs or frameworks as the entire source for a school's behavior system, and subsequently removing the faculty from co-creating any of the school's behavior targets and processes, would be a mistake. Engaging the faculty in collective inquiry about essential behaviors builds understanding and commitment to the school's behavioral processes.

In the next section, you will find the Tier 1 prevention cycle with the Plan–Do–Study–Act cycle similar to what you will find in chapters 4 and 5. However, because Tier 1 has two response levels—(1) schoolwide teaching of essential academic and social behaviors and (2) classroom-level teaching of essential academic and social behaviors—you will also find what we refer to as the *Tier 1 classroom prevention cycle*.

Tier 1 Prevention Cycle (Schoolwide)

The Tier 1 prevention cycle conceptualizes what we refer to as *functioning as a PLC with the focus on behavior* with regard to behavior at Tier 1 RTI schoolwide. It focuses your collaborative efforts on ensuring all students learn essential behaviors and providing Tier 1 prevention schoolwide based on student data. Figure 3.3 shows the cycle and where it exists in the RTI at Work pyramid.

The leadership team employs this cycle while referring to current schoolwide behavior data. From those data, the leadership team decides on the Tier 1 prevention supports needed schoolwide and in every classroom. The following sections highlight the plan, do, study, and act stages (Deming, 1993) in greater depth, as well as commonly asked questions about the stages and processes, tools, and resources to help in each. Reference the purposes, roles, and responsibilities for Tier 1 identified in chapter 2 (page 36) as you apply this cycle in your PLC.

The reproducible "Helpful Processes, Tools, and Forms" (page 58) is where you can record the tier and make notes about the processes, tools, and forms you find most helpful for each stage of the Plan–Do–Study–Act cycle. Also, remember, we have provided best practice processes, tools, and forms from our collective experiences, but you can incorporate others that will help you.

Plan: Select and align Tier 1 essential academic and social behavior standards based on Tier 1 schoolwide behavior needs and staff input.

Who is responsible? The leadership team, based on schoolwide data and teacher input

Act: Implement actions and continuously improve based on the data; begin the cycle at least monthly; and modify, add to, or strengthen schoolwide or classroom-level teaching of identified essential academic and social behavior standards.

Who is responsible? The leadership team and teachers

Tier 1 Prevention
Essential Academic and Social Behaviors

Academic Behaviors		
Metacognition	Self-concept	Self-monitoring
Motivation	Strategy	Volition

Social Behaviors
Responsible verbal and physical interactions with peers and adults
Appropriate language
Respect for property and materials
Independently staying on a required task
Regular attendance

Do: Teach the identified essential academic and social behavior standards schoolwide and in every classroom.

Who is responsible? The leadership team and classroom teachers, based on schoolwide data

Study: Analyze schoolwide academic and social behavior data, SMART goals, and the fidelity with which Tier 1 teaching of essential academic and social behavior standards is implemented schoolwide and at the classroom level.

Who is responsible? The leadership team, based on staff input

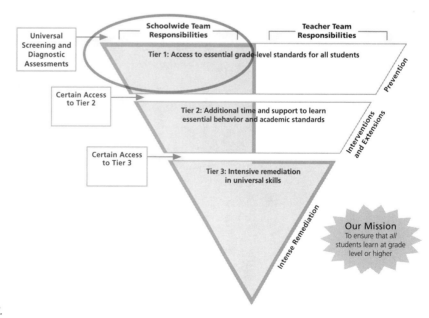

Source: Adapted from Buffum et al., 2018.

FIGURE 3.3: Tier 1 prevention cycle.

Helpful Processes, Tools, and Forms

Tier	
Plan	**Do**
Study	**Act**

Behavior Solutions © 2021 Solution Tree Press • SolutionTree.com

Visit **go.SolutionTree.com/RTIatWork** to download this free reproducible.

PLAN–Do–Study–Act

In the plan stage of the prevention cycle (highlighted in figure 3.4), you will learn how to develop a plan to carry out as a schoolwide team toward your intended outcomes.

▸ **Why:** To select and align Tier 1 essential academic and social behavior standards based on Tier 1 schoolwide and classroom behavior data and staff input

▸ **Who:** The leadership team with teacher team input

▸ **What:** Planning and coordinating the instruction of essential academic and social behavior standards schoolwide and in each classroom based on data

▸ **When:** At least monthly as a leadership team (potentially more based on schoolwide and classroom behavior data)

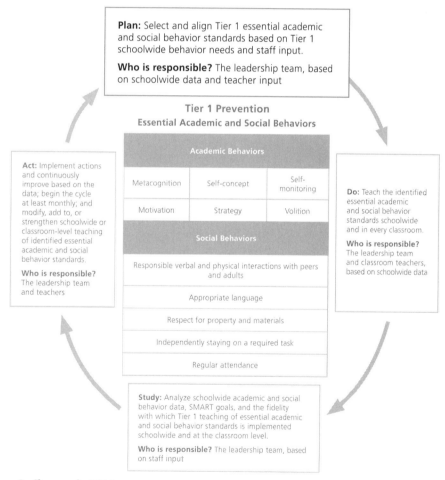

Source: Adapted from Buffum et al., 2018.

FIGURE 3.4: Tier 1 plan stage.

Commonly Asked Questions in the Plan Stage

Consider these questions.

▸ How do we decide which Tier 1 academic and social behavior standards to teach?

▶ How do we unwrap what these identified behavior standards look like?

▶ Who is responsible for coordinating and preparing the resources needed to teach these standards?

▶ What role do teachers play in teaching these standards?

▶ Do teachers have a voice in what is essential to the students in their classrooms?

▶ What if we already have a set of behavior expectations, SEL competencies, or character virtues identified as essential?

Tier 1 Plan Stage: Processes, Tools, and Forms

In this section, you will find processes, tools, and forms designed to help you begin the work in the plan stage.

Essential Academic and Social Behavior Standards Rubric

This rubric is where your teams identify and define what evidence they require for student mastery of academic and social behavior standards. The leadership team is responsible for creating a process, including faculty input, to do this. The leadership team alone may or may not initially determine this. The leadership team might create a task force or committee to first work on this, then bring recommendations to the faculty; or, they can use faculty meeting time for the whole staff to work on this. Each of the academic and social behavior standards listed also provides examples of some of the influences that accelerate to considerably accelerate student learning for which Hattie (2019) has determined effect sizes. Remember, an effect size of 0.5 is the equivalent of up to one year's growth in students' learning.

In the three blank columns on the right of figure 3.5, your leadership team, with input from teacher teams, will insert mastery indicators for the following levels.

▶ **Internalized mastery:** Student independently demonstrates

▶ **Emergent mastery:** Student demonstrates with prompt or cue

▶ **Minimal to no mastery:** Student inconsistently demonstrates or does not demonstrate

This rubric is blank to allow each leadership team to select developmentally appropriate mastery indicators reflective of its campus. For example, self-monitoring looks different for a kindergartener at an elementary school than it does for an alternative education student or for a senior in comprehensive high school.

Skills Connected to Each Standard (Hattie [2019] effect sizes)	Internalized Mastery Student independently demonstrates (2)	Emergent Mastery Student demonstrates with prompt or cue (1)	Minimal to No Mastery Student inconsistently demonstrates or does not demonstrate (0)
Academic behavior standard 1.1: Metacognition—knowledge and beliefs about thinking			
Transfer strategies = 0.86			
Elaboration and organization = 0.75			
Evaluation and reflection = 0.75			
Help seeking = 0.72			
Metacognitive strategies = 0.55			
Strategy monitoring = 0.58			
Self-verbalization and self-questioning = 0.59			
Self-regulation strategies = 0.52			
Academic behavior standard 1.2: Self-concept—a student's belief in his or her abilities			
Self-efficacy = 0.71			
Positive self-concept = 0.47			
Academic behavior standard 1.3: Self-monitoring—the ability to plan and prepare for learning			
Planning and prediction = 0.76			
Effort management = 0.77			
Strategy monitoring = 0.58			
Academic behavior standard 1.4: Motivation—the ability to initiate and maintain interest in tasks			
Effort = 0.77			
Deep motivation = 0.57			
Student expectations = 0.68			

Source for standard: Buffum et al., 2018.

continued →

FIGURE 3.5: Essential academic and social behavior rubric.

Visit go.SolutionTree.com/RTIatWork for a free reproducible version of this figure.

Academic behavior standard 1.5: Strategy—techniques for organizing and memorizing knowledge

Elaboration and organization = 0.75

Cognitive task analysis = 1.29

Academic behavior standard 1.6: Volition—the efforts and techniques needed to stay motivated and engaged in learning; also known as *grit*

Rehearsal and memorization = 0.73

Concentration, persistence, and engagement = 0.54

Deliberate practice = 0.79

Social behavior standard 2.1: Responsible verbal and physical interactions with peers and adults—social responsibility, honesty, compassion, respect, self-regulation, and self-control

Self-regulation strategies = 0.52

Self-verbalization and self-questioning = 0.59

Strategy monitoring = 0.58

Social behavior standard 2.2: Appropriate language—skills that demonstrate self-awareness, communication, civility, and character

Strategy monitoring = 0.58

Self-regulation strategies = 0.52

Social behavior standard 2.3: Respect for property and materials—skills that demonstrate empathy and respect

Strategy monitoring = 0.58

Social behavior standard 2.4: Independently staying on a required task—skills that demonstrate on-task behavior and self-monitoring

Time on task = 0.44

Concentration, persistence, and engagement = 0.54

Strategy monitoring = 0.58

Social behavior standard 2.5: Regular attendance—skills that demonstrate punctuality, time management, and accountability

Strategy monitoring = 0.58

To simplify the process of identifying and defining a universal set of Tier 1 essential academic and social behavior standards in this stage, we built on the essential academic and social behavior definitions from *Taking Action* (Buffum et al., 2018) and included examples of some influences that considerably accelerate student learning per Hattie's (2019) effect sizes. Remember that we use the essential academic and social behavior standards, but you can also use standards embedded in your pre-existing behavior initiatives. Figure 3.6 (page 64) shows one PBIS example using the schoolwide behavior expectation SOAR and its matrix outlined for all locations of the school. This is one example of how a schoolwide team identified—with the input from their teacher teams and other school staff stakeholders—the school's essential academic and social behavior standards in all locations. Although the SOAR matrix does not cover exactly the universal essential academic and social behavior standards we provide; it captures the purpose and aim of the schoolwide team in the plan stage as they have identified their schoolwide and classroom essential academic and social behavior standards. It also meets the cross-check criteria. In addition, this matrix serves as a teaching tool schoolwide and in every location of the school.

Academic and Social Behavior Priority Forced Rating Scale

The scale helps identify and prioritize the academic and social behavior standards educators will be teaching based on student, grade-level, or department need. Although this scale is designed to help prioritize the comprehensive list of academic and social behaviors based on your school's data and stakeholder input, it does not represent the only behaviors students will learn. This tool allows each teacher team to provide input to the leadership team as they organize the schoolwide efforts of teaching the prioritized essential behavior standards.

Follow these three steps.

1. Each team member gets a list of items and criteria to rank.

2. When team members are finished ranking independently, someone tallies the rankings for both the academic list and social behavior list.

3. The team finds consensus on what the highest-priority skill is. *The lowest total score is the highest priority.* Figure 3.7 (page 65) is an example.

SOAR in All Locations	Classroom	Hallway	Playground	Cafeteria	Bathroom	Library	Office	Technology
S Is for Self-Control	• Keep your hands and feet to yourself. • Use materials appropriately. • Use a quiet voice.	• Be aware of others. • Face forward in line. • Walk at all times.	• Keep your hands and feet to yourself. • Be aware of activities around you. • Listen for the whistle to stop.	• Walk at all times. • Stay seated with your feet on the floor. • Stand in line. • Wait patiently.	• Walk at all times. • Keep your hands and feet to yourself. • Use a quiet voice.	• Use space safely. • Keep shelves neat. • Use your own space. • Use a quiet voice.	• Walk quietly. • Sit silently and appropriately on office furniture. • Be polite to office staff.	• Use devices with clean hands. • Handle devices with care. • Only use technology as directed by the teacher.
O Is for On Task	• Be on time. • Follow directions. • Listen attentively. • Be willing to participate and answer questions.	• Listen to teachers' directions. • Be in the right place at the right time.	• Follow rules. • Line up when called. • Face forward in line. • Stay in line when walking in and out of buildings.	• Eat food carefully. • Throw away all trash and disposable trays. • Clean up your eating area.	• Use the facilities appropriately (water, soap, paper towel). • Quickly return to your previous location.	• Look at the speaker. • Ask questions for clarification. • Complete tasks.	• Listen to office staff. • Complete tasks or errands quickly.	• Attend to tasks on devices as assigned by the teacher. • Return devices to the appropriate location after use.
A Is for Achievement	• Give your best effort. • Be prepared and ready to learn. • Do your personal best.	• Go directly to your destination. • Walk with a purpose.	• Line up quickly to be able to return to class. • Be alert. • Strive to make friends with others.	• Raise your hand for help. • Leave your area as clean or cleaner than before.	• Quickly use the facilities to be able to return to class.	• Meet reading goals • Know your reading level. • Leave tables and shelves neat and tidy.	• Work quietly on all assignments or tasks.	• Be prepared to learn new technological activities or tasks. • Use devices for academic purposes only.
R Is for Respect	• Treat others as you want to be treated. • Use kind words. • Help and share with others.	• Use a quiet voice. • Keep your hands and feet to yourself. • Respect other students and staff.	• Put litter in the garbage can. • Use all equipment properly. • Invite others to join in. • Take turns. • Report problems to an adult.	• Use an inside voice. • Keep your hands and feet to yourself. • Use kind words.	• Keep the facilities clean. • Wait your turn. • Flush. • Wash your hands.	• Turn in all books on time. • Log off the computer when you're done. • Use a quiet voice.	• Enter quietly. • Wait patiently for an adult. • Use positive greetings, and say, "Thank you," after being helped.	• Share or take turns on devices. • Use all equipment properly. • Charge a device when the battery is low.

Source: Hannigan & Hauser, 2015.

FIGURE 3.6: Behavior matrix aligned with academic and social behavior standards—example.

Team or individual completing rating scale: *Grade 5 teacher team (four team members)*

Date: *September 21, 2020*

Academic Behaviors	Team member one	Team member two	Team member three	Team member four	Overall rank order score 1 = highest priority 6 = lowest priority
Metacognition	4	5	6	5	20
Self-concept	5	4	4	4	17
Self-monitoring	1	1	1	2	5
Motivation	2	3	2	1	8
Strategy	3	2	3	3	11
Volition (grit)	6	6	5	6	23

Highest priority academic behavior: *self-monitoring*

Social Behaviors	Team member one	Team member two	Team member three	Team member four	Overall rank order score 1 = highest priority 5 = lowest priority
Responsible verbal and physical interactions with peers and adults	2	2	1	3	8
Appropriate language	1	1	2	1	5
Respect for property and materials	3	4	3	2	12
Independently staying on a required task	4	3	4	5	16
Regular attendance	5	5	5	4	19

Highest priority social behavior: *Appropriate language*

FIGURE 3.7: Academic and social behavior priority forced rating scale—example.

Visit go.SolutionTree.com/RTIatWork for a free reproducible version of this figure.

Plan–DO–Study–Act

In the do stage of the prevention cycle (highlighted in figure 3.8), begin teaching the identified essential behavior standards based on student needs. In the do stage, it is important to note, you will find the information you need to include in the teacher team section of the reproducible "RTI at Work Pyramid: Tier 1" (page 117). Specifically, refer to the Tier 1 prevention cycle.

▸ **Why:** To teach identified essential academic and social behavior standards schoolwide and in every classroom

▸ **Who:** The leadership team and teacher teams

▸ **What:** Teaching identified essential academic and social behavior standards schoolwide and in every classroom through a variety of methods and ensuring up-to-date data are collected to make informed decisions about what standards need to be taught or reinforced

▸ **When:** At least monthly and potentially more based on the schoolwide and classroom data trends (such as a trend in hands-on behavior schoolwide that requires the schoolwide team to meet to develop an RTI prevention response prior to the next schoolwide team meeting)

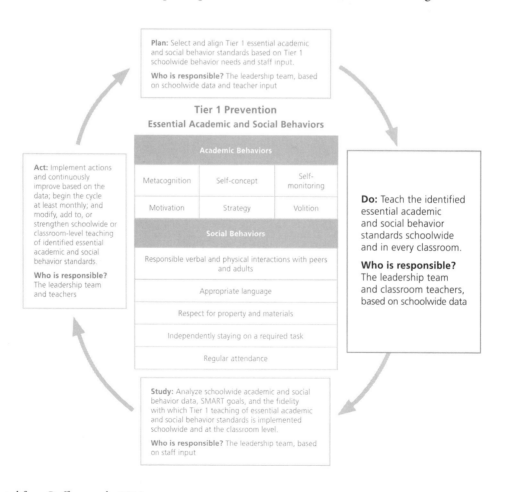

Source: Adapted from Buffum et al., 2018.

FIGURE 3.8: Tier 1 do stage.

Commonly Asked Questions in the Do Stage

Consider these questions.

▸ What does it look like in practice to meet the Tier 1 focus of providing all students access to essential academic and social behavior standards?

▸ Who teaches the essential standards schoolwide? Who teaches them in every classroom? How often do they teach them?

▸ What is the difference between schoolwide teaching or implementation and classroom teaching or implementation of these standards?

▸ What happens if we already have schoolwide behavior expectations selected?

Tier 1 Do Stage: Processes, Tools, and Forms

In this section, you will find processes, tools, and forms designed to help you begin the work in the do stage. They are not presented in order of importance, so we recommend reading through all of them and decide what process, tool, or form may help your school team.

What Teaching Essential Academic and Social Behavior Standards May Look Like

Essentially, Tier 1 schoolwide teaching and *booster* lessons (additional doses of teaching the standards that prevent the need for behavior interventions) are based on schoolwide data. Classroom teachers and others can deliver these lessons in a variety of formats. For example, teaching can look like any of the following.

▸ The leadership team ensures the school has a clearly defined process to teach the essential academic and social behaviors to all students across all school environments (including in non-classroom settings).

▸ The leadership team should create a process to push identified staff into the classroom level to teach or provide schoolwide teaching strategies such as videos, rallies, behavior teaching passport days, lessons, or classroom meetings.

▸ Classroom teachers can deliver and ensure teaching of essential academic and social behaviors expected in their classroom consistently. The leadership team should monitor this to ensure it is happening in every class. For example, if the schoolwide-identified need from figure 3.7 (page 65) centers on classroom respect, then the booster could involve teachers' developing and delivering a classroom respect agreement with student input and having all students sign the classroom respect agreement as their commitment to following it.

▸ Students can teach students by modeling expected academic and social behaviors.

Teaching behavior skills at the schoolwide level will look different from teaching them at the classroom level, of course. The leadership team coordinates and teaches *schoolwide* essential academic and social behavior standards with the following in mind.

▶ Schedule at least two intentional times yearly in all of a school's locations and additional reteaching based on schoolwide data trends.

▶ Include what is expected (how to treat each other) in all settings and the resources provided for schoolwide behavioral supports (such schoolwide teaching passport days, where schoolwide teaching stations are designed for learning and applying what is expected in all settings).

▶ Additional schoolwide suggestions follow.

• Course syllabi to include schoolwide essential academic and social behavior standards

• Schoolwide videos

• Announcements (such as those focused on identified schoolwide academic and social behavior needs)

• Newsletters

• Projects (such as service learning and schoolwide-need-focused campaigns, such as a digital citizenship)

• School challenges, such as a kindness or an upstander challenge

• Peer mediators for conflict resolution opportunities

• Students teaching students

• Social media campaigns

• Common schoolwide lessons based on schoolwide data needs (such as trend in hands-on behavior across the school)

With prevention content coordinated by the leadership team with staff input, classroom teachers teach classroom-level essential academic and social behavior standards with this in mind: frequently teach in every classroom as part of Tier 1 prevention and additional reteaching (booster sessions) based on schoolwide data trends. Table 3.2 lists and describes Tier 1 classroom-level behavior teaching opportunities.

We are often asked what the specific classroom role is in the schoolwide prevention cycle. Administrators face the frustration of teachers not feeling supported in situations with their most challenging students—situations where administrators may feel that teachers could have taken a few more preventative, rather than reactive steps. We also face the realization that beyond one classroom-management course in college teacher-preparation programs, teachers receive few tools that will support them.

TABLE 3.2: Tier 1 Classroom-Level Behavior Teaching Opportunities

Approach	Example or Explanation
Behavior-specific lessons	Short behavior lessons provided to classroom teachers by the schoolwide leadership team with direction and timeline for how and when to teach them
General lessons embedded with behavior teaching	Character and civic education components of general curriculum (such as discussions or assignments based on character development or civic responsibility)
Classroom meetings or circle time	Short meetings designed to encourage student voice for how to solve challenges at the classroom, school, or community levels
Homeroom or advisory	Designated time (commonly in secondary level) on developing relationships with students and practicing academic and social behaviors
Respect agreements	Behavior agreements co-developed jointly by students and teachers, with the focus on respect or expected behaviors in the classroom toward each other and the general community
Behavior standards review	Classwide review of classroom norms, expectations, or standards to focus on areas where additional teaching supports are needed (for example, how students work collaboratively on projects, how to respect other people's views, or how to practice being resilient when situations get tough)
Project-based learning	Can focus on essential behavior skills that are helpful for all students to practice applying when interacting with others (such as social media awareness, bullying prevention, or a kindness challenge)
Service learning projects	Teaching how to serve others in need at the school or community level, and often collaborative
Weekly behavior scenarios or role playing	Scenarios or role play designated for practicing academic and social behavior skills (such as students providing a scenario that they commonly face either at school or communitywide)

In this chapter, you learned about the *schoolwide* prevention cycle, which involves a schoolwide approach to teaching behavior in every location on your campus. In our work with schools, we've seen various factors that can impede a tight classroom system. It's quite possible for a school to have a tight schoolwide approach yet a high number of inconsistent classroom referrals to the office. This could be the case for a number of reasons; however, analyzing referral data is the only way to identify why this is occurring. For example, if a majority of referrals are coming from one classroom in particular, that doesn't mean all students who misbehave are in this particular classroom. It might indicate this particular teacher could benefit from support or procedures that will lead to fewer disruptions. Another reason could be the need for schoolwide calibration of the differences between a teacher-handled minor disruption and an office-handled major offense. From classroom to classroom, what one teacher deems major another regards as minor. This calibration would align expectations so everyone is speaking the same language when it comes to discipline.

Consider what a classroom focused on prevention looks like with academic content. The teaching-assessing cycle (figure 3.9) is the foundation of Tier 1 team core instruction. This powerful approach is based on the premise that the best intervention is prevention. Rather than waiting for students to struggle and *then* reacting by sending them off to someone else for Tier 2 support (reteaching), the collaborative team works together to *prevent* gaps in learning.

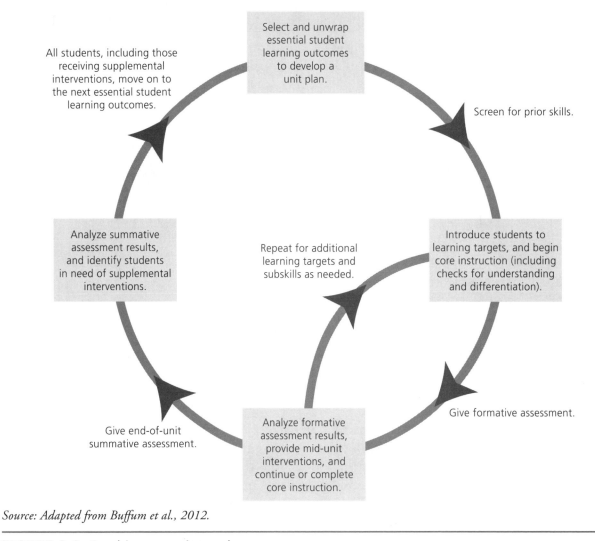

Source: Adapted from Buffum et al., 2012.

FIGURE 3.9: Teaching-assessing cycle.

The Tier 1 classroom prevention cycle is an adaptation of the teaching-assessing cycle with the exact premise of prevention for behavior. We've seen schools that are strong in supporting student academic needs with a focus on prevention yet are still in a reactionary response when it comes to student misbehavior.

How can we accept the responsibility that every student learns differently, *proactively* provide systematic interventions when he or she struggles to learn core instruction, and yet respond *reactively* and send the student out of the classroom on a referral when he or she struggles to behave appropriately? Often, the student returns to the classroom feeling more disconnected, disenfranchised, and rejected, and has a lasting fractured relationship with the teacher.

Furthermore, we wouldn't use students' second language, parents' educational background, or socioeconomic status as an excuse for students not learning at high levels, would we? How can we acknowledge that our students are coming into our classrooms with anxiety, depression, adverse childhood experiences, and other factors obstructing their ability to regulate their emotions, yet attempt to punish them into behaving properly? You can't punish anxiety; you can't punish depression; and you can't punish trauma. Students need to feel valued, loved, respected, and heard. There are ways to provide consequences for misbehavior *and* make connections so students don't engage in these behaviors again.

We have researched and tested best practices from highly effective classrooms and synthesized a process with a focus on prevention that has culminated with the Tier 1 *classroom* prevention cycle. The same logic that applies to the teaching-assessing cycle—of not waiting for students to struggle and *then* reacting by sending them off to someone else for Tier 2 support (reteaching)—applies to the Tier 1 classroom prevention cycle.

The Tier 1 classroom prevention cycle allows classroom teachers to accomplish two things: (1) establish a strong Tier 1 classroom environment focused on prevention and (2) have a consistent cycle of processing through behavior responses. You may change some of the responses or strategies—for example, to meet core component one, you can implement the Tier 1 four Cs highlighted in this book (page 72) or use another classroom design framework—highlighted in each component of the Tier 1 classroom prevention cycle based on grade-level needs, but the four core components of that cycle need to remain consistent. Figure 3.10 (page 72) shows the Tier 1 classroom prevention cycle, and table 3.3 (page 73) explains the components named in the figure. The "Teacher Audit of the Four Cs in a Classroom Tier 1 Behavior System" reproducible (page 80) can tell you if the components are present. Figure 3.11 (page 73) shows graphically where the cycle lives in the RTI at Work pyramid, and table 3.3 highlights that this Tier 1 classroom cycle is led by the teacher teams and implemented in their individual classrooms as a prevention to students needing Tier 2 behavior interventions. Its focus is on first best instruction and the classroom management system. Remember that the schoolwide prevention cycle is on the left side of the pyramid and led by the leadership team.

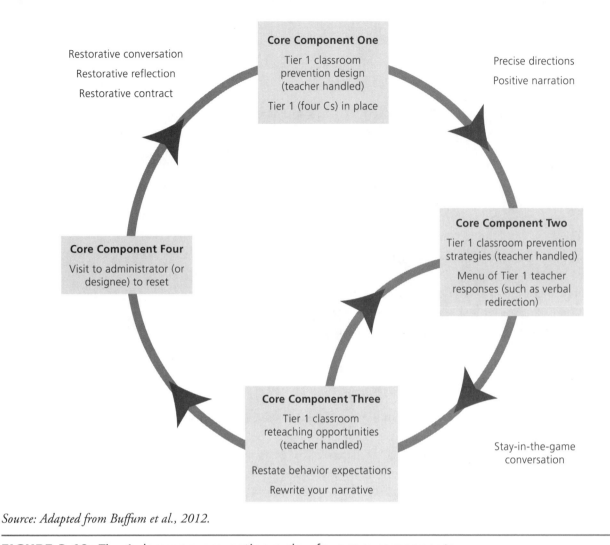

Restorative conversation
Restorative reflection
Restorative contract

Core Component One

Tier 1 classroom prevention design (teacher handled)

Tier 1 (four Cs) in place

Precise directions
Positive narration

Core Component Four

Visit to administrator (or designee) to reset

Core Component Two

Tier 1 classroom prevention strategies (teacher handled)

Menu of Tier 1 teacher responses (such as verbal redirection)

Core Component Three

Tier 1 classroom reteaching opportunities (teacher handled)

Restate behavior expectations

Rewrite your narrative

Stay-in-the-game conversation

Source: Adapted from Buffum et al., 2012.

FIGURE 3.10: Tier 1 classroom prevention cycle—four core components.

Best Practices of the Four Cs in a Tier 1 Classroom Behavior System

We believe that four Cs—(1) climate, (2) communication, (3) curriculum, and (4) culture—are critical for guiding your comprehensive Tier 1 classroom behavior system. Table 3.4 (page 75) identifies best practices for each of the four Cs. For prevention, teachers need to understand the best practices for each of the four Cs and agree to consistently implement those they determine are critical as a team. In table 3.4 (page 75), suggested best practices of the four Cs are provided based on our collective experiences, but please note additional best practices can be included in the four identified areas.

As you consider this work, look at your districtwide or schoolwide classroom observation (or walkthrough forms) and teacher evaluation criteria to see if they indicate what your teacher classroom behavior system should look like. For example, does it include classroom Tier 1 culture and climate? What observable evidence shows that it is taking place in the classroom and demonstrates teacher mastery toward creating a positive and engaging classroom culture and climate?

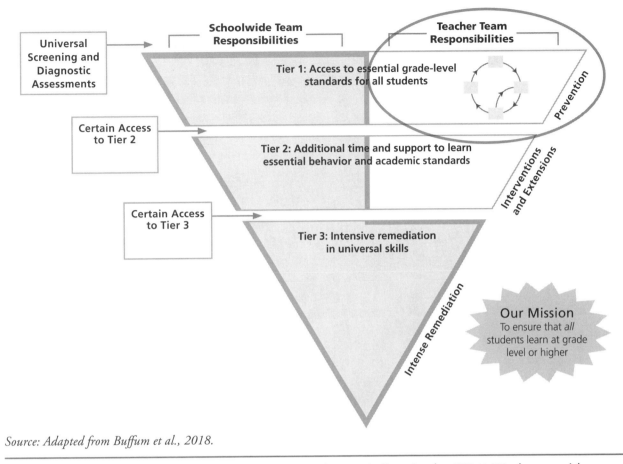

Source: Adapted from Buffum et al., 2018.

FIGURE 3.11: Where the Tier 1 classroom prevention cycle lives in the RTI at Work pyramid.

TABLE 3.3: Tier 1 Prevention Cycle Core Components

Core Component	Questions Teams Can Ask Themselves	Responses and Strategies Suggested for Each Component*
Core component one: Tier 1 classroom prevention design	"Have we set up a classroom designed for prevention?"	• **The four Cs:** The Cs include (1) climate, (2) communication, (3) curriculum, and (4) culture. Each of the four Cs (page 72) must be in place with evidence in order for a classroom to support and maintain positive relationships. Similar to first best classroom instruction as the best prevention, the four Cs support teachers as they develop and implement first best behavior prevention in the classroom. • **Precise directions:** Tell students what to do and how to do it. Precise directions communicate to students the movement, voice level, and participation expected of them. See *Every Student, Every Day: A No-Nonsense Nurturer® Approach to Reaching All Learners* (Borrero, 2019, p. 59). • **Positive narrations:** Positive narration gives off-task students an informal warning before they receive consequences. It is a simple, nonjudgmental description of the behavior you observe (providing examples of success for students to follow). See *Every Student, Every Day* (Borrero, 2019, p. 89).

Core Component	Questions Teams Can Ask Themselves	Responses and Strategies Suggested for Each Component˙
Core component two: Tier 1 classroom prevention strategies	"Do we have a menu of teacher-handled responses and classroom-level supports?"	• **Menu of Tier 1 teacher responses:** This is a best-practices list of Tier 1 teacher-handled classroom responses, such as a verbal redirection (see table 3.5, page 105).
Core component three: Tier 1 classroom reteaching opportunities	"Do we have a process for intentionally reteaching students desired classroom behaviors?"	• **Stay-in-the-game conversations:** These are ten- to thirty-second reminders for students to stay on task. See *Every Student, Every Day* (Borrero, 2019, p. 112). » Restate on- or off-task behaviors » Redirect for desired behavior and restate precise directions. » Encourage the student. » Extend support if needed. • **Restate behavior expectations:** Intentionally restate and reteach what is expected during classroom routines and procedures. • **Rewrite your narrative:** This short prompt facilitates a conversation between student and teacher and allows both to develop agreements and reteaching opportunities to start over the next period or day.
Core component four: Restorative or reset to administrator (or designee) to reset	"Do we have restorative opportunities with teacher, student, and the restorative designee?"	• **Restorative conversations:** Lengthier conversations must happen if you remove a student from class. The conversation can help you identify how to help the student succeed in your classroom. See *Every Student, Every Day* (Borrero, 2019, p. 112). » Restate the on- and off-task behaviors the student exhibited. » Redirect for desired behavior. » Listen to the student's perspective on why he or she is struggling. » Inquire or extend support to student. » Provide encouragement and let the student know he or she is welcome back into your classroom. • **Restorative reflections:** Scripted prompts facilitate student reflection on the misbehavior and reset for entry back into the classroom setting. • **Restorative contracts:** Restore and repair hurt relationships due to misbehavior in a classroom with agreed-on and monitored next steps to improve the relationships (page 158).

Note: You can use other responses and strategies.

TABLE 3.4: Best Practices of the Four Cs

Climate: The product of a classroom intentionally designed to foster and promote a safe, consistent, and positive environment	
Best Practice	**Example or Explanation**
Student voice	Students' input and expertise are embraced and help shape their classroom experience, including lessons, assignments, and interactions.
Classroom agreements or contracts	Classroom behavior agreements or contracts co-developed by students and the teacher ensure joint understanding and commitment between all stakeholders in the classroom.
Clear routines and procedures	The teacher develops and implements consistent, predictable routines and procedures.
Taught and reinforced classroom routines and procedures	The teacher intentionally teaches and reteaches the routines and procedures expected in the classroom (such as how to enter and exit the classroom, how to ask for help or take a bathroom break, and where to turn in assignments).
Teacher-managed minor infractions	The teacher understands the difference between teacher-handled and administrator-handled classroom infractions. The teacher also demonstrates ownership and autonomy when handling minor infractions within the classroom, and has adequate tools and resources when responding.
Brief transition times	Transition time between one task and another in the classroom is less than a minute. This requires teachers to intentionally organize lessons and next steps.
Active supervision	The teacher actively scans, moves, and has positive interactions with students in the classroom.
Communication: The product of a classroom intentionally designed to foster the ongoing interchange of expectations, ideas, commitments, voices, and behaviors among all stakeholders	
Best Practice	**Example or Explanation**
Positive teacher language (4:1 to 6:1)	The teacher uses positive (direct) language more often than negative language (four instances to one is the ideal ratio) and even more often for struggling students (six instances to one). Positive language, for example, focuses on what's desired and acknowledges students when they demonstrate appropriate skills.

continued ➡

Classroom management and communication or monitoring system	Classrooms are well managed with a system and have in place a communication or monitoring system to track behaviors for providing additional supports for students who need them.
Positive parent communication system	The teacher follows a process for positively communicating with parents or guardians (making five positive calls a week to different parents or guardians, for example). Contacting them with something positive when they are frequently called for negative reasons tremendously builds parent and guardian support.
Positive contacts	Multiple methods for making positive contact with students are employed: notes, affirmations, one-to-one conversations, fist bumps, and check-ins.
Substitute teacher behavior plans	An intentional preparation plan for substitute teachers helps stave off behavior challenges. Plans can provide appropriate information for substitutes on certain students who may need additional supports.
Updated seating charts	A seating chart is updated to include notes on what a student needs academically, behaviorally, and social-emotionally to access classroom instruction. This can provide a teacher—especially one with multiple class sessions—a quick visual reminder. Those reminders can be as simple as *504*, *IEP*, or *anxiety care plan*.

Curriculum: The product of a classroom intentionally designed to educate the whole child, including academics and beyond

Best Practice	Example or Explanation
Classroom meetings, circles, or check-ins	This intentionally created safe space provides opportunities for students to share and help each other or the community with concerns or challenges.
Alternative options for mastery	Students have opportunities to demonstrate their learning in different modalities. For example, if the physical act of writing triggers a student's sensory challenges, that student can present orally or create a speech-to-text response for an assignment; if a student has severe anxiety about classroom presentations, that student can demonstrate mastery other ways.
Universal design for learning (UDL)	The teacher understands and implements the three areas of UDL in the classroom: (1) engagement (stimulating interest and motivation via lessons), (2) representation (information is presented in different ways, for multiple modalities), and (3) action and expression (students can demonstrate what they learned or know in different ways; CAST, n.d.).

Engaging instruction	Ensuring that students find instruction meaningful and understand how it applies to their learning results in engagement.
Culturally responsive teaching	Student-centered, teacher-facilitated instruction reshapes the traditional curriculum to include instruction and teaching that respect culture, language, and racial identity. Focus on developing students' critical lens regarding injustices.
Embedded SEL core competencies	Developing students' self-awareness and self-management skills, which are essential in school and beyond, means embedding instruction into the classroom setting, assignments, lessons, and projects.
Behavior lessons	Students receive formal or informal behavior lessons in the classroom at least weekly. Lessons can range from actual behavior curriculum lessons (such as anti-bullying, respect, and digital citizenship), to discussing classroom text's character behaviors, to addressing real-life classroom, schoolwide, or community challenges around tolerance and empathy.
21st century skills	Intentionally incorporated instruction and application of 21st century skills includes opportunities to practice communicating and collaborating, as well as encouraging critical thinking and creativity. (The teacher might, for example, teach how to develop and adhere to group work norms so students know how to communicate differences and diversity of thought in a productive way, civil way.)

Culture: The product of a classroom intentionally designed to build and maintain relationships and community	
Best Practice	**Example or Explanation**
Structure for relationship building	Intentionally greeting students is the norm for the classroom teacher. The class creates and repeats mantras about respecting each other and developing a safe, loving classroom environment.
Classroom incentive system	Students can receive individual or classroom-level (team) acknowledgments for demonstrating appropriate behaviors they have learned. Incentives can be tangible or intangible based on student input and motivators.

continued →

| Trauma-informed practices | Understanding the impact traumatic childhood events have on a student's ability to regulate his or her behavior is trauma informed. Teachers shift their view from *This student is behaving poorly* to *This student is having a difficult time; what does she need?* The behavior is viewed through a lens of support and establishing a relationship rather than punishment and removing the student from class. |
| Character and service learning projects | At least once-monthly service learning projects provide opportunities to learn and implement character development. The focus is on being good citizens in and out of the classroom. |

*Visit **go.SolutionTree.com/RTIatWork** for a free reproducible version of this table.*

For prevention, teachers need to understand the best practices for each of the four Cs and agree to consistently implement those they determine are critical as a team. In table 3.4 (page 75), suggested best practices of the four Cs are provided based on our collective experiences, but please note additional best practices can be included in the four identified areas.

The four Cs best practice selection process is critical to the classroom's alignment and design of Tier 1. Follow these four steps to select best practices of the four Cs.

1. Select one best practice from each of the four Cs: (1) climate, (2) communication, (3) curriculum, and (4) culture. To decide which best practice from each to begin with, the team should use a selection rubric it has designed (or simply answer whether the best practice is beneficial for students, observable, and doable and select based on those criteria).

2. After agreement on the selected best practices, the team does the following.

    »   Identifies what the practice should look like operationally in each classroom

    »   Sets an implementation date (as well as provides training and modeling for teachers if needed)

3. The team holds monthly check-ins to ensure implementation success (evidence in place) and needed modifications.

4. After mastering each of the chosen best practices, the team adds more best practices from the four Cs and repeats the process.

Using this four Cs best practice selection process will help a faculty choose, define, and agree on success criteria for implementing the four Cs consistently. Using the reproducible "Teacher Audit of the Four Cs in a Classroom Behavior System" (page 80) will help you assess your current reality before beginning the steps.

Schedule of Application of Behavior Rounds With a Four Cs Focus

Use the Tier 1 behavior rounds process to monitor and continuously improve implementation of the selected four Cs or other essential academic and social behaviors that the faculty has decided on. Weekly Tier 1 classroom behavior rounds identify the non-negotiables or norms agreed on to be present in all classrooms as part of Tier 1 prevention. Use the information gathered from the behavior rounds similarly to how you use data from instructional rounds. Differentiate professional development or learning opportunities during staff meetings based on findings from the walkthroughs. The "Tier 1 Behavior Rounds: Four Cs Selection and Planning" reproducible (page 84) helps the leadership team plan how Tier 1 behavior rounds will relate to each identified best practice in each of the four Cs.

Here is an example of how to set up a behavior rounds schedule using the four Cs.

1. The leadership team, with the input from teacher teams, identifies a best practice from each of the four C categories. (See the "Tier 1 Behavior Rounds: Four Cs Selection and Planning" reproducible.)

2. Establish the *why* with staff, and train them on the four selected best practices.

3. Conduct twice-monthly Tier 1 behavior rounds using the reproducible "Tier 1 Behavior Rounds Observation Form" (page 85). Administrators or other identified members from the staff conducts these rounds. (Coverage is provided for other members of the leadership team to participate if need be.)

4. Share monthly behavior rounds data and observed trends with the leadership team—and with teacher teams and the intervention team as needed—and continuously provide, add, and adjust support based on the data and trends. For example, during classroom rounds someone might notice a general lack of consistency regarding instruction about and monitoring timeliness to class. Some teachers expect students to be seated, quiet, and ready to learn when the bell rings; others require their students to be in the room by that time; and still others are not carefully monitoring student tardiness. Sharing this observational data can lead to discussions regarding how the staff can be consistent and align teaching and reinforcing this essential social behavior.

5. Share behavior rounds information with the entire staff and elicit feedback.

6. Continue selecting four best practices at a time—one from each of the four Cs—and building until all best practices are in place.

Teacher Audit of the Four Cs in a Classroom Tier 1 Behavior System

Circle the score that best describes the presence of each of the four Cs best practices in your classroom system. Be honest. This audit will help you assess the current state of your behavior system and learn what areas you most need to focus on.

Best Practice	Score 0 = Not present 1 = In progress 2 = In place	Evidence or Next Steps For any best practice scored in place (2), list evidence that it is in place or in progress (1). Next steps to put it in progress if scored 0?
Climate: The product of a classroom intentionally designed to foster and promote a safe, consistent, and positive environment		
I allow for student voice in my classroom.	0 1 2	
I maintain a safe, predictable classroom.	0 1 2	
I have consistent, clear classroom procedures and routines in place.	0 1 2	
I teach and reinforce my classroom routines and procedures.	0 1 2	
I engage in active classroom supervision (scanning, moving, and having positive interactions).	0 1 2	
I have a process for handling minor misbehaviors in my classroom.	0 1 2	
I have transition times of one minute or less.	0 1 2	
I teach and reinforce clear classroom behavior expectations, agreements, rules, and standards.	0 1 2	
Total climate score	_____ of 16 points (Goal: 13 points or more)	

page 1 of 4

Communication: The product of a classroom intentionally designed to foster the ongoing interchange of expectations, ideas, commitments, voices, and behaviors among all stakeholders

I use positive teacher language and tone in my classroom.	0 1 2
I have and reinforce a classroom management system.	0 1 2
I have a behavior communication and monitoring system with parents and guardians.	0 1 2
I have a behavior communication and monitoring system with students.	0 1 2
I have a behavior communication and monitoring system with administrators and other stakeholders (such as support providers).	0 1 2
I make at least five positive contacts with parents and guardians per week.	0 1 2
I have a clear alternate plan for when I am out of the classroom, including for students who require special accommodations or interventions.	0 1 2
I have updated seating charts based on student voice and needs.	0 1 2
Total communication score	_____ of 16 points (Goal: 13 points or more)

Behavior Solutions © 2021 Solution Tree Press • SolutionTree.com
Visit **go.SolutionTree.com/RTIatWork** to download this free reproducible.

Curriculum: The product of a classroom intentionally designed to educate the whole child, including academics and beyond							
I embed social-emotional competencies in my teaching.	0 1 2						
I incorporate 21st century skills in my classroom.	0 1 2						
I have at least one scheduled weekly slot for teaching behavior expectations, lessons, or standards.	0 1 2						
I have at least one scheduled weekly classroom meeting, circle, or check-in time with students.	0 1 2						
I provide students multiple options to learn and demonstrate mastery.	0 1 2						
I provide daily engaging, meaningful instruction based on student voice and input.	0 1 2						
I embed culturally responsive teaching practices in my classroom.	0 1 2						
I implement all the special education and other accommodations and interventions designed for student success.	0 1 2						
Total curriculum score	_____ of 16 points (Goal: 13 points or more)						

page 3 of 4

Culture: The product of a classroom intentionally designed to build and maintain relationships and community

Item	Score
I have a daily routine for greeting students.	0 1 2
I offer positive classroom incentives.	0 1 2
I invest in relationship building and restore or repair relationships when needed.	0 1 2
My classroom is a welcoming space for students.	0 1 2
My classroom is a welcoming space for families and other stakeholders.	0 1 2
I have a system for ensuring students feel safe asking for help.	0 1 2
I embed community-based service learning projects.	0 1 2
I use trauma-informed practices.	0 1 2
Total culture score	_____ of 16 points (Goal: 13 points or more)
Total four Cs score	Total score: _____ of 64 points (Goal: 52 of 64 points or more, or 80 percent)
Focus **Any C with a score of less than 13 points**	Corresponding Next Steps

Tier 1 Behavior Rounds: Four Cs Selection and Planning

The leadership team should select one best practice from each of the four Cs and record it in the first column. Then, the team should answer the three questions to plan how Tier 1 behavior rounds will relate to each identified best practice.

	What will we see and hear in classrooms that is evidence of agreed-on observable success criteria for each of the four Cs?	What resources or training should we provide prior to the Tier 1 behavior rounds?	What is the goal of each behavior round for each identified component? **Example:** By January, the selected Tier 1 critical classroom components will be in place in every classroom as demonstrated by the observable evidence listed in the second column.
Climate Best practice:			
Communication Best practice:			
Curriculum Best practice:			
Culture Best practice:			

Tier 1 Behavior Rounds Observation Form

In each of the four Cs constructs—(1) climate, (2) communication, (3) curriculum, and (4) culture—identify a best practice and evidence of the best practice implemented in the classroom you will observe. If it is helpful, you can list what the evidence will look like prior to the rounds and circle, tally, or check off those you see during rounds. For example, if you have selected greeting students at the beginning of the day as a best practice and expectation for culture, then you could list and then tally the following evidence: teacher verbally greeting students at the door; teacher greeting students with a check-in process; teacher giving a high five, hand shake, or fist bump at the door. For this example, it makes sense for the walkthrough to occur at the start of the day.

This is not an evaluative tool. This is a quick method to get a schoolwide snapshot of the classroom environments supported across a campus. Compile these data and use them with the leadership team's focus on prevention and support. This is a method for getting a more comprehensive picture of your school's Tier 1 system.

Observer:			
Observed:			
Date:			
Climate chosen best practice:	**Communication** chosen best practice:	**Curriculum** chosen best practice:	**Culture** chosen best practice:
This practice is implemented in a classroom when:	This practice is implemented in a classroom when:	This practice is implemented in a classroom when:	This practice is implemented in a classroom when:
Notes			

Plan–Do–STUDY–Act

In the study stage of the prevention cycle (highlighted in figure 3.12), the leadership team studies multiple schoolwide data points and identifies SMART goals and implementation needs. One or more designated leadership team members push into the teacher team meetings to help identify essential academic and social behavior trends that need prevention.

- ▶ **Why:** To analyze schoolwide and classroom academic and social behavior data and stakeholder input, develop SMART goals, and ensure implementation fidelity

- ▶ **Who:** The leadership team with teacher team input

- ▶ **What:** Developing precise problem statements based on data and next-step solutions and identifying action steps

- ▶ **When:** At least monthly and potentially more based on the schoolwide and classroom behavior data

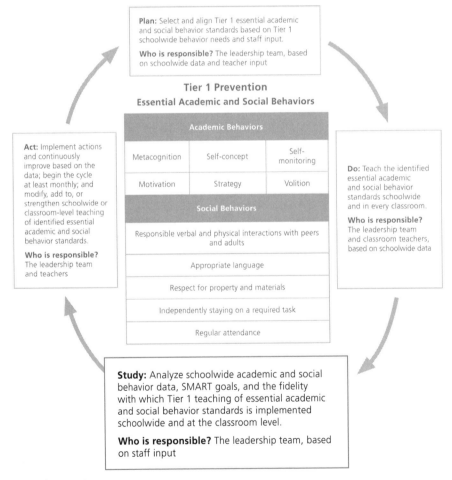

Source: Adapted from Buffum et al., 2018.

FIGURE 3.12: Tier 1 study stage.

Commonly Asked Questions in the Study Stage

Consider these questions.

- ▶ How do we function as a PLC with the focus on behavior, including steps and data points with a focus on behavior data?

- ▶ What type of behavior data will we use to decide what our students need schoolwide and in every classroom, and how do we get the data?

- ▶ What data do we utilize to identify problem statements?

- ▶ How can a designated member of the leadership team push into each teacher team meeting at least monthly to get additional information on how students are doing with Tier 1 essential academic and social behavior standards?

Tier 1 Study Stage: Processes, Tools, and Forms

In this section, you will find processes, tools, and forms designed to help you begin the work in the study stage.

Tier 1 Study Stage Three-Step Guide

This three-step guide reminds educators of the critical points and possible data needed to make informed decisions about what standards need teaching.

1. Identify schoolwide or classroom-level precise problem statements based on multiple data points.

2. Determine what essential standard or standards need to be taught or retaught at the school, grade, department, or classroom level based on student needs and data.

3. Design SMART goals, action steps, and timelines around the problem statements.

Data Collection

The leadership team needs processes and structures in place to collect up-to-date behavior data for its monthly meetings. If you have a process or structure for collecting these data, you should be able to chart what the process looks like. Figure 3.13 (page 88) shows one process flowchart, with collected schoolwide data that the leadership team can use.

Make a flowchart showing how your schoolwide team identifies trends (such as classroom minor misbehaviors that result in catching students prior to escalation or an uptick in problematic behaviors in a specific location on campus or at a specific time of day) and overall social-emotional needs (such as an increase in anxiety or depression).

The leadership team might use the following data in the study stage.

- ▶ Minor and major discipline referrals (ensuring minor and major misbehaviors are distinguished and staff understand there is a documentation process for both)

If a student engages in repetitive minor misbehavior (three or more of the same or similar behaviors continue after the teacher has put supports in place) or engages in a major behavior, the teacher completes an office referral. That referral includes information such as location, time of day, type of incident, possible perceived function of the misbehavior, and other students or stakeholders involved. The student goes to the office for administrator assistance and documentation purposes.

After the administrator handles the referral incident and fills out the disciplinary outcome section of the form, which includes suggested supports, the information is logged into the school's data system and communicated with the teacher.

A designated person (often the administrator) from the leadership team ensures that all discipline data are put into the data system and up to date prior to leadership team meetings.

FIGURE 3.13: Sample data-collection flowchart.

- Detention, suspension, and expulsion data

- Universal screeners of social-emotional supports (teacher-completed or student-completed self-assessments on social-emotional needs)

- Student and teacher culture check-in surveys

- Behavior rounds (four Cs data)

- Teacher team monthly input given to the leadership team member who pushes into teacher team meetings

- Teacher lead input via a monthly report by grade level or department, and also an informal process through which teachers can bring up needs (if they, for example, notice a lot of cheating or online bullying behavior issues spilling into classrooms)

- Input from classified staff (including but not limited to liaisons and playground, cafeteria, and office staff)

- Adverse childhood experiences data (indicating traumatic events such as violence or neglect; Centers for Disease Control and Prevention, 2019)

Problem Statements

Figure 3.14 shows examples of precise problem statements that a leadership team may derive from the study stage and use to come up with data-based actions for solving the problems. After the team creates problem statements (like those in the Schoolwide Precise Problem Statement rows), it can complete the rest of the form.

Having the completed essential academic and social behavior priority focused rating scale (figure 3.7, page 65) on hand during this meeting can help members decide what standards to implement to address the problems.

Essential Academic or Social Behavior Standard to Teach in Response to the Problem	Actions That Will Solve the Problem	Goal and Timeline for Solving the Problem	Person Responsible for the Goal
Schoolwide precise problem statement: Disrespectful student behavior toward adults has doubled this year. Many students are contributing, and the problem seems to occur during the afternoon more than the morning. We are not sure why.			
Social behavior standard 2.1: Responsible verbal and physical interactions with peers and adults	Address respect in the newsletter, model respect, and reteach expected respectful behavior in the classroom setting.	Decrease the frequency of disrespectful behavior referrals to no more than five per grade level per month by the end of the school year.	Designated members of the leadership team and all teachers
Schoolwide precise problem statement: Threats and hands-on behavior referrals have increased for all grade levels in the month of November. Students from all grade levels are contributing, and the problem seems to occur in the classroom and on the playground. We are not sure why this is happening and what time of day this behavior is happening most often.			
Social behavior standard 2.1: Responsible verbal and physical interactions with peers and adults	Teach Stop, Walk, and Talk schoolwide; do a Hands-Off Academy school challenge; reteach expected behavior in every class; give "This is a hands-off school" announcements; provide active supervision.	Decrease the frequency of threats and hands-on behavior referrals to no more than two per grade level per month by the end of the school year.	Designated members of the leadership team and all teachers
Schoolwide precise problem statement: Profanity referrals have increased for fifth grade in the month of November. We are not sure why this is happening and what time of day this behavior is happening most often.			
Social behavior standard 2.2: Appropriate language	Fifth-grade students can help reteach appropriate language.	Decrease the frequency of vulgarity and profanity referrals to no more than two per month among fifth-grade students by the end of the school year.	Identified students and teachers

FIGURE 3.14: Schoolwide precise problem statements and solutions form—examples.   continued →

Schoolwide precise problem statement: Tardies have increased for all grade levels in the month of November. Students from all grade levels are contributing, and the problem seems to occur in the classroom. We are not sure why this is happening and what time of day this behavior is happening most often.			
Social behavior standard 2.5: Regular attendance	Play a schoolwide tardy project video, possibly play a musical reminder to get to class, provide active supervision, and have school-improvement incentives.	Decrease the frequency of tardies to no more than three per grade level per month by the end of the school year.	Designated members of the leadership team and all teachers
Schoolwide precise problem statement: Cell phone referrals have increased for all grade levels in the month of November. Students from all grade levels are contributing, and the problem seems to occur in the classroom. We are not sure why this is happening and what time of day this behavior is happening most often. Teachers from all grade levels are concerned because cell phones are becoming a distraction and contributing to off-task behaviors in class.			
Social behavior standard 2.4: Independently staying on a required task	Reteach proper cell phone use schoolwide.	Decrease the frequency of cell phone referrals to no more than three per grade level per month by the end of the school year.	Identified teachers and students from each grade level to help develop and teach lessons

Source for standard: Buffum et al., 2018.

*Visit **go.SolutionTree.com/RTIatWork** for a free reproducible version of this figure.*

Study Agenda Form

After receiving the necessary data, the leadership team determines how close it is to reaching its previously set SMART goals, sets new SMART goals (O'Neill & Conzemius, 2006), and completes the Schoolwide Behavior Study Agenda form. You can use components of the form or add them to an existing PLC agenda or minutes format. Figure 3.15 features sample text from leadership team minutes.

Tier 1 Teacher Input Collection

Data collected by the leadership team at this point include both quantitative and qualitative teacher input.

The leadership team collects teacher team input at the following frequencies as part of this cycle.

> ▸ **Monthly:** A designated representative from the leadership team pushes into every teacher team meeting once a month to collect input on Tier 1 needs. Essentially, the designated leadership team member can schedule times to go into each teacher team meeting to gather input on what the classroom and schoolwide behavior needs are and the leadership team can use that input to help guide the school's study stage in the prevention cycle.

> ▸ **Ongoing:** The leadership team and teacher teams share a Google document of data on a continuous basis. An example of these data are meeting minutes that have a space for teacher input and are gathered at every teacher team meeting.

Meeting date: *October 15*	

Team members present: *Janea, Bob, LaShawn, Kenneth, and Maria*

Top priorities for this meeting:
- *Revisiting how teachers keep track of minor misbehaviors in their classrooms*
- *Addressing the spike in hands-on behavior schoolwide and in the classroom settings due to what is referred to as the necking game, where students slap each other on the back of the neck when they least expect it*

Data reviewed, including the dates of the data:
- *August: All grade levels—twenty-five incidents of outside the classroom hands-on behavior*
- *September: All grade levels—thirty incidents of outside of the classroom hands-on behavior*
- *October: All grade levels as of October 15—five incidents of outside of the classroom hands-on behavior*

Achievement status of the previous meeting's designated SMART goals:

Last month, focus was on hands-on behavior outside of the classroom, which has significantly decreased from August 15 to October 15. In August, it was twenty-five incidents outside of the classroom. Currently it's at five incidents outside of the classroom. We have enforced active supervision and added structured games during free time. However, the team has noticed the hands-on trend inside of the classroom has increased with both seventh- and eighth-grade students.

Next meeting date: *November 15*

Write a precise problem statement based on the data. Include what, when, where, who, and why.

Students are having trouble keeping their hands to themselves inside of the classroom. Minor discipline referrals for inappropriate physical interactions during class time have doubled for seventh- and eighth-grade students when compared with this time last year (October 2018 compared with October 2019 trends).

Possible function (why): A new hands-on tag game has become popular on social media, so students could be doing it during class to get peer attention.

Write a SMART (strategic and specific, measurable, attainable, results oriented, and time bound; Conzemius & O'Neill, 2014) goal based on the precise problem statement.

Minor discipline referrals for inappropriate physical interactions will decrease to no more than three minor referrals per month for seventh- and eighth-grade students by November 2019.
- *Seventh-grade baseline: Thirty minor referrals per month on average*
- *Eighth-grade baseline: Twenty-eight minor referrals per month on average*

What essential academic and social behavior standard or standards need prevention, teaching, reteaching, or correction?

Standard 2.1 (responsible verbal and physical interactions with peers and adults)

At what level should this be implemented? Schoolwide? At the classroom level?

All students in middle school A will be taught social behavior standard 2.1 (responsible verbal and physical interactions with peers and adults) for prevention purposes.

Who will be responsible, and what will they do?
- *The leadership team will allow for scheduled time for teachers to teach (that is, homeroom time).*
- *The leadership team will provide the quick sample scenario lessons around self-control. (See a sample simple and short classroom teaching titled "Sample 1".)*
- *Homeroom teachers will provide students these opportunities to learn skills every Monday morning from 9:00 a.m. to 9:30 a.m. for the next four weeks.*

Source for standard: Buffum et al., 2018.

FIGURE 3.15: Schoolwide behavior study agenda form—example.

*Visit **go.SolutionTree.com/RTIatWork** for a free reproducible version of this figure.*

This maintains channels of consistent communication between the teacher teams and the leadership team so decisions about Tier 1 prevention are based on both schoolwide data and teacher input.

The following reproducibles can help the leadership team and teacher teams collect teacher team input, along with the school's Tier 1 behavior data, during the study stage. Although we highlighted a push-in process prior to this tool that also promotes ongoing communication, we want to make clear the purpose of including Tiers 1, 2, and 3 boxes in the PLC teacher team minutes.

▶ "Behavior Standard Feedback Form for Teacher Team Push-In" (page 95)

▶ "Classroom Behavior Needs Identification Form" (page 96)

▶ "Push-In for Tier 1, 2, or 3: Elementary Teacher Team Input" (page 97)

Ongoing Shared Meeting Minutes

The shared meeting minutes form, shown in figure 3.16, is a practical method for ongoing communication about RTI needs between the teacher teams and the leadership team or intervention team. Because they can write their contributions in this form, teachers do not have to wait for the monthly push-in to communicate needs or updates if something arises.

The leadership team or intervention team completes the Comments section of the ongoing shared meeting minutes form in response to the notes the teacher teams leave in the Tiers 1, 2, and 3 columns. You can add this section to the bottom of your meeting minutes or agenda, or you can use it separately where teachers can go to their grade-level or department shared document and insert notes or a request for additional supports. This shared minutes process should include a protocol that requires the leadership team to respond within a few days.

Possible scenarios when this might apply follow.

▶ A teacher team noticed a group of students struggling with hands-off behavior, and the teachers have exhausted the Tier 1 teaching components of that essential social behavior. They enter notes in the Tier 2 box asking for supports in reteaching this group of students. The schoolwide team designee in charge of the school's Tier 2 supports responds to the teacher team and helps develop and coordinate a Tier 2 response.

▶ A new grade-level trend arises that needs to be addressed right away. The teacher team needs support or ideas for what that teaching would look like, so it enters that information in the Tier 2 box. The schoolwide team designee (in this case, likely the administrator) will arrange a time to meet with the teacher team to help with coordinating a timely schoolwide response).

▶ Teachers identify a student in crisis who needs support right away, and they insert that information in the Tier 3 box. The administrator who is notified connects with the Tier 3 intervention team member for a timely response. The intervention team designee will arrange a time to meet with the teacher team to help with coordinating a timely Tier 3 remediation plan for the student in need.

Grade level or department:			
Teacher team meeting date:			
Tier 1			
What Tier 1 academic or social behavior needs are there?	How is Tier 1 classroom implementation going?	What resources do we need?	What behavior support help do we need?
Leadership team comments:			

Tier 2		
How is Tier 2 implementation going?	What new behavior trends require reteaching?	Do we need the lead from the leadership team Tier 2 subset to push into a teacher team meeting to discuss Tier 2 behavior needs?
Leadership team comments:		

Tier 3		
How is Tier 3 intervention plan implementation going?	What resources do we need from the intervention team?	Do we need the Tier 3 intervention team lead to push into a teacher team meeting to discuss Tier 3 behavior needs? (Next meeting date: _____)
Intervention team comments:		

FIGURE 3.16: Ongoing shared meeting minutes form.

*Visit **go.SolutionTree.com/RTIatWork** for a free reproducible version of this figure.*

Behavior Support Form

The "Behavior Support Form" reproducible (page 98) is another example of how teachers can communicate on an ongoing basis regarding their classroom, grade level, or department's RTI needs. This form goes directly to the leadership team lead, who is often the principal. The teacher team or an individual teacher uses this form if a situation urgently requires assistance. A teacher can pick up the "Behavior Support Form" from the office or use an easily accessible online version of the form (shared via Google Drive, for instance) to submit a support request. The online form should be set up to go directly to the leadership team lead. If the request is for Tier 3 support, the leadership team lead should forward the request to the intervention team lead within twenty-four hours.

Who handles the response varies by tier need.

> ▸ **Tier 1 support request:** The leadership team responds.

> ▸ **Tier 2 support request:** The leadership team responds.

> ▸ **Tier 3 support request:** The intervention team responds.

However, we urge teacher teams to work together first, sharing classroom management suggestions and supports at the Tier 1 level.

Leadership Team Data Point Numbers by Month

The leadership team can use the "Leadership Team Data Point Numbers by Month" reproducible (page 99) at its monthly meetings. The totals help leadership team members notice trends and address schoolwide behavior needs; they also serve as meeting minutes.

Behavior Standard Feedback Form for Teacher Team Push-In

Team members vote on which two standards—one academic and one social—they prefer to focus on schoolwide. Enter the total vote for each in the row under each option. In the row under Why?, explain the rationales teachers share for each option. After completing the form, the leadership team push-in designee takes the information back to the leadership team for action.

Date of teacher team push-in:

Leadership team designee:

Teacher team grade level or department:

Essential **Academic Behavior** Standards					
What essential standard would you prefer to focus on schoolwide?					
Metacognition	Self-concept	Self-monitoring	Motivation	Strategy	Volition
Why?					

Essential **Social Behavior** Standards				
What essential standard would you prefer to focus on schoolwide?				
Responsible verbal and physical interactions with peers and adults	Appropriate language	Respect for property and materials	Independently staying on a required task	Regular attendance
Why?				

Classroom Behavior Needs Identification Form

Individual teachers or teacher teams can use this form to identify areas of academic and social behavior need by class and by student. They can use this form once a month individually and share the information with their teacher teams or the designated leadership team member who pushes into their teacher team meetings once a month. This helps ensure that adequate teaching opportunities and prevention supports are put into place.

Identify the essential *academic behavior* standards that the *majority of the class* needs support mastering with an *X*.					
Metacognition	Self-concept	Self-monitoring	Motivation	Strategy	Volition

Identify the essential *academic behavior* standards that *individual students* need support mastering by writing their names in the corresponding columns.					
Metacognition	Self-concept	Self-monitoring	Motivation	Strategy	Volition

Identify the essential *social behavior* standards that the *majority of the class* needs support mastering with an *X*.				
Responsible verbal and physical interactions with peers and adults	Appropriate language	Respect for property and materials	Independently staying on a required task	Regular attendance

Identify the essential *social behavior* standards that *individual students* need support mastering by writing their names in the corresponding columns.				
Responsible verbal and physical interactions with peers and adults	Appropriate language	Respect for property and materials	Independently staying on a required task	Regular attendance

Push-In for Tier 1, 2, or 3: Elementary Teacher Team Input

The designated leadership team members complete this form when pushing into each teacher team meeting (at least once monthly) to collect teacher input on behavior. This designee shares the gathered information with the leadership team at least once a month to help with the study stage of the Tier 1 prevention cycle; in addition, he or she shares tier-specific behavior information in the following ways.

▸ *The designee shares the Tier 1 Needs column information with the entire leadership team.*

▸ *The designee shares the Tier 2 Needs column information with the leadership team subset that focuses on the school's Tier 2 implementation.*

▸ *The designee shares the Tier 3 Needs column information with the intervention team that focuses on the school's Tier 3 remediation implementation.*

Subject or Grade Level	Push-In Month and Participant	Tier 1 Needs *Grade-level or schoolwide behavior teaching needs*	Tier 2 Needs *Grade-level behavior reteaching needs*	Tier 3 Needs *Intensive individual student behavior needs*
How well are existing Tier 2 interventions working? Please give examples, data, and other evidence.				
How well are existing Tier 3 interventions working? Please give examples, data, and other evidence.				

Behavior Support Form

Please complete all the sections of this form if you need behavior support from the schoolwide team.

Referring teacher (for individual classroom or student support):
Referring teacher team (for team referrals that impact all team members):
Referral date:
The referral is for (underline one):   • Tier 1 support (The leadership team responds.)   • Tier 2 support (The leadership team responds.)   • Tier 3 support (The intervention team responds.)
Areas of concern (describe using data):
Suggested resolution:
Other essential information:
For leadership team or intervention team use: Response date: _____ Response person: _____ RTI actions: _____ Revisited by: _____

Leadership Team Data Point Numbers by Month

	August	September	October	November	December	January	February	March	April	May	June	July
Minor referrals												
Major referrals												
In-school suspensions												
Out-of-school suspensions												
Alternative discipline assignments												
Expulsions												
Re-entries following admittance to behavioral health institutions												
Detentions												
Behavior conferences												

Behavior Solutions © 2021 Solution Tree Press • SolutionTree.com

Visit **go.SolutionTree.com/RTIatWork** to download this free reproducible.

page 1 of 2

	August	September	October	November	December	January	February	March	April	May	June	July
Monthly teacher-team push-in visits for Tier 1 input												
Tier 1 schoolwide teaching of standards												
Tier 1 behavior rounds conducted												
"Behavior Support" forms submitted												
Student surveys conducted on perception of school culture												
Teacher surveys conducted on perception of school culture												
Community surveys conducted on perception of school culture												
Administrator surveys conducted on perception of school culture												
Support professionals surveys conducted on perception of school culture												
Number of threat assessments conducted at the school												

Plan–Do–Study–ACT

In the act stage of the prevention cycle (highlighted in figure 3.17), the leadership team brings together behaviors it identified during the plan stage and adjusts as needed to meet established goals.

- ▸ **Why:** To implement actions and continuously review and improve based on schoolwide behavior data and teacher team input; begin the prevention cycle again, starting with the plan stage, at least monthly; and modify, add to, or strengthen schoolwide or classroom-level teaching of identified essential academic and social behavior standards

- ▸ **Who:** The leadership team and teacher teams

- ▸ **What:** Implements the actions and timelines

- ▸ **When:** At least monthly schoolwide based on schoolwide data trends and every day in every classroom as part of the Tier 1 prevention design

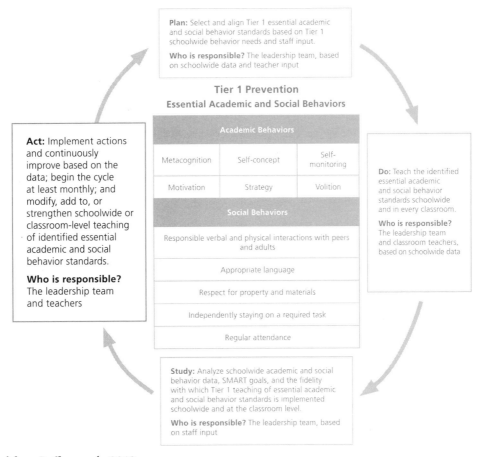

Source: Adapted from Buffum et al., 2018.

FIGURE 3.17: Tier 1 act stage.

Commonly Asked Questions in the Act Stage

Consider these questions.

▸ Who is in charge of implementing the actions?

▸ What is the lesson guide?

▸ What do we do if the plan does not work?

▸ How do we communicate and receive input from stakeholders about our actions?

Tier 1 Act Stage: Processes, Tools, and Forms

In this section, you will find processes, tools, and forms designed to help you begin the work in the act stage.

Classroom Lesson Guide

The classroom lesson guide (figure 3.18) helps the teachers deliver the lessons for agreed-on essential behavior standards. The leadership team leads the process to create the guide before addressing the identified challenge from the study session based on schoolwide data; see the "Leadership Team Data Point Numbers by Month" reproducible (page 99). The guide's purpose is to prevent behaviors from escalating to the next level of behavioral support.

Teachers take the following steps to fill out the guide and determine how they will deliver lessons for agreed-on behavior standards.

1. In the Teaching Topic column, identify the standard.

2. In the Teaching Options column, list and select options.

3. In the Student Work Outcome (Evidence) column, select from the list of evidence options.

Essential Behavior Skill: Matching Exercise

This matching exercise is an easy way for students to learn and begin applying their new behavior skills. The exercise instructions follow. Visit **go.SolutionTree.com /RTIatWork** for a free reproducible version of these instructions.

1. Have students independently, in partners, or in groups look up definitions of two behavior skills using appropriate online searches each week for four weeks (for eight skills total). On one index card, they should write a definition of the skill and what it should look like in the school setting and in the community. On another index card, they should write the name of the skill. At the end of the four weeks, the students should have a total of eight skill definition cards with examples and eight skill name cards.

2. Allow students to play a memory game. Have them spread out their cards face down on a table and take turns turning over two cards at a time,

Date	Teaching Topic	Teaching Option (Circle one.)	Student Work Outcome (Evidence)
September 2	Essential social behavior standard 2.1: Responsible verbal and physical interactions with peers and adults	Tier 1 essential standard matching exercise (figure 3.19, page 104, for an example) Classroom discussion Preset curriculum SEL lessons Second Step SEL lesson Olweus anti-bullying lessons Scenario practice Writing prompt ⟨Service learning project connected to the school or community (that is, a schoolwide student campaign on self-control or bullying prevention)⟩ Student-developed project or initiative Other: _____	Circle one of the options: ⟨Student journal entries around the discussed topic⟩ Student online portfolio of resources Writing products Student service projects Student behavior work wall Student choice products Student presentations Other: _____
September 3	Essential social behavior standard 2.1: Responsible verbal and physical interactions with peers and adults	⟨Tier 1 essential standard matching exercise (figure 3.19)⟩ Classroom discussion Preset curriculum SEL lessons Second Step SEL lesson Olweus anti-bullying lessons Scenario practice Writing prompt Service learning project connected to the school or community (that is, a schoolwide student campaign on self-control or bullying prevention) Student-developed project or initiative Other: _____	Student journal entries around the discussed topic Student online portfolio of resources Writing products Student service projects Student behavior work wall Student choice products ⟨Student presentations⟩ Other: _____

Source for standard: Buffum et al., 2018.

FIGURE 3.18: Classroom lesson guide.

Visit go.SolutionTree.com/RTIatWork for a free reproducible version of this figure.

trying to get a match. The student with the most matched cards at the end of the game is the winner. Either all the students choose from everyone's cards, or students play in their pairs or groups from step 1 so this game goes more quickly.

3. When they're done playing, provide a prompt for them to talk or write about their learning (for example, To what extent did this matching exercise help you learn the importance of mastering this schoolwide essential standard—self-monitoring?)

The sample matching exercise cards in figure 3.19 focus on academic behavior standards of self-control and self-monitoring. Self-monitoring skills can include showing self-control, self-regulation, accountability, and patience, as well as asking for help, solving problems, and correcting oneself.

Instead of the matching exercise, or in addition to it, you can give students the autonomy to create a video, give a presentation, or write a skit demonstrating their mastery.

Self-Control
Definition:
The ability to control myself, in particular emotions and desires or the expressions of them in one's behavior, especially in difficult situations
The definition in your own words:
To control your emotions and behavior
What it should look like at school:
Hands to yourself
What it should look like in the community:
Hands to yourself
Why practicing self-control is important:
To stop getting into trouble and hurting others
Self-Monitoring
Definition:
The ability to respond to the ongoing demands of life experiences with a range of emotions in a manner that is socially tolerable and sufficiently flexible
The definition in your own words:
You are working on controlling your emotions.
What it should look like at school:
Take deep breaths and think if a situation upsets you; take a walk (to get a drink of water or oxygen).

What it should look like in the community:
Not lashing out at someone who took your parking spot even though you want to.

Why practicing self-monitoring is important:
For the future, you do not want to grow up to be a person with escalating behavior—you want good mental health for the rest of your life.

FIGURE 3.19 Matching exercise cards—example.

*Visit **go.SolutionTree.com/RTIatWork** for a free reproducible version of this figure.*

Tier 1 Teacher-Managed Minor Responses

One of the four Cs, climate, focuses on best practices for responding to minor misbehaviors in the classroom—teacher-managed minor responses. It is essential that teachers have an effective repertoire of minor responses to use in class and other school settings that includes those in table 3.5.

TABLE 3.5: Tier 1 Teacher-Managed Minor Responses

Teacher Response	What It Looks Like
Review classroom behavior expectations and rules.	Review the classroom behavior expectations and rules one-on-one with the student. Have the student give examples of appropriate and inappropriate behaviors.
Provide a verbal or nonverbal prompt.	Provide a signal, visual, or prompt to help the student remember to get back on task.
Review classroom agreements or commitments.	Review classroom agreements or commitments and assign a classroom agreement progress-monitoring sheet.
Contact the student's parent or guardian.	Contact the parent or guardian and let him or her know how to also help with the behavior.
Have the student contact his or her parent or guardian.	Have the student call his or her parent or guardian and explain what behaviors he or she is demonstrating and how he or she is going to correct them.
Use proximity.	Seat the student closer to the teacher, or regularly walk by the student.
Require restitution.	Use a community service (figure 3.20, page 107) or restitution log (figure 3.21, page 108) to give the student an assignment.

continued →

Teacher Response	What It Looks Like
Require an apology.	Assign an apology letter (figure 3.22, page 108) for the student to write to the stakeholders.
Use precorrection.	Identify context and predictable behavior with student input. Remind the student of behavior expectations prior to a context where the likelihood of misbehavior increases.
Use behavior rehearsals.	Ask the student to recall the appropriate behavior, model the behavior, or keep a checklist as a reminder of the behavior.
Try redirection.	Promptly remind the student of the appropriate behavior.
Use the teacher team assistance process.	Request the assistance of the grade-level or department teacher team for identifying or helping with possible Tier 1 prevention or response suggestions.
Assign a safe seat or location.	Provide a safe seat or location for the student in the classroom or another safe setting.
Use a structured break.	Set up a structured break opportunity with a break pass for the student.
Invite the student's parent or guardian to sit in on class.	Contact the parent or guardian and invite him or her to sit in the classroom with the student.
Conference with the student.	Have a one-on-one conference to reason with the student and identify the function of the behavior.
Assign a behavior think sheet.	Assign a behavior think sheet (figure 3.23, page 109, and figure 3.24, page 110).
Assign a reflection sheet.	Assign a reflection sheet (figure 3.26, page 112), aligned with the schoolwide or classroom expectations and rules.
Cosign a behavior contract or restorative agreement (figure 3.25, page 111) or assign a restorative assignment.	Complete a restorative agreement with actions identified to help restore relationships.
Assign detention.	Require the student to complete an actual behavior task during the detention.
Require a behavior assignment.	Assign a behavior homework sheet or assignment.
Revoke a privilege.	Take away classroom or schoolwide privileges.

Teacher Response	What It Looks Like
Change the seating chart.	Discuss with the student which seating location he or she believes would result in better choices.
Partner with a teacher.	With a partner teacher, agree that the student will go to that teacher's room to work, which provides the student a setting change.

*Visit **go.SolutionTree.com/RTIatWork** for a free reproducible version of this table.*

The community service form in figure 3.20 is for students. At the end of the assigned community service (restitution), the student submits a reflection on what he or she learned from this experience, along with the completed restitution form and log in figure 3.21 (page 108). An administrator, the restitution (community service) supervisor, the student's parent or guardian, and the student sign the form.

Student name:				
Grade:				
Date service begins:				
Total hours or days assigned:				
Community service job description:				
Community service supervisor:				
Date	Location	Amount of Time	Staff Initials	Comments

FIGURE 3.20: Community service form.

*Visit **go.SolutionTree.com/RTIatWork** for a free reproducible version of this figure.*

Name: Grade:		Restitution supervisor:	
Date restitution begins: _____ Hours or days assigned: _____		Total hours of restitution assigned: _____ Total days of restitution assigned: _____	
Restitution job description		Why you are assigned restitution	
Restitution Log				

Date	Restitution Location	Time or Days	Staff Initials	Additional Comments

Administrator signature:
Restitution supervisor signature:
Parent or guardian signature:
Student signature:

FIGURE 3.21: Restitution form and log.

Directions: Write an apology letter. When you write it, do the following things.

- Address the stakeholders you have impacted due to your behavior.
- Identify and own the behavior that put you in this position.
- Acknowledge the hurt you caused due to your behavior.
- Identify the function of your behavior.
- Apologize to the stakeholders.
- Give three examples of what you have learned from this experience.
- Give three examples of what will prevent you from choosing this behavior again.
- Assure the stakeholders that this will never happen again.
- Sign the letter as a contract to your apology.

FIGURE 3.22: Apology letter student directions.

*Visit **go.SolutionTree.com/RTIatWork** for a free reproducible version of this figure.*

Figures 3.23 and 3.24 (page 110) show elementary and secondary behavior think sheets. Visit **go.SolutionTree.com/RTIatWork** for another elementary think sheet option. Figure 3.25 (page 111) shows the secondary-student contract.

Figure 3.26 (page 112) helps students make plans for showing self-control. Visit **go.SolutionTree.com/RTIatWork** to download free reproducibles that help students make plans for showing respect, achieving, and being on task.

I was feeling . . .

| Sad | Silly | Mad | Embarrassed | Afraid or worried | Bossy |

I wanted . . .

_____ attention   _____ to have fun   _____ to get my own way

_____ to be left alone   _____ someone to listen to me   _____ to show I was already mad

_____ something else: _____

I hurt _____ 's   _____ body   _____ feelings

_____ friends or reputation   _____ property   when I _____

_____

_____.

I could have _____ instead.

Student signature: _____   Date: _____

Parent signature: _____   Date: _____

Please return this sheet to the school office tomorrow.

FIGURE 3.23: Think sheet—elementary.

Visit **go.SolutionTree.com/RTIatWork** *for a free reproducible version of this figure.*

Student name:
Date:
Period:
What behavior did you demonstrate?
Why was that behavior not a good decision?
Who did you hurt?
What were you trying to accomplish?
Next time you have that goal, how will you meet it without hurting anybody? What behavior will you demonstrate instead?

FIGURE 3.24: Think sheet—secondary.

*Visit **go.SolutionTree.com/RTIatWork** for a free reproducible version of this figure.*

Student name:					
Focus behavior:					
Goal:					

Day	Monday	Tuesday	Wednesday	Thursday	Friday
Period one					
Period two					
Period three					
Period four					
Period five					
Period six					
Period seven					
Period eight					
Period nine					

Daily reward:	Was it earned? Yes No
Friday reward:	Was it earned? Yes No

Parent signature: _____   Date: _____

FIGURE 3.25: Student restorative contract—secondary.

*Visit **go.SolutionTree.com/RTIatWork** for a free reproducible version of this figure.*

Student name:
What is your plan for showing self-control?
What could happen when you do not show self-control?
Why should you show self-control?
Write three rules that help everyone show self-control.
What consequences should be in place for students who don't show self-control?
What are some examples of things that *are* and *are not* showing self-control?
On the back of this page, make a drawing about showing self-control.

FIGURE 3.26: Self-control reflection sheet.

Visit **go.SolutionTree.com/RTIatWork** *for a free reproducible version of this figure.*

PLC and Tier 1 RTI Integration Criteria Guide

Take a critical look at the four priority criteria outlined in figure 3.27 to help your school function as a PLC and to use the essential academic and social behavior standards and your school's behavior data to assign Tier 1 RTI (prevention) schoolwide and in every classroom. These priority criteria will help you prevent the systemic behavior gap that too often contributes to failure of implementation and will be your evidence of success criteria when completing the BIA. The rightmost column has the systemic behavior gap elements to focus on.

PLC and Tier 1 RTI Integration Criteria	Tier 1 Evidence Indicators	Reflect on These Evidence Indicators and the Systemic Behavior Gap They Will Address
Establish and operate an effective leadership team to address schoolwide prevention for behavior.	The school mission statement includes behavior.	
	Norms are established.	
	School goals and resource funding align.	
	Team purposes, roles, and responsibilities are clear.	
	The principal is an active member of the leadership team.	
	Teams meet monthly.	
	Teams utilize the Tier 1 prevention cycle stages at meetings with up-to-date data.	
	The leadership team considers multiple data points when identifying precise problem statements, developing actions, and deciding timelines.	
	The leadership team establishes schoolwide SMART goals and bases them on school data, prevention needs, and schoolwide and districtwide goals.	
	A leadership team member is designated for monthly teacher team push-in to receive teacher team input.	
	Teacher teams are educated on the once-monthly push-in process.	
	The teacher team push-in schedule and data are created with staff.	
	A team lead is identified to help ensure team-meeting fidelity.	
	Teacher teams have the coordination, design, and resources needed to implement preventions in their classrooms.	

continued →

FIGURE 3.27: PLC and Tier 1 RTI integration guide.

Visit go.SolutionTree.com/RTIatWork for a free reproducible version of this figure.

Essential academic and social behavior standards are identified and aligned to the school needs and mastery needs.	Clear responsibilities and roles for prevention are established for teacher teams.	A minor and major behavioral intervention process is defined.
Students and staff can identify and articulate the *why* of the teaching and learning of the essential academic and social behavior standards.	Each teacher team meeting includes an opportunity for teachers to assist each other with RTI needs and use the teacher team minutes or agenda to communicate RTI needs to the leadership team.	Flowcharts are available to guide the process and responses. These responses are research or evidence-based practices proven to teach and improve positive student behavior.
Sample processes, resources, and tools used schoolwide and in classrooms (slideshows, videos, matching games, role playing, announcements, passport days, and so on) are based on data for schoolwide teaching.	Teacher ongoing training and materials are provided based on need.	A behavioral intervention referral form aligns with the identified process.
Teachers understand their role in prevention in the classroom.	Staff are surveyed regularly to gather their feedback and input.	The school has clearly articulated teacher-managed and administrator-managed student behaviors.
Teachers have clear expectations of what a Tier 1 classroom should look like to support mastery of the essential academic and social behaviors.	Teachers review student work and other evidence of schoolwide and classroom teaching of essential behaviors.	The school has ongoing staff training on behavioral support procedures.
	A classroom walkthrough process ensures Tier 1 prevention best practices, the four Cs, and a classroom management system are in place in every classroom.	The school has a process for entering minor and major data, and other behavior data are clear and identified.
		A designated leadership team member ensures he or she collects data from the teacher teams regarding RTI needs.
		Collaborative teacher teams have a process to communicate needs prior to the push-in meeting if needed.
Identify and teach schoolwide essential academic and social behavior standards.	**Establish teacher teams' roles and responsibilities in ensuring Tier 1 prevention is in place in every classroom, invest in building their capacity, and maintain their commitment to their role and responsibilities.**	**Establish effective procedures for collecting multiple adequate levels of Tier 1 schoolwide data and provide ongoing training and support for how to use those data for decision making.**

Behavior Integration Assessment: Tier 1

How do you measure the implementation of the integration criteria? With the BIA. The comprehensive assessment tool is for all three tiers of integration criteria designed to address and prevent the systemic behavior gap. This assessment is designed for the leadership team to utilize as a guide to ensuring the criteria is in place to avoid the systemic behavior gap.

Keep in mind that the evidence indicators from each of the four criteria in figure 3.27 (page 113) provides your team with tangible evidence to justify your score. We've seen teams score themselves high on rubrics or say "We're doing all those things" when criteria are broadly written or lacking specificity. For this reason, we created the evidence indicators in the integration guide that allow teams to hold themselves accountable with artifacts and other evidence to justify a score of 2 (in place). It also gives teams a target toward mastery to put in place so they can achieve a score of 2 on the BIA.

Complete the following reproducibles as a schoolwide team.

▸ "Behavior Integration Assessment: Tier 1" (page 116)

▸ "RTI at Work Pyramid: Tier 1" (page 117)

▸ "Reflection One" (page 118)

Behavior Integration Assessment: Tier 1

With your schoolwide team, indicate what best describes your school's behavior tiered system RTI and PLC integration. Be honest. This assessment is designed to help you monitor your integration and reveal what tier and construct you need to focus on to improve.

Criteria	Score	Next Steps and Evidence
PLC at Work and Tier 1 of RTI at Work	Circle one. 0 = Not in place 1 = In progress 2 = In place	For any item scored 0 or 1, list next-step processes, tools, or forms that will help your school meet this criterion. For any item scored 2, list evidence (processes, tools, and forms) it is in place.
Establish and operate an effective leadership team to address schoolwide prevention for behavior.	0 1 2	
Identify and teach schoolwide essential academic and social behavior standards.	0 1 2	
Establish teacher teams' roles and responsibilities in ensuring Tier 1 prevention is in place in every classroom, invest in building their capacity, and maintain their commitment to their role and responsibilities.	0 1 2	
Establish effective procedures for collecting multiple adequate levels of Tier 1 schoolwide data and provide ongoing training and support for how to use those data for decision making.	0 1 2	

RTI at Work Pyramid: Tier 1

Use information from chapters 2 and 3 to complete the three indicated sections on the RTI at Work pyramid. Use the Plan–Do–Study–Act graphic (figure 3.3, page 57) as a visual guide to all the processes, tools, and forms shared in each of the stages of Tier 1. As a schoolwide team, complete the sections indicated in the RTI pyramid, with the focus on Tier 1.

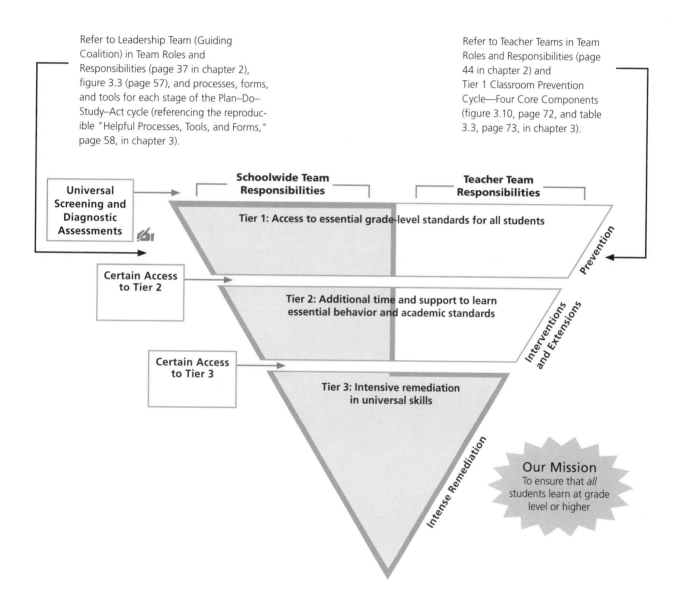

Refer to Leadership Team (Guiding Coalition) in Team Roles and Responsibilities (page 37 in chapter 2), figure 3.3 (page 57), and processes, forms, and tools for each stage of the Plan–Do–Study–Act cycle (referencing the reproducible "Helpful Processes, Tools, and Forms," page 58, in chapter 3).

Refer to Teacher Teams in Team Roles and Responsibilities (page 44 in chapter 2) and Tier 1 Classroom Prevention Cycle—Four Core Components (figure 3.10, page 72, and table 3.3, page 73, in chapter 3).

Universal Screening and Diagnostic Assessments

Schoolwide Team Responsibilities

Teacher Team Responsibilities

Tier 1: Access to essential grade-level standards for all students

Certain Access to Tier 2

Tier 2: Additional time and support to learn essential behavior and academic standards

Certain Access to Tier 3

Tier 3: Intensive remediation in universal skills

Prevention

Interventions and Extensions

Intense Remediation

Our Mission
To ensure that *all* students learn at grade level or higher

Source: Buffum, A., Mattos, M., & Malone, J. (2018). Taking action: A handbook for RTI at Work. *Bloomington, IN: Solution Tree Press.*

Reflection One

We know this is hard work. Take a minute to reflect and celebrate your learning with your team.

_____

_____

_____

Ask yourselves the following questions.

- "How are we feeling about Tier 1 implementation?"

- "What can we commit to as a team before delving into Tier 2?"

Record your responses here and date them so you log your RTI at Work journey with the focus on behavior.

Date:

_____

_____

_____

_____

_____

_____

_____

_____

_____

_____

_____

_____

_____

_____

_____

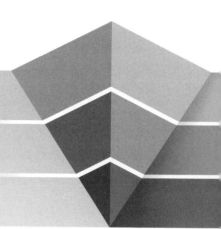

CHAPTER 4

Implementing Behavior Solutions at Tier 2—Intervention

In regard to behavior skills, Tier 2 focuses on reteaching the identified essential academic and social behavior standards. We will answer the following questions and others in this chapter.

- How do we identify who needs Tier 2 reteaching opportunities?

- How do we know what behavior standard to reteach?

- What does *function as a PLC* and *assign RTI for Tier 2* mean?

- What are everyone's roles and responsibilities in Tier 2 implementation?

- Where do we start?

- How will implementation help address the systemic behavior gap?

No matter what Tier 2 intervention you select or believe is best for identified students, it has to include a reteaching component. Tier 2 interventions commonly—and erroneously—require a student check-in procedure without intentionally reteaching the essential behavior standards, resulting in further need for Tier 2 intervention.

In this chapter, we provide the Tier 2 intervention cycle intentionally designed to help schools learn how to utilize behavior data to continuously identify targeted reteaching needs and to intervene. In addition, this chapter helps your teams head off and overcome the challenges of Tier 2 implementation. This starts by building a Tier 2 system of interventions (including entry and exit criteria and behavior academies).

Tier 2 Implementation Challenges

Tier 2 presents some challenges that appear in all tiers, and some that are specific to it. Common Tier 2 implementation challenges include the following, and each is discussed here in turn.

- ▸ What to do with struggling students

- ▸ What team roles are

- ▸ How Tier 2 interventions that occur in class differ from those outside class

- ▸ What to do as a classroom teacher who must develop or implement a Tier 2 intervention

Many educators struggle with knowing what to do for the students who are not consistently demonstrating essential academic and social behaviors standards. For example, a teacher may begin by using classroom management strategies (Tier 1 classroom response) for a student who repeatedly blurts out and interrupts class instruction. However, if the student's behavior continues to escalate resulting in out of classroom referrals (even with all the Tier 1 classroom supports in place), then this student should be identified to receive additional Tier 2 behavioral support.

Educators also struggle to understand how to leverage the PLC process so they can use behavior data to identify, create, and help implement reteaching of Tier 2 academic and social behavior needs. On the behavior side of (intervention) reteaching, the leadership team is tasked with coordinating and providing the Tier 2 interventions for students who are not responding to Tier 1 teaching. This differs from the academic side, on which teacher teams are the experts of their content, grade level, or department and therefore take lead responsibility for identifying, developing, and reteaching their students who did not respond to their Tier 1 academic instruction. The intervention team does not have a primary role in Tier 2 intervention support; this is the leadership team's primary function, and often a subset of the leadership team is designated for schoolwide Tier 2 implementation and support.

In addition to these challenges, the difference between Tier 2 interventions provided *outside* the classroom setting, not by the classroom teacher (such as social skills groups or Hands-Off Academy), and Tier 2 interventions that *include* the classroom teacher's collaboration and coordination (including monitoring and positive feedback, such as check-in/check-out) can be confusing.

Another challenge arises when the leadership team asks teachers to develop and implement Tier 2 interventions on their own. Being involved with several Tier 2 interventions can overwhelm a classroom teacher, who is probably not trained in developing and implementing behavior interventions, and whose school may also have poor implementation in Tier 1. Therefore, it is best practice that the leadership team helps support teacher teams when it comes to Tier 2 behavior intervention needs. For an example of the latter, consider the following scenario.

An elementary school teacher, Mrs. Jones was frustrated about her school's implementation of a Tier 2 intervention called *check-in/check-out* (*CICO*). Her frustration stemmed from the fact that her school was not implementing Tier 1 prevention with fidelity, yet was attempting to provide a Tier 2 intervention. Specifically, according to this teacher, no essential behavior skills were consistently identified and taught schoolwide, the school had no process for drilling into schoolwide behavior data (since no data were consistently collected), and no structure existed for identifying students who needed additional behavior reteaching opportunities. In fact, administration told staff they were expected to handle all Tier 1 and Tier 2 behavior challenges in their classrooms and the leadership team would only be available to provide support for Tier 3 behaviors. Given this current state, teachers were already frustrated with the lack of support from administration, which only worsened once they received the following email from the behavior specialist at their school.

> Dear Teachers,
>
> We will be implementing the CICO behavior intervention starting Monday. Please email me the names of the students with behavior needs in your class and exactly what behaviors you would like me to focus on as I check in with them in the morning and after school.
>
> Sincerely,
> Behavior Specialist

The teachers received no context or training prior to this email, ultimately leaving the behavior specialist with more than sixty-five students beginning the intervention. As you can imagine, implementation failed. Students were all over the place as they arrived for their check-in on Monday, teachers did not know their roles in the intervention, no one retaught skills, and behaviors continued escalating. The leadership team threw out CICO as an option after two weeks.

What went wrong? Why does this happen? What should have happened instead? How do you match Tier 2 reteaching opportunities based on data, and what do you provide during these opportunities?

Often, schools provide some sort of social skills group but lack a structured school-wide system of designing and implementing Tier 2 interventions based on student data. The site leadership team's responsibility is to create a subcommittee that will serve as the school's Tier 2 behavior team. This team, comprised of some leadership team members and staff members trained in research-based behavioral supports, will lead the school's efforts to do the following.

- Create Tier 2 behavior intervention criteria to assist teachers with identifying students for Tier 2 behavior interventions.

- Design interventions based on a behavior's identified function.

- Ensure reteaching of the Tier 1 behaviors that students haven't mastered.

- Coordinate and communicate with the staff that will provide Tier 2 behavior supports for each identified student.

Ultimately, a lack of this structure contributes to the systemic behavior gap, and it often leads to misconceptions about intervention effectiveness and to resentment between teachers and those assigning teachers' roles in providing Tier 2 interventions they are not trained to implement. This also results in poor communication and compliance-based, unreliable Tier 2 implementation.

Why should Tier 2 require us to reteach essential academic and social behaviors? Why is this where we need to begin? Because providing strategic Tier 2 intervention based on student needs (student behavior data, stakeholder input, intervention data, and so on) will ultimately help prevent these students' behaviors from escalating and requiring Tier 3 remediation supports.

The PLC and RTI Processes for Behavior in Tier 2

Tier 2 provides additional reteaching opportunities and supports to help students learn and demonstrate the taught essential academic and social behavior standards. We will provide the *how* for this work later in the chapter, but it starts with identifying why you are considering Tier 2 at your school, the criteria for which students will receive it, and what they will receive in the intervention. Consider the team roles outlined in chapter 2 (page 39) as you read this chapter.

Similar to academic interventions, there is a need for behavior interventions. Although the leadership team leads this process, the staff must work together to establish the behaviors and conditions for students in need to receive reteaching opportunities for the essential academic and social behavior standards as part of Tier 2.

Some Tier 2 interventions—or reteaching opportunities—are implemented *outside* the classroom, and some are implemented inside *and* outside the classroom. It is critical that teacher teams understand their roles and responsibilities in both cases. For example, a teacher-student contract is sometimes identified as a Tier 2 classroom intervention. However, members of the leadership team's Tier 2 subset do not necessarily have to address it. That does not necessarily require direct participation from the leadership team's Tier 2 subset members. On the other hand, a CICO intervention requires the collaboration, coordination, and collective responsibility of the leadership team's Tier 2 subset members and the teacher or teachers of that student.

The stronger the Tier 2 focus, the fewer the students who will need additional Tier 3 support. In order to strengthen this focus, the leadership team with input from the teacher teams, must determine, in a timely manner, which students need supplemental behavior support and provide them with help that targets the skills they are lacking. We also recommend that, whether the Tier 2 intervention is provided inside or outside the classroom, communication remain open among the individual teachers, the teacher teams, the leadership team Tier 2 subset lead, and the leadership team.

By the end of this chapter, you will learn how to complete the circled empty spaces shown in figure 4.1 as part of the culminating activity for Tier 2. Specifically, you will insert into the reproducible "RTI at Work Pyramid: Tier 2" (page 172) the Tier 2 behaviors, conditions, and the schoolwide team and teacher teams' responsibilities. In the next section, you will learn about the Tier 2 intervention cycle, which the Tier 2 subset of the leadership team should use.

Tier 2 Intervention Cycle

The Tier 2 intervention cycle will help you conceptualize and guide your school's Tier 2 behavior interventions based on targeted student behavior data. Members of the leadership team's Tier 2 subset use this cycle as they refer to current behavior data each time they meet (at least twice monthly) to identify, design, and help monitor implementation fidelity and effectiveness. Essentially, the leadership team's Tier 2 subset focuses on identifying students based on behavior data and stakeholder feedback and providing them with Tier 2 intervention (reteaching) opportunities for the essential academic and social behavior standards.

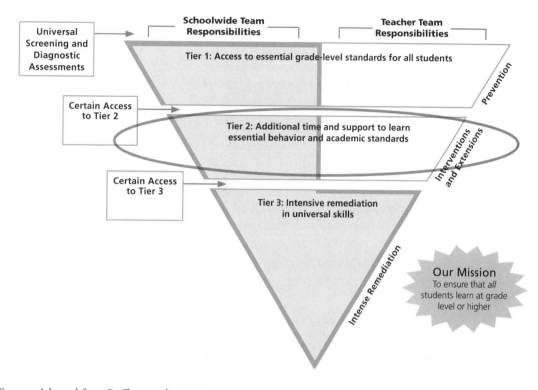

Source: Adapted from Buffum et al., 2018.

FIGURE 4.1: Culminating pyramid reference (Tier 2).

It is important to remember the key difference between academic (skill) and behavior (will) interventions.

▸ **For *academics*:** Teacher teams take lead responsibility for reteaching the essential academic standards and for extending learning for students who have mastered essentials. Other support staff can assist teacher teams with these academic interventions, but teacher teams are ultimately responsible for guiding the process.

▸ **For *behavior*:** The leadership team works with the entire faculty to identify, teach, and reinforce essential behaviors for all students. For students who are identified as needing additional support to master essential behaviors, the leadership team—through the subset Tier 2 behavior team—leads supplemental behavior interventions. Teachers and teacher teams help by identifying students for behavior support, implementing interventions that impact their classroom, monitoring student progress, and providing feedback to the leadership team. Figure 4.2 (page 124) illustrates the Tier 2 intervention cycle and where it exists in the RTI at Work pyramid.

Plan: Identify students who are not demonstrating mastery of the essential academic and social behavior standards based on schoolwide behavior data and criteria and develop targeted Tier 2 interventions (such as behavior academies) with entry and exit criteria based on their reteaching needs.

Who is responsible? The leadership team Tier 2 subset, based on schoolwide data and teacher input

Screen for prior skills and determine an appropriate supplemental academic or social behavior reteaching opportunity.

Tier 2 Intervention
Essential Academic and Social Behaviors

Academic Behaviors		
Metacognition	Self-concept	Self-monitoring
Motivation	Strategy	Volition

Social Behaviors
Responsible verbal and physical interactions with peers and adults
Appropriate language
Respect for property and materials
Independently staying on a required task
Regular attendance

Act: Implement actions and continuously improve based on the data; begin the cycle at least monthly; and modify, add to, or strengthen schoolwide or classroom-level teaching of identified essential academic and social behavior standards.

Who is responsible? The leadership team Tier 2 subset, based on staff input

Continue to monitor students receiving or exiting Tier 2.

Do: Introduce students to the Tier 2 behavior learning targets and begin reteaching academic and social behavior standards based on students' identified area of need (including self-monitoring checks). At least six to eight weeks of at least one reteaching session a week is recommended.

Who is responsible? The leadership team Tier 2 subset, in coordination with teachers, based on schoolwide data and teacher input

Give formative skill-building checks for mastery and generalization of the learned behavior standards (such as SMART goal, self-monitoring, and stakeholder feedback check-ins).

Study: Analyze behavior data, stakeholder feedback, student feedback, SMART goals, and the fidelity of implementation results, and adjust and modify Tier 2 intervention based on the data.

Who is responsible? The leadership team Tier 2 subset, based on schoolwide data and teacher input

Give a summative academic or social behavior mastery assessment at the end of supplemental intervention.

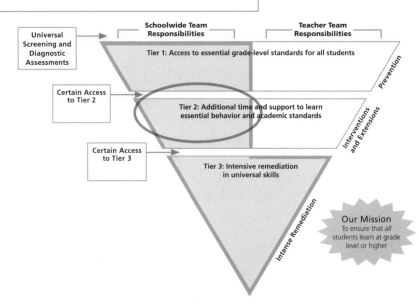

Source: Adapted from Buffum et al., 2018.

FIGURE 4.2: Tier 2 intervention cycle.

The leadership team employs this cycle while referring to current schoolwide behavior data. From those data, the leadership team decides on the Tier 2 intervention supports needed. The following sections highlight the Plan–Do–Study–Act stages (Deming, 1993) in greater depth, as well as commonly asked questions about the stages and processes, tools, and resources to help in each. Reference the purposes, roles, and responsibilities for Tier 2 identified in chapter 2 (page 39) as you apply this cycle in your PLC.

The reproducible "Helpful Processes, Tools, and Forms" (page 58) is where you can record the tier and make notes about the processes, tools, and forms you find most helpful for each stage of the Plan–Do–Study–Act cycle. We have provided best practices from our collective experiences, but you can incorporate others that will help you.

PLAN–Do–Study–Act

In the plan stage of the intervention cycle (highlighted in figure 4.3), students are identified and matched to Tier 2 interventions (reteaching) opportunities of essential academic and social behavior standards based on behavior data and teacher team input.

Plan: Identify students who are not demonstrating mastery of the essential academic and social behavior standards based on schoolwide behavior data and criteria and develop targeted Tier 2 interventions (such as behavior academies) with entry and exit criteria based on their reteaching needs.

Who is responsible? The leadership team Tier 2 subset, based on schoolwide data and teacher input

Screen for prior skills and determine an appropriate supplemental academic or social behavior reteaching opportunity.

Tier 2 Intervention
Essential Academic and Social Behaviors

Academic Behaviors		
Metacognition	Self-concept	Self-monitoring
Motivation	Strategy	Volition

Social Behaviors
Responsible verbal and physical interactions with peers and adults
Appropriate language
Respect for property and materials
Independently staying on a required task
Regular attendance

Act: Implement actions and continuously improve based on the data; begin the cycle at least monthly; and modify, add to, or strengthen schoolwide or classroom-level teaching of identified essential academic and social behavior standards.

Who is responsible? The leadership team Tier 2 subset, based on staff input

Continue to monitor students receiving or exiting Tier 2.

Do: Introduce students to the Tier 2 behavior learning targets and begin reteaching academic and social behavior standards based on students' identified area of need (including self-monitoring checks). At least six to eight weeks of at least one reteaching session a week is recommended.

Who is responsible? The leadership team Tier 2 subset, in coordination with teachers, based on schoolwide data and teacher input

Give formative skill-building checks for mastery and generalization of the learned behavior standards (such as SMART goal, self-monitoring, and stakeholder feedback check-ins).

Study: Analyze behavior data, stakeholder feedback, student feedback, SMART goals, and the fidelity of implementation results, and adjust and modify Tier 2 intervention based on the data.

Who is responsible? The leadership team Tier 2 subset, based on schoolwide data and teacher input

Give a summative academic or social behavior mastery assessment at the end of supplemental intervention.

Source: Adapted from Buffum et al., 2018.

FIGURE 4.3: Tier 2 plan stage.

> ▸ **Why:** To use schoolwide data and teacher team input to formalize Tier 2

> ▸ **Who:** The Tier 2 subset of the leadership team with teacher team input

> ▸ **What:** Planning and coordinating reteaching of Tier 2 essential academic and social behavior standards based on schoolwide data and teacher team input; identifying students who have not demonstrated mastery of the essential behavior standards

> ▸ **When:** At least twice monthly

Commonly Asked Questions in the Plan Stage

Consider these questions.

> ▸ How do we decide which academic and social behavior standards we should reteach?

> ▸ Who is responsible for coordinating and preparing these Tier 2 opportunities?

> ▸ When does this reteaching take place?

> ▸ What happens during the reteaching sessions?

> ▸ What data should we utilize to decide which students need additional reteaching of the essential behavior standards?

Tier 2 Plan Stage: Processes, Tools, and Forms

In this section, you will find processes, tools, and forms designed to help you begin the work in the plan stage.

Tier 2 Intervention Will and Skill Reference

Table 4.1 compares will-based versus skill-based Tier 2 interventions. The left side of the table is will based, and the right side is skill based.

Menu of Tier 2 Intervention Response Options

Table 4.2 lists Tier 2 intervention response options and clarifies some of the differences between leadership team (Tier 2 subset led) and teacher teams (teacher led).

TABLE 4.1: Will-Based and Skill-Based Tier 2 Interventions

Will-Based Tier 2 Interventions *Won't Do*	Skill-Based Tier 2 Interventions *Can't Do*

• *Will interventions* target students who have or could have mastered the essential standard but lack the essential social behavior to master it.*
 	
• Often, schoolwide team-led (Tier 2 subset) Tier 2 interventions fit in this category.
 	
• Possible will-based Tier 2 interventions:
  » Anger management group
  » Social skills group
  » Upstander Academy
	• *Skill interventions* target students who have not mastered how to do academic essential standards.*
	
	• Often, teacher-led Tier 2 interventions fit in this category.
	
	• Possible skill-based Tier 2 interventions:
	  » Embedded time in the master schedule for teacher teams to collectively intervene and extend student learning (sometimes called *What I Need time* or *WIN time*)
	  » Time management
	  » Organization

*See pages 161–162 in *Taking Action* (Buffum et al., 2018).

TABLE 4.2: Tier 2 Menu of Response Options

Tier 2 Intervention (Will or Skill)	Example or Explanation*	Led By
Social Skills Academy	Social Skills Academy is for reteaching essential behavior skills needed to ensure students demonstrate appropriate behaviors in a variety of settings, including hallways, classrooms, and the playground.	Leadership team (Tier 2 subset)
Anger management	Anger management is designed to help students struggling with anger learn new skills to self-monitor, self-regulate, and process their emotions in a healthy way.	Leadership team (Tier 2 subset)
Upstander Academy	Upstander Academy is for reteaching essential behavior skills, such as courage and leadership, to ensure students do not bully other students.	Leadership team (Tier 2 subset)
Hands-Off Academy	Hands-Off Academy is for reteaching essential behavior skills needed to ensure students keep their hands to themselves.	Leadership team (Tier 2 subset)
Organizational skills	Organizational skills are retaught so students learn the essential behavior skills needed to demonstrate self-discipline in school.	Leadership team (Tier 2 subset)
Peer mediation	Peer mediation is a method of additional peer-to-peer support opportunities using conflict resolution skills.	Leadership team (Tier 2 subset)

continued →

Structured play or recess (page 144)	Structured play or recess helps students internalize their learned skills during play or recess in an organized fashion. For example, a student who is learning how to take turns may have a structured recess intervention designed to help him apply these skills during an activity or game that requires their application.	Leadership team (Tier 2 subset)
CICO Academy skill teaching component (page 137)	CICO Academy is in addition to the traditional check-in/check-out intervention procedures. CICO Academy is designed for reteaching essential social behavior skills (often pulling out students) needed to ensure students can access their education by learning the skills they need to meet their CICO goals. It is best for students with repeated minor misbehaviors such as blurting out or having difficulty staying on task.	Leadership team (Tier 2 subset)
Small groups or out-of-classroom circles	Circle groups are another way of helping students process common areas of challenges or concerns, including grief, anxiety, depression, and trauma.	Leadership team (Tier 2 subset)
Behavior support plans	Behavior support plans are written with the focus on improving one or two focus social behaviors and include a teaching component of the skills necessary to master the identified social behaviors in the plan.	Leadership team (Tier 2 subset)
Friendship groups (page 145)	Friendship groups teach how to establish and maintain relationships and how to resolve conflicts.	Leadership team (Tier 2 subset)
Civility Academy	Civility Academy is for reteaching students how to interact civilly and how to coexist in peace with each other. In this academy, students are taught how to practice empathy, tolerance, and learn how to listen to other perspectives respectfully.	Leadership team (Tier 2 subset)
Mentoring (page 142)	Mentoring can include the support from a teacher, staff member, community member, or older student who checks in with a student about an identified area of focus.	Leadership team (Tier 2 subset)
Structured break system (development and teaching social behavior skill component)	A structured break system is for reteaching the essential behavior skills needed to ensure students demonstrate appropriate behaviors in a variety of settings, including hallways, classrooms, and the playground.	Leadership team (Tier 2 subset)
Cognitive behavior therapy group	Cognitive behavior therapy (CBT) is designed to help students who need to learn skills to help combat anxiety and depression.	Leadership team (Tier 2 subset)
Classroom circles or meetings	Classroom circles or meetings are for learning skills from each other on academic essential standards (including, for example, growth mindset strategies).	Teacher team

Structured break system (classroom teacher monitored component)	A structured break system is for reteaching essential behavior skills needed to ensure students demonstrate appropriate behaviors in a variety of settings, including hallways, classrooms, and the playground. The teachers role is to help provide the student the opportunity to take their breaks accordingly and monitor use of the plan in their classroom.	Teacher team
CICO (teacher monitored)	A CICO Tier 2 intervention requires teachers to complete a monitoring chart throughout parts of the day or class periods and to provide the student feedback regarding why the student does or does not receive points.	Teacher team
Restorative teacher or student contracts (teacher followed and monitored)	A restorative teacher or student contract requires co-developing a contract and ongoing monitoring by the teacher and student to ensure they are following their commitments to each other for classroom academic behaviors.	Teacher team
Tier 2 classroom contract	A Tier 2 classroom contract focuses on one or two academic behaviors that need improvement.	Teacher team
Homework Club	This academic standards-based support has students focus on one or two skills that help them complete homework, learn how to ask for help, and self-monitor when feeling overwhelmed.	Leadership team
Organizational skills	This academic standards-based support teaches one or two skills that aid organization.	Leadership team
Time management	This academic standards-based support teaches on one or two skills that help students manage their time effectively.	Leadership team

*Some of these leadership team-led interventions require teachers to help monitor and provide input on how students apply their learning.

*Visit **go.SolutionTree.com/RTIatWork** for a free reproducible version of this table.*

Tier 2 Intervention-Planning Data Check

To provide adequate reteaching opportunities for students who are not demonstrating appropriate academic and social behaviors, it is essential that the leadership team (specifically the Tier 2 leadership team subset) identify the story behind the Tier 2 behavior data. This way, it can ensure the Tier 2 interventions match the behavior needs. The team should do a twice-monthly Tier 2 intervention-planning data check, completing the form in figure 4.4 (page 130). The planning data check helps ensure everyone is using behavior data to serve schoolwide Tier 2 needs. Refer to the section Data Collection (page 87) for examples of the kinds of data the team can reference during this process.

Twice-monthly meeting: *September 3*	
What Tier 2 interventions are currently offered at the school?	*CICO*
How many students are currently receiving Tier 2 behavior supports at the school, and for what essential behaviors are they receiving it?	*CICO: Four sixth-grade students need help learning self-control.*
What are the schoolwide behavior data trends?	*Three students in fourth grade and five students in fifth grade are demonstrating repeated minor classroom referrals and meet the CICO Tier 2 criteria.* *Three students in third grade are demonstrating repeated referrals for hands-on behavior in and out of the classroom.*
What input do the collaborative teacher teams have for Tier 2 RTI needs?	*Based on the monthly teacher team push-in input, the third-grade team noted needing reteaching opportunities for its identified students who are receiving repeated minor hands-on behavior referrals.*
Which essential academic or social behavior standards need reteaching?	*CICO: Self-monitoring* *Hands-Off Academy: Self-control*
What additional Tier 2 intervention is needed? When is the start date?	*Hands-Off Academy for the three third-grade students* *Adding students who meet the CICO criteria into CICO starting Monday, March 1*

FIGURE 4.4: Tier 2 intervention-planning data check example.

*Visit **go.SolutionTree.com/RTIatWork** for a free reproducible version of this figure.*

Tier 2 Intervention Description and Entry and Exit Criteria

A Tier 2 intervention description and criteria reference sheet (figure 4.5) summarizes the offered Tier 2 interventions at the school and provides the criteria for a student to receive (and cease needing to receive) a specific intervention (How do students access the Tier 2 intervention? How do they get in? How do they get out?). This is a great resource for both the leadership team Tier 2 subset and the entire staff to reference if they need additional supports for students. Table 4.3 (page 136) offers methods for monitoring student progress in Tier 2.

Tier 2 Intervention Snapshot

The Tier 2 intervention snapshot in figure 4.6 (page 133) helps organize Tier 2 interventions based on data. The Tier 2 leadership team subset completes this form, reviewing it twice monthly.

Tier 2 Intervention	Intervention Description	Entry Criteria for the Intervention	Exit Criteria for the Intervention (Must meet at least one)
Social skills reteaching	Students will learn appropriate social skills. They will receive opportunities to generalize the newly learned skills in appropriate settings.	• The student has challenges getting along with peers inside and outside the classroom. • The student has three or more minor referrals. • A teacher or administrator writes a referral. • Other (such as a parent request or support provider request)	• The student uses taught skills most of the time with peers, inside and outside the classroom setting. • The student has no more than two minor referrals for this behavior for a minimum of six weeks. • The Tier 2 leadership team subset and stakeholder recommend exit.
CICO	Students will experience additional positive adult interactions throughout the day to help monitor and give feedback on appropriate behaviors. They will learn the skills they need to meet their CICO goals.	• The student has repeated minor misbehavior challenges following rules in the classroom setting. • The student has three or more minor referrals. • A teacher or administrator writes a referral. • Other (such as a parent request or support provider request)	• The student uses taught skills most of the time in the classroom setting. • The student has no more than two minor referrals for this behavior for a minimum of six weeks. • The student meets all CICO goals for at least six weeks at 80 percent compliance or higher. (Adjust this percentage as needed.) • The Tier 2 leadership team subset and stakeholder recommend exit.
Hands-Off Academy	Students will receive instruction on how to keep their hands to themselves. They will keep their behaviors in mind by completing the "Hands-Off Academy: Weekly Student Self-Monitoring Sheet" reproducible (page 153). They will learn how to assess their anger triggers and have opportunities to practice appropriate replacement behaviors.	• The student has challenges keeping his or her hands to himself or herself. • The student has three minor physical contact referrals or has one major physical contact referral or incident. • A teacher or administrator writes a referral. • Other (such as a parent request or support provider request)	• The student uses taught skills to calm down when angry in all settings. • The student has fewer than two minor or major referrals for this behavior for a minimum of six weeks. • The student meets Hands-Off Academy goals for at least six weeks at 80 percent compliance or higher. (Adjust this percentage as needed.) • The Tier 2 leadership team subset and stakeholder recommend exit.

continued →

FIGURE 4.5: Tier 2 intervention description and entry and exit criteria reference sheet.

Behavior contract	Students will work with an adult to develop and monitor a behavior contract. They will learn how to meet the requirements on the behavior contract.	• The student has challenges with a specific behavior (such as tardiness or incomplete homework). • The student has three or more incidents of the same addressed behavior. • A teacher or administrator writes a referral. • Other (such as a parent request or support provider request)	• The student follows the contract agreement with no referrals for a minimum of six weeks. • The student has no more than two minor or major referrals (or combination of the two) for this behavior for a minimum of six weeks. • The student has met his or her contract goals for a minimum of six weeks. • The Tier 2 leadership team subset and stakeholder recommend exit.
Class break	Students will learn strategies to calm down when they perceive an unfair situation in the classroom setting. They will learn how to use a class break process and their newly learned skills to calm down and return to class without escalating their behavior.	• The student demonstrates challenges calming down when upset. • The student has three-plus minor or major referrals (or a combination) resulting from escalated behavior when upset. • A teacher or administrator writes a referral. • Other (such as a parent request or support provider request)	• The student uses appropriate retaught skills to self-monitor and self-regulate emotions. • The student has no more than two minor referrals for this behavior for a minimum of six weeks. • The student uses the class break system appropriately for at least six weeks. • The Tier 2 leadership team subset and stakeholder recommend exit.

Visit **go.SolutionTree.com/RTIatWork** for a free reproducible version of this figure.

Tier 2 Intervention: *CICO*	Method to Improve or Maintain Implementation
Date: *February 27*	
What are the entry criteria for this Tier 2 intervention?	*The criteria to place students on CICO are three classroom minor referrals.* *Teacher or collaborative teacher team input on students who may benefit may also be considered for CICO.* *A grade-level administrator makes contact with the students' parents and explains everyone's responsibilities for this Tier 2 intervention to be successful. In addition, the administrator sends a letter home to the parents that reiterates the phone conversation.* *The Tier 2 subset also notifies teachers that they will have a student on CICO and reviews their responsibilities. It informs the teachers that it will collect data, and if a student meets the goal of 80 percent compliance for six to eight weeks, the student will exit the Tier 2 intervention.*
How often does this Tier 2 leadership team subset meet?	*The behavior intervention teacher (or the school's best trained staff member in the area of behavior interventions) meets with the students and explains the student responsibilities and rewards for achieving the targeted behavior goals.* *Students meet briefly with a designated adult every morning for a check-in send-off and at the end of school for a check-out debrief.* *Groups of four or five meet weekly on Thursdays to learn and practice skills they need in order to master their CICO goals (that is, CICO Academy). This is provided by a designated staff member identified by the Tier 2 leadership team subset.*
What supports do students receive in this Tier 2 intervention?	*Behavior contracts* *CICO behavior forms (pages 147 and 148)* *CICO Academy* *Peer-group role playing and discussion*
How many students are currently in this Tier 2 intervention?	*Seven students:* *• Two in grade 4* *• Two in grade 5* *• Three in grade 6*
Do students in this Tier 2 intervention have academic and social behavior goals? Is there an incentive plan built into the behavior goals?	*Yes, they have goals. By April 18, we will reduce the number of CICO students receiving classroom kickouts (referrals out of the classroom) by at least 80 percent. Currently, the reflection center has documented an average of three kickouts per week for students receiving CICO.* *Students in this plan haven't been consistently receiving their daily and weekly CICO incentives. We met with each student and had them take a brief motivator survey to ensure the incentives we align to their CICO are meaningful for them. We will report on the incentives at the next meeting.*

FIGURE 4.6: Tier 2 intervention snapshot—CICO example.

continued →

How are these students monitored, and how often?	*Daily check-ins and check-outs* *Weekly session groups* *Google check-in surveys (weekly teacher and student)* *Reflection center frequency check-ins*
How are these Tier 2 intervention progress-monitoring data shared with the leadership team, and how often?	*Shared monthly with our leadership team by the Tier 2 leadership team subset lead in a shared Google document*
How is this Tier 2 intervention information shared with the school staff, and how often?*	*Shared twice monthly with our whole staff*
What are the exit criteria for this Tier 2 intervention?	*Six consecutive weeks of 80 percent compliance or higher and zero classroom kickouts*
How should the Tier 2 leadership team subset react when a student is not responding to this intervention?	*Put the student in a Tier 3 system of identifying barriers and specific triggers that anger the student or distract him or her from achieving goals. Systems are in place to answer the following questions.* • *What does the problem behavior look like?* • *How often does the problem behavior occur?* • *How long does the problem behavior last when it does occur?* • *What is the problem behavior's intensity or level of danger?* *Identify the behavior's function, triggers, and settings to help predict when the behavior may occur. The focus is to minimize class kickouts and increase the level of student achievement at Tier 2.*

*Teachers during a staff meeting get a brief update from the leadership team Tier 2 subset on how many of the students in the school receiving this intervention are responding and meeting their goals.

Visit **go.SolutionTree.com/RTIatWork** for a free reproducible version of this figure.

Plan–DO–Study–Act

In the do stage of the intervention cycle (highlighted in figure 4.7), begin providing Tier 2 reteaching to the identified students based on schoolwide data and teacher team input.

▶ **Why:** To provide the planned Tier 2 intervention by reteaching the identified essential academic and social behavior standards

▶ **Who:** The Tier 2 subset of the leadership team with teacher team input

▶ **What:** Reteaching identified essential academic and social behavior standards and giving opportunities for self-monitoring, generalization, and mastery assessment

Plan: Identify students who are not demonstrating mastery of the essential academic and social behavior standards based on schoolwide behavior data and criteria and develop targeted Tier 2 interventions (such as behavior academies) with entry and exit criteria based on their reteaching needs.

Who is responsible? The leadership team Tier 2 subset, based on schoolwide data and teacher input

Screen for prior skills and determine an appropriate supplemental academic or social behavior reteaching opportunity.

Tier 2 Intervention
Essential Academic and Social Behaviors

Academic Behaviors		
Metacognition	Self-concept	Self-monitoring
Motivation	Strategy	Volition
Social Behaviors		
Responsible verbal and physical interactions with peers and adults		
Appropriate language		
Respect for property and materials		
Independently staying on a required task		
Regular attendance		

Act: Implement actions and continuously improve based on the data; begin the cycle at least monthly; and modify, add to, or strengthen schoolwide or classroom-level teaching of identified essential academic and social behavior standards.

Who is responsible? The leadership team Tier 2 subset, based on staff input

Continue to monitor students receiving or exiting Tier 2.

Do: Introduce students to the Tier 2 behavior learning targets and begin reteaching academic and social behavior standards based on students' identified area of need (including self-monitoring checks). At least six to eight weeks of at least one reteaching session a week is recommended.

Who is responsible? The leadership team Tier 2 subset, in coordination with teachers, based on schoolwide data and teacher input

Give formative skill-building checks for mastery and generalization of the learned behavior standards (such as SMART goal, self-monitoring, and stakeholder feedback check-ins).

Study: Analyze behavior data, stakeholder feedback, student feedback, SMART goals, and the fidelity of implementation results, and adjust and modify Tier 2 intervention based on the data.

Who is responsible? The leadership team Tier 2 subset, based on schoolwide data and teacher input

Give a summative academic or social behavior mastery assessment at the end of supplemental intervention.

Source: Adapted from Buffum et al., 2018.

FIGURE 4.7: Tier 2 do stage.

▶ **When:** At least one session of reteaching weekly for six to eight weeks (approximately thirty minutes a session)

Commonly Asked Questions in the Do Stage

Consider these questions.

▶ Who reteaches the academic behaviors, and who reteaches the social behaviors?

▶ How long are these students in Tier 2?

▶ Who is responsible for providing Tier 2 interventions?

Tier 2 Do Stage: Processes, Tools, and Forms

In this section, you will find processes, tools, and forms designed to help you begin the work in the do stage.

TABLE 4.3: Methods for Monitoring Student Progress in Tier 2

Method	Explanation
Intervention session attendance	Number of days receiving Tier 2 reteaching opportunities (present for the intervention)
Academic and behavior goals	Student goals set around academic and behavior success to help demonstrate the impact of the academic and social behavior intervention
Number of behavior incidents monitored on a weekly basis	Logged number of minor and major school referrals
Daily check-ins and check-outs	If Tier 2 intervention has a CICO component, data sheets logging participation of CICO collected and utilized
Weekly session groups	Topic and participation of weekly group reteaching opportunities
Check-in surveys	Student or teacher check-in surveys based on perception of student progress
Reflection center frequency check-ins	Number of reflection center forms completed

Visit **go.SolutionTree.com/RTIatWork** *for a free reproducible version of this table.*

Tier 2 Behavior Academies: Structure for Organizing and Delivering Reteaching Opportunities

A *behavior academy* is a practical, effective, and doable format for providing reteaching to students. The Tier 2 leadership subset will designate staff who can administer an academy to a group or individual students. Refer back to table 4.2 (page 127) for a description of some academies' purposes.

We have effectively implemented this five-step approach, but it is not the only Tier 2 reteaching format you can employ in your system. Behavior academies align with the schoolwide essential academic and social behavior standards. We designed their implementation structure to work, with some modifications, for all grade levels and practitioners.

1. Academic and social behavior skill preassessment

2. Introduction, goal setting, and self-monitoring weekly check-ins

3. Behavior skill rehearsals—reteaching—based on skill needs (see appendix B, page 237, for behavior rehearsal cards); for between six and eight weeks, target skills related to the academic or social behavior skill deficit

4. Reflection journal entry and commitment (ask student what mastery looks like for the academic or social skill the academy focuses on); homework practice component at every session

5. Summative behavior standard assessment mastery

Table 4.4 pairs behavior academies with the academic and social behavior skills that they address. Figure 4.8 (page 138) pairs Tier 2 problem statements with Tier 2 behavior academies that address the problems. Refer back to the Problem Statements section (page 88) for more about that topic.

The "Behavior Academy: Secondary Student Goal Setting and Progress Monitoring" reproducible (page 149) and "Behavior Academy: Elementary Student Goal Setting and Progress Monitoring" reproducible (page 151) will help students set goals and monitor their progress.

CICO Academy

CICO Academy is a common approach, and here are the usual steps.

1. Each student has a CICO folder, which holds copies of the "CICO Daily Check-In" reproducible (page 147).

2. The student checks in with staff at the office every morning before school. Together, student and staff quickly review the student's expectations and goals. The student picks up the folder and returns the signed form from the day before to the designated check-in staff.

TABLE 4.4: Matching Essential Skill Needs to Tier 2 Behavior Academies

Academic Behavior Skill	Tier 2 Reteaching Opportunity
Metacognition	Mindfulness Academy
Self-concept	Self-Efficacy Academy
Self-monitoring	Self-Discipline Academy
Motivation	Self-Efficacy Academy
Strategy	Organizational Skills Academy
Volition (grit)	Self-Discipline Academy
Social Behavior Skill	**Tier 2 Reteaching Opportunity**
Responsible verbal and physical interactions with peers and adults	Hands-Off Academy
Appropriate language	Social Skills Academy
Respect for property and materials	Civility Academy
Independently staying on a required task	CICO Academy
Regular attendance	Attendance Academy

Problem Statement	Solution Action
A group of boys constantly gets into trouble for not keeping their hands to themselves during unstructured time at school. They have been suspended in the past for the same behavior but continue to have difficulty keeping their hands to themselves.	Hands-Off Academy
Three students are having difficulty with the way they respond to other students both in and out of the classroom when they do not agree with the other students' opinions or beliefs. It has resulted in not hands-on behavior but inappropriate discourse.	Civility Academy
A group of students are failing in school. They do not display disruptive behaviors in class, but they do not complete any work, and they do not seem motivated to their teachers. Their teachers have talked to them, but they continue putting forth no effort in class.	Organizational Group Academy
A group of students is having a difficult time establishing positive relationships with other students. They constantly invade the personal space of other students and make inappropriate comments to get attention.	Social Skills Academy
A group of girls has been bullying other students for months. During structured and unstructured times, they send mean text messages to other girls they do not like. The administrator has talked to them several times, but they continue to engage in this behavior.	Upstander Academy
A group of students gets sent to the office daily for disruptive behaviors in the classroom. Their teachers are frustrated and feel like the students are getting away with their behavior. The students have repeatedly received suspensions for disruptive classroom behavior, but they continue to demonstrate similar behaviors.	CICO Academy

FIGURE 4.8: Matching Tier 2 problem statements to Tier 2 behavior academies.

3. The student's teacher rates behaviors during allotted periods throughout the day.

4. After school, the student meets with teacher in the office with the filled-out daily form. The teacher helps the student calculate the score and gives a daily progress report to have signed by a parent or guardian. Students who meet their daily goal earn a small incentive.

5. The check-out teacher collects folders and staples the progress report in the student agenda for a parent or guardian signature.

The following is an example of incentives a school might offer for different point totals (out of fifty) that students earn on their "CICO Daily Check-In" reproducible.

40 points:	Principal's assistant for the day	**20 points:**	Morning announcement guest speaker
25 points:	Extra recess pass with friend	**20 points:**	Lunch with friends
		20 points:	Lunch with the staff
25 points:	Gym assistant trainer for thirty minutes	**10 points:**	Ice pop
25 points:	Free computer time for thirty minutes	**10 points:**	Popcorn
		10 points:	Fun pencil, eraser, or folder
25 points:	Free art time for thirty minutes	**5 points:**	Get-out-of-homework-free pass

Figure 4.9 is a template addressed to parents and guardians when a team decides to implement CICO. Figure 4.10 (page 140) is an example of a CICO-specific student goal-setting form. In this example, the intervention CICO is indicated. The "CICO Daily Check-In" (page 147) and "CICO Contract" reproducible (page 148) help maintain the CICO intervention. Visit **go.SolutionTree.com/RTIatWork** to download a free reproducible version of a CICO daily report to send to parents for signing.

To the parent or guardian of ___Toby Smith_____

Your child has been recommended for a daily check-in/check-out (CICO) intervention. CICO helps students meet our schoolwide expectations in a positive way. Your child will be assigned a coordinator and be responsible for checking in with that person each morning and checking out at the end of each day.

Your child's teacher will fill out a report daily, and the assigned coordinator will review the report at check-in and check-out time. *Please review and sign the report each night.* Your child will earn incentives and rewards for appropriate behavior. As parents, you are responsible for making sure your child arrives on time each day for check-in and for reviewing and signing the daily report card. Together, we can make this a positive experience for your child.

Thank you. You are an important part of your child's success. Please contact the assigned coordinator at _____555-7721_____ if you have any questions.

Please check only one:

__✓__ I do give consent for my child to participate.

____ I do not give consent for my child to participate.

Parent or guardian signature: ___Julie Smith_____ Date: __February 1__

Please return signed form to the front office

FIGURE 4.9: CICO intervention letter to parents and guardians.

*Visit **go.SolutionTree.com/RTIatWork** for a free reproducible version of this figure.*

Student name: Toby Smith
Mentor name: Mr. Jaylen
Date starting CICO: February 2
I am enrolled in CICO so I can improve the following behavior skills. Doing my work and not interrupting people
My daily CICO goal is _____30_____ out of _____50_____ points. I earn a privilege at the end of each day if I meet this goal.
My weekly CICO goal is _____150_____ out of _____250_____ points. I earn something at the end of the day on Friday if I have met my daily goal.
I am going to continue earning my points by doing these things. Keep hands to self, try to breathe when I want to talk to someone (during work time)
I commit to trying my best every day. Student signature: ___Toby Smith___ Mentor signature: ___Mr. Jaylen___

FIGURE 4.10: Student goal-setting form—CICO example.

*Visit **go.SolutionTree.com/RTIatWork** for a free reproducible version of this figure.*

Tier 2 Behavior Rehearsal Cards

Tier 2 behavior rehearsal cards are a simple way to reteach unmastered skills aligned with the identified academic and social behavior standards. We designed them to address practitioners' need for a simple and efficient reteaching tool for students receiving or needing Tier 2 behavior interventions. Figure 4.11 shows the Hands-Off Academy behavior rehearsal cards. The remainder of the cards for behavior academies are in appendix B (page 237).

Students can do the following with the Tier 2 behavior rehearsal cards.

▶ Look up definitions of the behavior term first.

▶ Come up with their own scenarios.

▶ Draw the wrong way and right way to exercise the behavior.

Why: We are a hands-off school.

What: I will learn skills to help keep my hands to myself.

How: Print the cards on card stock, cut them out, and distribute them to students so they can role-play one-on-one with you or in pairs or triads with other students.

Additional suggestions: After students rehearse, have them complete their self-monitoring sheet. Then have them complete a journal entry (or share verbally or by another preferred modality) explaining what they rehearsed and commit to further practicing the skills. Assign practice at home and in the school setting, and have students share how they did so at the next session.

Show Self-Control You are having a difficult time keeping your hands to yourself when you perceive something to be unfair or you feel angry. What is the right way? What is the wrong way?	**Get Calm** You are having a difficult time calming yourself down when something or someone upsets you. You decide to use your hands to react instead of walking away and trying to calm down. What is the right way? What is the wrong way?
Show Self-Regulation You notice you are getting angry at a student or situation, but you decide to ignore your trigger signs and continue to escalate to hands-on behavior. What is the right way? What is the wrong way?	**Hold Yourself Accountable** You have received a consequence for putting your hands on another student. You are very upset and argue with the administrator or teacher that it was not your fault and you will not accept responsibility for your behavior. What is the right way? What is the wrong way?
Ask for Help You have a disagreement with another student over the rules of a game. Instead of asking for help from an adult, you decide to use your hands to solve the disagreement. What is the right way? What is the wrong way?	**Show Patience** You consistently push students out of your way so you can be first walking into or out of class. What is the right way? What is the wrong way?
Solve Problems You are so upset at a student or situation that you do not consider other ways you can solve the problem without using your hands. What is the right way? What is the wrong way?	**Self-Monitor and Self-Correct** You notice you are having trouble keeping your hands to yourself during a recess game, but you decide to continue engaging in the behavior because you believe you are already going to get into trouble. What is the right way? What is the wrong way?

FIGURE 4.11: Hands-Off Academy behavior rehearsal cards.

- ▶ Define the behavior at the start of a unit based on their background knowledge.

- ▶ Give examples of mastery in an exam format.

- ▶ Finish a writing prompt aligned with the skills.

- ▶ Complete homework demonstrating using the skills in multiple settings.

- ▶ Identify a problem in the school or community similar to the scenarios.

- ▶ Construct a service learning project to address the behavior challenge.

- ▶ Help design and teach a lesson around the behavior topic.

- ▶ Present to a younger group on the behavior.

- ▶ Engage in role playing.

- ▶ Get a stakeholder to sign off on his or her skill demonstration.

- ▶ Film a video demonstrating the appropriate ways to demonstrate each skill.

- ▶ Develop a how-to guide for others who need help with these skills.

You can adjust the eight-step process explained in appendix B (page 237) for use as a Tier 1 prevention with the whole class, and more often for Tier 2 reteaching in smaller groups or one-on-one with students.

- ▶ **Whole class:** When the purpose is Tier 1 prevention, teachers base how often they use the cards on classroom behavior need. For example, a teacher may decide to use them once a week or once a month.

- ▶ **Small groups or individual students:** When the purpose is reteaching targeted skills or behaviors, teachers hold rehearsals at least once a week, thirty minutes per session, for between six and eight weeks. For example, the behavior cards work if a student is receiving CICO and needs to relearn self-monitoring skills in all settings.

Academy students complete a weekly self-monitoring sheet; see the "Hands-Off Academy: Weekly Student Self-Monitoring Sheet" reproducible (page 153) for an example. Visit **go.SolutionTree.com/RTIatWork** to download a free reproducible version of a customizable version that works for all academies.

Mentor Logs

A mentor is selected based on a student's input when asked what adult at the school he or she is comfortable checking in with and asking for help. This person is the student's advocate and support system at the school. Often, students can ask mentors to attend meetings—student success team meetings, behavior plan meetings, IEP meetings, for example—for the student. The student and mentor complete a mentor log like the one in figure 4.12 during meetings.

When a mentor and student meet, often it is an authentic occurrence, but the following steps help ensure intentionality and focus on what the student needs in order to master the essential skills.

Student name: Maddox

Mentor name: *Mr. Wallace*

Mentor checklist:

☑ Establish a relationship with the student.

☑ Check in at least once a week.

☑ Use data when having discussions with the student.

☑ Help the student set SMART goals.

☑ Help teach the student how to monitor progress toward goals.

☑ Log discussions.

☑ Attend meetings and be a liaison for the student.

☑ Reteach the student essential skills needed to succeed.

☑ Be consistent.

Meeting date:
March 4, 2020

Next meeting date:
March 9, 2020

Student behavior focus:
Interacting with peers without getting angry

What Is Going Well About the Specific Behavior (Give details.)	What Can Improve About the Specific Behavior (Give details.)	Student Next Steps	Mentor Next Steps
I am focusing on social interactions with peers. What is going well is I have decided to join the debate team where I am interacting with other students and learning how to understand their points of view without getting angry.	I am still feeling myself get angry at times, but now I am better at removing myself from the situation. However, I still do obsess about the person who made me angry even if I remove myself. I want to work on being able to let that go and understand it is ok to have different opinions.	My next step is to continue using my skills to calm myself down when I get upset and try to stay in the space without removing myself when I am angry. This will help me build some resilience skills and process some of my anger. The more I practice using my skills when I get triggered, the better I will be able to handle it.	*My next step is to check in with the school counselor, with your permission, to ask her to re-invite you to practice some of the anger-management skills you received from her at the beginning of the school year per your permission. She has a permission slip still on file, and it will be a good idea to continue practicing the skills.*

FIGURE 4.12: Mentor log.

Visit go.SolutionTree.com/RTIatWork for a free reproducible version of this figure.

1. Greet the student and ask how the student is doing.

2. Ask specifically how the student is doing academically and socially.

3. Ask how you can support the student.

4. End by writing at least one next-step action for both the student and yourself, and by choosing a follow-up meeting date.

Structured Recess

A structured recess plan is designed to provide a student with a structured setting where they can practice and generalize their skills. See the reproducible "Structured Recess Plan" (page 154) for a template. Before-school, morning, and lunch recess require a student to do the following.

▶ Check in with a designated person (who can be an administrator, support staff designee, or liaison).

▶ Eat in the designated location.

▶ Have recess in a designated area and do structured activities with supervision nearby. (For example, the student may play basketball with a friend who is a good role model; student choice is fine as long as the chosen activity is structured.)

▶ Report to a designated person who escorts the student to class when recess is over.

Make sure the school has a bathroom plan for during recess and an alternate plan for rainy or physical education days.

At the end of each day, the student and staff are required to do the following.

▶ After being released, the student goes to the office a few minutes before dismissal.

▶ An administrator or designated person records the daily intervention data on the reproducible "Structured Recess Progress-Monitoring Chart" (page 156).

▶ The administrator or designated person provides the student a small incentive if he or she reached a daily goal. The incentive might be something like positive verbal acknowledgment or something from the office schoolwide prize box, for example.

▶ Once weekly, an administrator or office staff member allows the student to choose an additional incentive (such as thirty minutes to work on a computer or to draw) if he or she has met goals on at least four days. This usually is given at the end of the day on a Friday or other designated time agreed on by the leadership team and involved teachers.

Discuss the student's interests and decide on incentives prior to completing the progress-monitoring chart. Ensure that everyone involved knows what incentives to offer and that the school has a plan for when the designated check-in or incentive person is absent.

Everyone who supports this plan needs to be on the same page with the schedule. You can see a sample plan in figure 4.13. Keep the "Structured Recess Plan" (page 154) and "Structured Recess Progress-Monitoring Chart" (page 156) reproducibles on a clipboard in the office so all team members have access to them and so the designated person can fill out the monitoring chart daily.

Intervention dates: Week of March 2 through week of April 6 (six weeks)

Intervention daily goals:

• Follow the structured recess plan.

• Have no behavior incidents reported during recess.

(Note: The student has a daily incentive for meeting daily goals. The student comes to the office a few minutes before release daily to get it if goals are met.)

Intervention weekly goals:

Meet daily goals for four out of five days in a week.

(Note: The student has a weekly incentive for meeting the weekly goal. The student comes to the office a few minutes before release weekly to get it if the goal is met.)

Intervention behavior teaching component:

Six weekly behavior academy lessons, each thirty minutes, focus on how to be successful during recess. (In addition to the weekly lessons, the student should get opportunities in the recess setting to practice learned skills under the supervision of the adult supporting that component of the intervention.)

Intervention behavior academy sessions completed:

Check off and date sessions as they are completed.

FIGURE 4.13: Structured recess intervention plan—example.

*Visit **go.SolutionTree.com/RTIatWork** for a free reproducible version of this figure.*

Friendship Group Intervention

This Tier 2 intervention is designed to help students learn how to coexist, and a restorative agreement is their commitment to doing so. Follow these five steps when creating a restorative agreement. The administrator will lead the process.

1. Explain to the students that they will participate in a friendship group for the next six weeks (or up to eight weeks, depending on teacher team input) and, if they meet their goals and work together, they will earn a lunch with the principal and a friend of each of their choice.

2. Give them one folder and time to decorate it together. The folder will hold the agreement and the reproducible "Friendship Group Check-In Form" (page 157).

3. Staple the form to the inside the folder after students sign the agreement.

4. Decide on check-in dates. For example, consider a weekly check-in every Wednesday during morning recess when the group can fill in the form and give a rating.) And establish the following with students about the process.

   » Teach the students how to ask for help if group members are not following the agreement.

   » Ensure that office staff know the students will be coming in.

   » Put the folder in a spot that is easy for the students to access.

   » Show them where the folder is and where in the office they can fill it out.

   » Explain that they should be able to complete the form in ten minutes.

   » Ask each student to give you a thumbs-up before leaving the office if everything is OK.

5. After students have met their goals for the established time frame (such as six weeks), give them the promised lunch. Consider also giving them certificates or positive notes congratulating them for successfully resolving their problems and participating in a friendship group, and let their classroom teachers know they have met their goals.

The "Friendship Group Check-In" (page 157) and "Restorative Agreement" (page 158) reproducibles can help with this intervention.

CICO Daily Check-In

Student name:

Directions: Write today's date in the Date cell. In each column, circle the number that indicates how well the student met the goal during the time period.

Date:	Be respectful	Be safe	Work peacefully	Strive for excellence	Follow directions	Teacher initials
Classroom	0 1 2	0 1 2	0 1 2	0 1 2	0 1 2	
Morning recess	0 1 2	0 1 2	0 1 2	0 1 2	0 1 2	
Classroom	0 1 2	0 1 2	0 1 2	0 1 2	0 1 2	
Lunch	0 1 2	0 1 2	0 1 2	0 1 2	0 1 2	
Classroom	0 1 2	0 1 2	0 1 2	0 1 2	0 1 2	

Total points: _____ out of 50

Today: _____ % Goal: _____

0 = Bummer. You can do it!

1 = So-so!

2 = You did it!

Check-in time:

Office initials:

Check-out time:

Office initials:

CICO Contract

Goal: To assist _____ in behavioral and academic progress so this student can be more successful in school.

Strive for Five

Be Respectful – Be Safe – Work Peacefully – Strive for Excellence – Follow Directions

This plan will help you manage your behavior better. An academic or behavior progress report will help you meet the schoolwide expectations for behavior.

Student responsibilities:

▶ *Check in with an office staff member every morning before class to go over your daily goals.*

▶ *Bring the progress report to class and have your teacher fill it out throughout the day at each designated time period.*

▶ *Check out with your coordinator near the end of every day, and also bring your progress report with you for review.*

▶ *Have your daily report card signed every night by your parent or guardian.*

Parent or guardian responsibilities:

▶ *Review the contract with your child and sign it.*

▶ *Discuss the goals with your child and support your child's efforts.*

▶ *Sign the report card nightly.*

▶ *Accept the evaluations of the teachers and staff.*

▶ *Reward your children when they meet their goals.*

Teacher responsibilities:

▶ *On the progress report, evaluate the student's progress toward meeting goals.*

▶ *Provide the student with positive, constructive, and specific feedback throughout the day.*

Coordinator responsibilities:

▶ *Facilitate check-in and check-out.*

▶ *Provide student with positive, constructive, and specific feedback.*

▶ *Inform the student ahead of time if you are going to be absent.*

▶ *Track student progress.*

I have read the expectations of this contract. By signing this contract, I accept my responsibilities to Strive for Five.

Student signature: _____ Date: _____

Parent or guardian signature: _____ Date: _____

Teacher initials: _____ Coordinator initials: _____ Date: _____

Behavior Academy: Secondary Student Goal Setting and Progress Monitoring

Leave the second Goal row blank if you have just one goal.

Student:	
Leadership team Tier 2 subset designee:	
Behavior academy name:	
Start date:	

Circle the academic and social behaviors you will focus on.

Academic Behavior Skills

Metacognition	Self-concept	Self-monitoring	Motivation	Strategy	Volition

Social Behavior Skills

Responsible verbal and physical interactions with peers and adults   Appropriate language   Respect for property and materials

Independently staying on a required task   Regular attendance

Define *proficiency* for mastering the identified academic or social behavior skill. What would this skill look like if demonstrated appropriately?

Key for Rating Progress

NP = No progress
MP = Minimal progress
AP = Adequate progress

	Session One Date and Progress Rating	Session Two Date and Rating	Session Three Date and Rating	Session Four Date and Rating	Session Five Date and Rating	Session Six Date and Rating	Session Seven Date and Rating	Session Eight Date and Rating
Goal:								
Goal:								
Additional notes or comments:								

Behavior Academy: Elementary Student Goal Setting and Progress Monitoring

Name:
Date:
What behavior are you working on?
Describe it in your own words or draw a picture.
Draw a picture here.
What is your behavior goal?
How will you use your learned skill?
Did you meet your goal from last week? Circle Yes or No.   Yes   No

If No, put a check next to why you chose that behavior:

☐ I wanted attention from other people.

☐ I wanted to be in control.

☐ I did not want to do my work.

☐ I wanted to cause problems because I am sad and frustrated inside.

☐ I wanted to cause problems because someone does not like me.

☐ I wanted (fill in the blank): _____

Did you get what you wanted? Circle Yes or No.	Yes	No

What could you do instead?

Draw the wrong way to get what you want.	Draw the right way to get what you want.

What skill can we practice that will help?

What is your commitment this week?

Hands-Off Academy: Weekly Student Self-Monitoring Sheet

Student directions: Self-reflect on how you are doing with the learned essential skill and then complete this form. Please be honest about what has worked and what has not worked for you so far. That helps us give you all the support you need to master this skill. Your form is specific to the behavior skills you are practicing, so *first do the Previous Week column* (circle one option for each behavior) and then explain what worked and what did not work for you this week.

Student name:	
Date:	
Behaviors	**Previous Week**
How often did I show respect to adults and students?	Circle one: Most of the time Sometimes Not often
How often did I keep my hands to myself?	Circle one: Most of the time Sometimes Not often
What worked for me?	
What didn't work for me?	

Contract for this week

I, _____ , will work on _____ this week so I can meet my behavior goal.

Administrator signature:

Student signature:

Structured Recess Plan

Student:	
Teacher:	
Date:	
Before-school recess	
Designated check-in person: Alternate check-in person:	
Designated breakfast location:	
Designated recess zone 1:	
Designated recess zone 2:	
Recess activities:	
Nearby supervisor:	
Designated check-out and escort:	
Morning recess	
Designated check-in person:	
Designated snack location:	
Designated recess zone 1:	
Designated recess zone 2:	
Recess activities:	
Nearby supervisor:	

page 1 of 2

Designated check-out and escort:
Lunch recess
Designated check-in person:
Designated lunch location:
Designated recess zone 1:
Designated recess zone 2:
Recess activities:
Nearby supervisor:
Designated check-out and escort:
End of the day
Designated check-out and progress-monitoring logger:
Designated daily incentive giver:
Designated weekly incentive giver:
Designated possible incentives:

Structured Recess Progress-Monitoring Chart

In the column asking Did I follow the plan with fidelity today, *please answer only for yourself*. The student met the structured recess goal if he or she followed the structured recess plan and had no behavior incidents reported during recess.

Week of: _____	Did the student meet a structured recess goal today? (Circle one.)	Did I follow the plan with fidelity today?		
		Student	Teacher	Zone	Administrator
Monday	Yes or No	Yes or No	Yes or No	Yes or No	Yes or No
Tuesday	Yes or No	Yes or No	Yes or No	Yes or No	Yes or No
Wednesday	Yes or No	Yes or No	Yes or No	Yes or No	Yes or No
Thursday	Yes or No	Yes or No	Yes or No	Yes or No	Yes or No
Friday	Yes or No	Yes or No	Yes or No	Yes or No	Yes or No
Week of: _____	Did the student meet a structured recess goal today? (Circle one.)	Student	Teacher	Zone	Administrator
Monday	Yes or No	Yes or No	Yes or No	Yes or No	Yes or No
Tuesday	Yes or No	Yes or No	Yes or No	Yes or No	Yes or No
Wednesday	Yes or No	Yes or No	Yes or No	Yes or No	Yes or No
Thursday	Yes or No	Yes or No	Yes or No	Yes or No	Yes or No
Friday	Yes or No	Yes or No	Yes or No	Yes or No	Yes or No
Week of: [	Did the student meet a structured recess goal today? (Circle one.)	Student	Teacher	Zone	Administrator
Monday	Yes or No	Yes or No	Yes or No	Yes or No	Yes or No
Tuesday	Yes or No	Yes or No	Yes or No	Yes or No	Yes or No
Wednesday	Yes or No	Yes or No	Yes or No	Yes or No	Yes or No
Thursday	Yes or No	Yes or No	Yes or No	Yes or No	Yes or No
Friday	Yes or No	Yes or No	Yes or No	Yes or No	Yes or No

Friendship Group Check-In

Check-In Date	How We Are Doing With Our Goals (Circle one.)	Student Signatures
	☺ ☹	
	☺ ☹	
	☺ ☹	
	☺ ☹	
	☺ ☹	
	☺ ☹	
If we can complete _____ weeks of positive check-in ratings, we get to have a special lunch with the principal, and each of us can invite a friend.	☺ ☹	

Restorative Agreement

Date of meeting:
Disputants:
Who is the referral source? Circle an option.   Administrator   Teacher   Student   Self   Other (name)

Conflict Information

What is the conflict about?
Did we recognize an injustice or violation? Circle Yes or No: Yes   No If neither, explain:
Did we restore equity? Circle Yes or No: Yes   No
If equity was restored, circle how.   This meeting   An apology was made for injustices or violations   Other (explain)

Future Intentions

We agree to prevent the problem from happening again by: Student signatures:

Follow-Up Meeting

We agree to meet again. We will meet on this date:

Student signatures:

What were our follow-up meeting results?

Plan–Do–STUDY–Act

In the study stage of the intervention cycle (highlighted in figure 4.14), the Tier 2 subset of the leadership team studies the Tier 2 implementation data and teacher teams' input and develops collective SMART goals. The Tier 2 leadership team subset gets together to study Tier 2 needs and progress.

▸ **Why:** To analyze Tier 2 implementation data and interpret Tier 2 SMART goals

▸ **Who:** The Tier 2 subset of the leadership team

▸ **What:** Developing data-based precise problem statements and identifying next-step Tier 2 intervention solutions and action steps

▸ **When:** At least twice monthly

Plan: Identify students who are not demonstrating mastery of the essential academic and social behavior standards based on schoolwide behavior data and criteria and develop targeted Tier 2 interventions (such as behavior academies) with entry and exit criteria based on their reteaching needs.

Who is responsible? The leadership team Tier 2 subset, based on schoolwide data and teacher input

Screen for prior skills and determine an appropriate supplemental academic or social behavior reteaching opportunity.

Tier 2 Intervention
Essential Academic and Social Behaviors

Academic Behaviors		
Metacognition	Self-concept	Self-monitoring
Motivation	Strategy	Volition
Social Behaviors		
Responsible verbal and physical interactions with peers and adults		
Appropriate language		
Respect for property and materials		
Independently staying on a required task		
Regular attendance		

Do: Introduce students to the Tier 2 behavior learning targets and begin reteaching academic and social behavior standards based on students' identified area of need (including self-monitoring checks). At least six to eight weeks of at least one reteaching session a week is recommended.

Who is responsible? The leadership team Tier 2 subset, in coordination with teachers, based on schoolwide data and teacher input

Give formative skill-building checks for mastery and generalization of the learned behavior standards (such as SMART goal, self-monitoring, and stakeholder feedback check-ins).

Act: Implement actions and continuously improve based on the data; begin the cycle at least monthly; and modify, add to, or strengthen schoolwide or classroom-level teaching of identified essential academic and social behavior standards.

Who is responsible? The leadership team Tier 2 subset, based on staff input

Continue to monitor students receiving or exiting Tier 2.

Study: Analyze behavior data, stakeholder feedback, student feedback, SMART goals, and the fidelity of implementation results, and adjust and modify Tier 2 intervention based on the data.

Who is responsible? The leadership team Tier 2 subset, based on schoolwide data and teacher input

Give a summative academic or social behavior mastery assessment at the end of supplemental intervention.

Source: Adapted from Buffum et al., 2018.

FIGURE 4.14: Tier 2 study stage.

Commonly Asked Questions in the Study Stage

Consider these questions.

▶ How do we function as a PLC with an emphasis on Tier 2 behavior data?

▶ What data points do we use?

▶ How do we get the data, and what type of data will we use?

▶ What Tier 2 data do we use to identify problem statements?

▶ How can we access input from the teacher teams?

▶ Do we connect with the leadership team designee who pushes in monthly, or do we wait until the teacher teams provide input using the "Behavior Support Form" (page 98)?

Tier 2 Study Stage: Processes, Tools, and Forms

In this section, you will find processes, tools, and forms designed to help you begin the work in the study stage.

Tier 2 Teacher Input Collection

The leadership team collects teacher team input at the following frequencies as part of this cycle.

▶ **At least monthly:** The leadership team representative who pushes into every teacher team meeting monthly to gather Tiers 1, 2, and 3 input shares the information regarding Tier 2 with the designated representative from the leadership team's Tier 2 subset.

▶ **When requested:** The designated representative of the leadership team's Tier 2 subset pushes into a teacher team meeting based on receipt of any completed "Behavior Support Form."

▶ **Ongoing:** The leadership team and teacher teams share a Google document of data; it might include meeting minutes with a space for teachers' Tier 2 behavior input and student identification gathered at every teacher team meeting.

Exit Tickets for Teacher Input Collection

Most teachers are familiar with exit tickets as a way to formatively assess students' understanding about a day's unit: they might ask students to write down one or two things they don't currently comprehend. For example, at the end of each staff meeting or department meeting, teacher teams group together and provide information (in the form of exit tickets) on how the implemented Tier 2 interventions are working for their grade or department and in what areas they need more support. They can share these answers in bulleted form, as shown in figure 4.15 (page 162). Teams can repeat this quick communication and input process for each RTI tier.

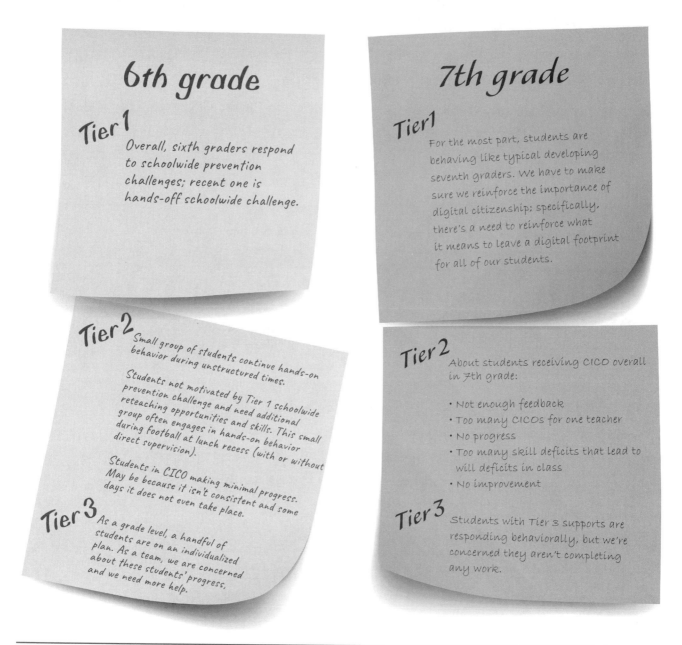

6th grade

Tier 1
Overall, sixth graders respond to schoolwide prevention challenges; recent one is hands-off schoolwide challenge.

Tier 2
Small group of students continue hands-on behavior during unstructured times.

Students not motivated by Tier 1 schoolwide prevention challenge and need additional reteaching opportunities and skills. This small group often engages in hands-on behavior during football at lunch recess (with or without direct supervision).

Students in CICO making minimal progress. May be because it isn't consistent and some days it does not even take place.

Tier 3
As a grade level, a handful of students are on an individualized plan. As a team, we are concerned about these students' progress, and we need more help.

7th grade

Tier 1
For the most part, students are behaving like typical developing seventh graders. We have to make sure we reinforce the importance of digital citizenship; specifically, there's a need to reinforce what it means to leave a digital footprint for all of our students.

Tier 2
About students receiving CICO overall in 7th grade:

- Not enough feedback
- Too many CICOs for one teacher
- No progress
- Too many skill deficits that lead to will deficits in class
- No improvement

Tier 3
Students with Tier 3 supports are responding behaviorally, but we're concerned they aren't completing any work.

FIGURE 4.15: Exit tickets—example.

SMART Goals Monitoring

At this stage in the intervention cycle, individual teachers or teacher teams identify areas of academic and social behavior need by class and by specific student. Teachers can use the SMART goals monitoring form (figure 4.16) for their own classrooms and share it with their teacher team or the leadership team member who pushes into teacher team meetings once a month.

Tier 2 intervention: CICO				
Tier 2 Intervention SMART Goals	**Twice-Monthly SMART Goal Check**			
	Date: *November 6*	**Date:** *November 20*	**Date:** *December 4*	**Date:** *December 18*
CICO academic behavior goal: At least 80 percent of the students participating in the CICO Tier 2 intervention will maintain a C average. (Average GPA will be reviewed twice monthly; the baseline average prior to starting the CICO intervention is D.)	*4 of 10 met goal*	*4 of 10 met goal*	*5 of 10 met goal*	*5 of 10 met goal*
CICO social behavior goal: At least 80 percent of the students participating in the CICO Tier 2 intervention will not be suspended from the classroom for two weeks. (Average classroom suspensions will be reviewed twice monthly; the students' baseline average of classroom suspensions prior to starting the CICO intervention was two a week.)	*2 of 10 met goal*	*4 of 10 met goal*	*6 of 10 met goal*	*7 of 10 met goal*

FIGURE 4.16: Tier 2 SMART goals monitoring form for teachers—example.

*Visit **go.SolutionTree.com/RTIatWork** for a free reproducible version of this figure.*

Plan–Do–Study–ACT

In the act stage of the intervention cycle (highlighted in figure 4.17, page 164), the leadership team's Tier 2 subset brings together the actions it identified during the plan stage based on data and adjusts as needed to meet set goals.

- ▶ **Why:** To implement the modifications and adjustments based on the study stage to get the desired Tier 2 results

- ▶ **Who:** The Tier 2 subset of the leadership team

- ▶ **What:** Implementing modified actions and timelines and restarting the cycle on an ongoing basis

- ▶ **When:** At least twice monthly

Plan: Identify students who are not demonstrating mastery of the essential academic and social behavior standards based on schoolwide behavior data and criteria and develop targeted Tier 2 interventions (such as behavior academies) with entry and exit criteria based on their reteaching needs.

Who is responsible? The leadership team Tier 2 subset, based on schoolwide data and teacher input

Screen for prior skills and determine an appropriate supplemental academic or social behavior reteaching opportunity.

Tier 2 Intervention
Essential Academic and Social Behaviors

Academic Behaviors		
Metacognition	Self-concept	Self-monitoring
Motivation	Strategy	Volition
Social Behaviors		
Responsible verbal and physical interactions with peers and adults		
Appropriate language		
Respect for property and materials		
Independently staying on a required task		
Regular attendance		

Act: Implement actions and continuously improve based on the data; begin the cycle at least monthly; and modify, add to, or strengthen schoolwide or classroom-level teaching of identified essential academic and social behavior standards.

Who is responsible? The leadership team Tier 2 subset, based on staff input

Continue to monitor students receiving or exiting Tier 2.

Do: Introduce students to the Tier 2 behavior learning targets and begin reteaching academic and social behavior standards based on students' identified area of need (including self-monitoring checks). At least six to eight weeks of at least one reteaching session a week is recommended.

Who is responsible? The leadership team Tier 2 subset, in coordination with teachers, based on schoolwide data and teacher input

Give formative skill-building checks for mastery and generalization of the learned behavior standards (such as SMART goal, self-monitoring, and stakeholder feedback check-ins).

Study: Analyze behavior data, stakeholder feedback, student feedback, SMART goals, and the fidelity of implementation results, and adjust and modify Tier 2 intervention based on the data.

Who is responsible? The leadership team Tier 2 subset, based on schoolwide data and teacher input

Give a summative academic or social behavior mastery assessment at the end of supplemental intervention.

Source: Adapted from Buffum et al., 2018.

FIGURE 4.17: Tier 2 act stage.

Commonly Asked Questions in the Act Stage

Consider these questions.

▸ Who is in charge of implementing the actions?

▸ What do we do if the plan does not work?

▸ How do we communicate and receive input from stakeholders about our actions?

Tier 2 Act Stage: Processes, Tools, and Forms

In this section, you will find processes, tools, and forms designed to help you begin the work in the act stage.

Tier 2 Behavior Data Wall

A *behavior data wall* is a display showing a school's students at their respective tiers of interventions and supports (Hannigan & Hannigan, 2018a). It should reside in a safe, confidential location. Often, a data wall lives with the designated representative of the leadership team. It is updated at the following frequencies.

▸ Monthly by the entire leadership team

▸ Twice monthly by the Tier 2 subset of the leadership team

▸ Weekly by the intervention team lead (leads team that addresses the school's Tier 3 needs)

Figure 4.18 shows a sample behavior data wall.

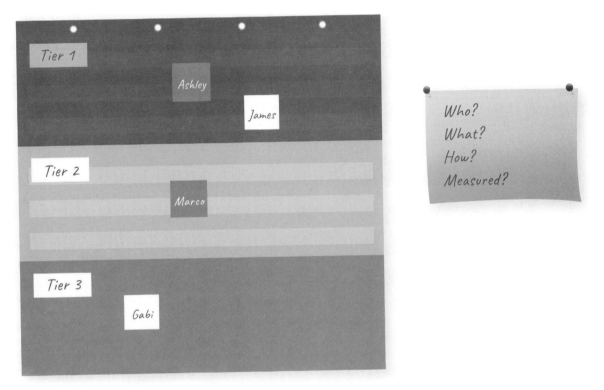

Source: Adapted from Hannigan & Hannigan, 2018a.

FIGURE 4.18: Behavior data wall—example.

The leadership team's Tier 2 subset follows these steps to use a behavior data wall and monitor students' progress in receiving Tier 2. These instructions apply to both Tier 2 and Tier 1; however, chapter 5 (page 175) will include additional Tier 3 information.

1. Buy a colored pocket chart and post it in a confidential setting. Each colored row on the chart represents a different tier, such as green for Tier 3, yellow for Tier 2, and red for Tier 3.

2. Identify all students receiving a Tier 2 or Tier 3 intervention at your school, and put each name on a note card. For further confidentiality, the cards can show the students' ID numbers.

3. For students receiving Tier 2 interventions, place their name on a yellow card and insert it in the yellow pocket section; for students receiving Tier 3

remediation, place their name on a red card and insert it in the red pocket section.

4. As a team, decide whether each student will remain at the current level, move to another level, exit the intervention, or receive other supports. Move cards to the corresponding tier pocket color.

5. You can move name cards to Tier 1 when the intervention data consistently show a student has responded to the Tier 2 or Tier 3 intervention *and* is responding at Tier 1. For example, a student on a Tier 3 special education behavior support plan who is responding to the Tier 3 intervention and not getting into any trouble can move to the Tier 1 (green) section of the pocket chart for that week. The subset can go further and put a green dot sticker on the student's card in the red pocket to indicate the student is responding to the behavior support plan.

6. Placing this student's card in the green (top) section of this pocket chart does not mean taking the student off the intervention he or she is responding to. It means the student is responding that week without getting into trouble. If the student is in green for months, that may indicate that the individualized education program (IEP) team needs to discuss whether a behavior goal on an IEP would suffice instead of a behavior support plan. However, teams should discuss each student on a case-by-case basis. Also, *Tier 3* does not mean *special education.* Tier 3 could very well apply to a general education student in need of intensive supports.

7. As a team, log student progress weekly, using any progress-monitoring tool you prefer. Make sure the log is also available for all stakeholders involved with the Tier 3 remediation so they can reference it and provide input.

Figure 4.19 is an example of a Tier 2 intervention at-a-glance form that the leadership team Tier 2 subset uses to identify how the Tier 2 interventions at the school are working compared to identified goals.

The leadership team Tier 2 subset can use a progress-monitoring log as they discuss students receiving Tier 2 interventions. This is one method of logging your behavior data wall visual group discussions. In discussing each student, the leadership team subset that created the customized log in figure 4.20 decided to focus on the number of minor and major classroom referrals and days of suspensions, and whether the team should continue with an intervention. The log shows data sets that one team might find important, but your team can log additional data sets as part of this process. This log is designed to help the team decide and act on next steps based on progress-monitoring data.

Intervention	Total Students	Total Students Meeting Goal	Percentage of Students Meeting Goal
CICO	25	20	80 percent
Social skills groups	30	27	90 percent
Anger management	15	5	33 percent
Homework club	35	25	71 percent

FIGURE 4.19: Interventions at a glance—example.

*Visit **go.SolutionTree.com/RTIatWork** for a free reproducible version of this figure.*

Twice-Monthly Progress Review Date	Student Name	Tier 2 Intervention	Number of Minor Behavior Referrals	Number of Major Behavior Referrals	Status in Meeting Individual Tier 2 Intervention Goals for Behavior (Yes or No)	Number of Days Suspended	Determination to Continue, Change, or Exit the Intervention

FIGURE 4.20: Behavior data wall—progress-monitoring log example.

*Visit **go.SolutionTree.com/RTIatWork** for a free reproducible version of this figure.*

PLC and Tier 2 RTI Integration Criteria Guide

Take a critical look at the four priority criteria outlined in figure 4.21 (page 169) to help your school function as a PLC and to use the essential academic and social behavior standards and your school's behavior data to assign Tier 2 RTI (intervention) schoolwide. These criteria will help you prevent the systemic behavior gap that too often contributes to failure of implementation and will be your evidence of success criteria when completing the behavior integration assessment (BIA).

Remember, the schoolwide team is primarily responsible for the Tier 2 schoolwide organization and implementation, however, the teacher teams do have a role in their classroom systems to support Tier 2 interventions; specifically, for academic behavior-based Tier 2 interventions (skill not will). Please consider both as you are completing the RTI pyramid sections.

Behavior Integration Assessment: Tier 2

Again, you measure the implementation of the integration criteria with the BIA. The comprehensive assessment tool is for all three tiers of integration criteria designed to address and prevent the systemic behavior gap. This assessment is designed for the leadership team to utilize as a guide to ensuring the criteria is in place to avoid the systemic behavior gap.

Keep in mind that the evidence indicators from each of the four criteria in figure 4.21 (PLC and Tier 2 RTI integration guide) provides your team with tangible evidence to justify your score. We've seen teams score themselves high on rubrics or say "We're doing all those things" when criteria are broadly written or lacking specificity. For this reason, we created the evidence indicators that allow teams to hold themselves accountable with artifacts and other evidence to justify a score of 2 (in place). It also gives teams a target toward mastery to put in place so they can achieve a score of 2 on the BIA.

Use information from chapters 2 (page 33) and 4 (page 119) to complete the three indicated sections on the RTI at Work pyramid. Use the Plan–Do–Study–Act graphic (figure 4.2, page 124) as a visual guide to all the processes, tools, and forms shared in each of the stages of Tier 2.

Complete the following reproducibles as a schoolwide team.

- ▶ "Behavior Integration Assessment: Tier 2" (page 171)

- ▶ "RTI at Work Pyramid: Tier 2" (page 172)

- ▶ "Reflection Two" (page 173)

PLC and Tier 2 RTI Integration Criteria	Tier 2 Evidence Indicators	Reflect on These Evidence Indicators and the Systemic Behavior Gap They Will Address
Establish and operate an effective Tier 2 subset of the leadership team to address Tier 2 intervention needs.	Team purposes, roles, and responsibilities are clear. The principal is an active member of the leadership team. The Tier 2 subset has twice-monthly meetings and completed agendas or minutes. The Tier 2 subset has a data-based process for identifying students for Tier 2. The Tier 2 subset utilizes the intervention cycle stages and up-to-date data at meetings. The Tier 2 subset considers multiple data points when identifying precise problem statements and developing and implementing Tier 2. An identified leadership team member conducts monthly teacher team push-ins to gather teacher input on RTI. An identified team lead helps ensure the fidelity of team meetings. The Tier 2 subset establishes SMART goals for Tier 2 implementation based on intervention needs. The Tier 2 subset coordinates, designs, and provides resources that teacher teams need to support implementation of Tier 2 interventions in their classrooms. Tier 2 interventions are in place with fidelity.	
Identify students who need Tier 2 interventions (reteaching) for the essential academic and social behavior standards.	Students and staff can identify and articulate the *why* of designing and implementing Tier 2. The Tier 2 subset uses processes, resources, and tools to gather Tier 2 implementation data. The Tier 2 subset establishes entry and exit criteria for Tier 2 interventions. Teachers clearly understand how to ask for help with students they identify who may benefit from Tier 2. Students receive Tier 2 interventions in a timely fashion. Evidence of Tier 2 reteaching lessons and different teaching methods is apparent.	

FIGURE 4.21: PLC and Tier 2 RTI integration guide.

continued →

Establish teacher teams' roles and responsibilities in ensuring Tier 2 implementation, and invest in building their capacity and maintaining their commitment to their role and responsibilities.	Clear Tier 2 responsibilities and roles are established for teacher teams. Teachers understand and feel equipped to meet their role in Tier 2 (that is, following and monitoring Tier 2 interventions in the classroom). Each teacher team meeting includes an opportunity for teachers to assist each other with RTI needs and use the teacher team minutes or agenda to communicate Tier 2 needs to the leadership team. The Tier 2 subset provides Tier 2 teacher training materials based on need. Staff emails and memos are based on Tier 2 data trends and updates. Staff feedback and input on Tier 2 implementation is regularly gathered (every all-staff meeting). Student work or evidence of Tier 2 reteaching is collected and shared regularly. Tier 2 interventions are in place with fidelity in the classroom. The Tier 2 subset establishes a Tier 2 incentive program based on individual students' motivation and behavior goal mastery.	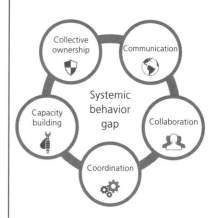
Establish effective procedures for collecting multiple adequate levels of Tier 2 intervention data and provide ongoing training and support on how to use those data for decision making.	The Tier 2 subset establishes and maintains staff's commitment to Tier 2 implementation. The Tier 2 subset maintains an up-to-date data-based Tier 2 process (that is, a behavior data wall and progress-monitoring log). The Tier 2 subset has a Tier 2 data-entry procedure and review plan in place; at least twice a month, it intentionally reviews the progress of individual students receiving Tier 2 and the intervention's collective progress. Staff understand the difference between Tier 1 prevention and Tier 2 intervention in regard to behavior. Staff receive ongoing training on how to ask for support and how to monitor progress using Tier 2 intervention forms. The school has an established system for monitoring the Tier 2 plan and communicating it to all stakeholders. A designated leadership team member ensures he or she collects data from the teacher teams regarding Tier 2 behavior needs and provides them to the Tier 2 subset of the leadership team at least monthly. Teachers provide more urgent Tier 2 intervention requests directly to the Tier 2 subset of the leadership team. Collaborative teacher teams have a process to communicate with the Tier 2 subset lead and request Tier 2 supports prior to the push-in meeting if needed.	

*Visit **go.SolutionTree.com/RTIatWork** for a free reproducible version of this figure.*

Behavior Integration Assessment: Tier 2

With your schoolwide team, indicate what best describes your school's behavior tiered system RTI and PLC integration. Be honest. This assessment is designed to help you monitor your integration and reveal what tier and construct you need to focus on to improve.

Criteria	Score	Next Steps and Evidence
PLC at Work and Tier 2 RTI at Work	Circle one. 0 = Not in place 1 = In progress 2 = In place	For any item scored 0 or 1, list next-step processes, tools, or forms that will help your school meet this criterion. For any item scored 2, list evidence (processes, tools, and forms) it is in place.
Establish and operate an effective Tier 2 subset of the leadership team to address Tier 2 intervention needs.	0　1　2	
Identify students who need Tier 2 interventions (reteaching) for the essential academic and social behavior standards.	0　1　2	
Establish teacher teams' roles and responsibilities in ensuring Tier 2 intervention is in place and invest in building their capacity and maintaining their commitment to their role and responsibilities.	0　1　2	
Establish effective procedures for collecting multiple adequate levels of Tier 2 intervention data and provide ongoing training and support on how to use those data for decision making.	0　1　2	

RTI at Work Pyramid: Tier 2

Use information from chapters 2 and 4 to complete the three indicated sections on the RTI at Work pyramid. Use the Plan–Do–Study–Act graphic (figure 4.2, page 124) as a visual guide to all the processes, tools, and forms shared in each of the stages of Tier 2.

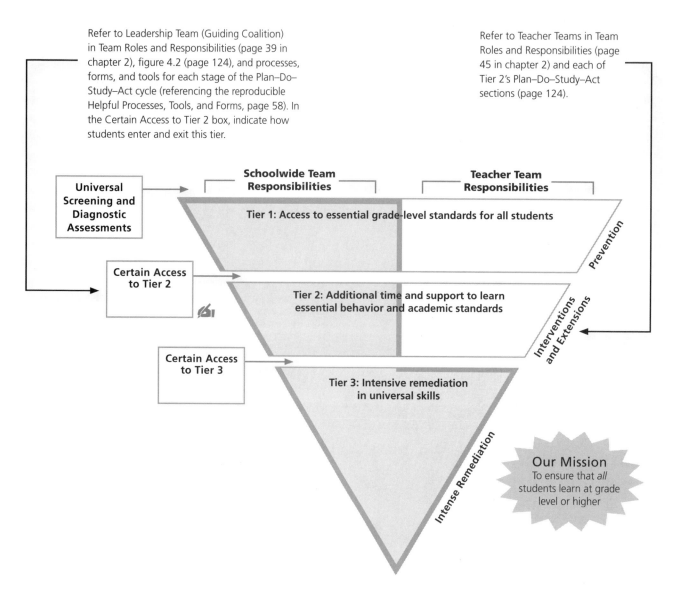

Refer to Leadership Team (Guiding Coalition) in Team Roles and Responsibilities (page 39 in chapter 2), figure 4.2 (page 124), and processes, forms, and tools for each stage of the Plan–Do–Study–Act cycle (referencing the reproducible Helpful Processes, Tools, and Forms, page 58). In the Certain Access to Tier 2 box, indicate how students enter and exit this tier.

Refer to Teacher Teams in Team Roles and Responsibilities (page 45 in chapter 2) and each of Tier 2's Plan–Do–Study–Act sections (page 124).

Universal Screening and Diagnostic Assessments

Schoolwide Team Responsibilities

Teacher Team Responsibilities

Tier 1: Access to essential grade-level standards for all students

Certain Access to Tier 2

Tier 2: Additional time and support to learn essential behavior and academic standards

Certain Access to Tier 3

Tier 3: Intensive remediation in universal skills

Prevention

Interventions and Extensions

Intense Remediation

Our Mission
To ensure that *all* students learn at grade level or higher

Source: Adapted from Buffum, A., Mattos, M., & Malone, J. (2018). Taking action: A handbook for RTI at Work. *Bloomington, IN: Solution Tree Press.*

Reflection Two

We know this is hard work. Take a minute to reflect and celebrate your learning with your team.

_____

_____

_____

Ask yourselves the following questions.

- "How are we feeling about Tier 2 implementation?"

- "What can we commit to as a team before delving into Tier 3?"

Record your responses here and date them so you log your RTI at Work journey with the focus on behavior.

Date:

_____

_____

_____

_____

_____

_____

_____

_____

_____

_____

_____

_____

_____

_____

_____

_____

CHAPTER 5

Implementing Behavior Solutions at Tier 3—Remediation

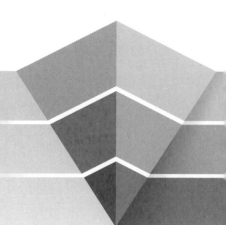

In regard to behavior skills, Tier 3 focuses on intensive, individualized remediation and supports for identified students. These supports should be provided in addition to Tier 1 and Tier 2 behavior supports. We will discuss the following questions and others in this chapter.

▸ How do we identify who needs Tier 3 remediation opportunities?

▸ How do we know what behavior standards to remediate?

▸ What does *remediation* mean?

▸ What are everyone's roles and responsibilities in Tier 3 implementation?

▸ Where do we start?

▸ How will implementation help address the systemic behavior gap?

Tier 3 implementation challenges will arise. The questions proposed in this chapter are intentionally designed to identify and help avoid PLC and Tier 3 RTI implementation challenges. We also highlight ways to remediate behaviors that show a lack of proficiency in the identified essential academic and social behavior standards and provide a Tier 3 remediation cycle. This starts by building the foundation of Tier 3 (remediation).

Tier 3 Implementation Challenges

Tier 3 presents some challenges that appear in all tiers, and some that are specific to it. Common Tier 3 implementation challenges include the following, and each is discussed here in turn.

▸ How to support Tier 3 intensive behavior interventions for students most at risk

- ▶ What team roles are

- ▶ How to identify what students need and what intensive supports are available to help students stabilize their behavior

Many educators struggle with how to support Tier 3 intensive behavior interventions for students who are most at risk. The behaviors can be a function of many variables, so it is critical that educators plan and implement an individualized response to lessen these behaviors' frequency and severity. But ultimately, educators need to *teach the positive behaviors* needed to thrive. This requires time for coordination and implementation and an all-hands-on-deck culture that supports all students, whether they are in general education or special education.

Educators often are unsure how to leverage the collaborative structures of a PLC to implement Tier 3 remediation. The school intervention team's essential responsibilities at Tier 3 are to diagnose, target, prioritize, and monitor Tier 3 interventions (Buffum et al., 2015).

Similar to academic interventions, behavior interventions require the staff members best trained in this area take lead responsibility in Tier 3. To this end, we highly recommend that the staff with the most expertise in intensive behavior supports or intervention development—the school counselor, special education teacher, school psychologist, or social worker, for example—help develop, implement, and monitor the individualized plans. The leadership team must allocate the resources—staff, money, and time—to ensure the staff can successfully implement each student's intensive intervention plan.

Educators can have difficulty identifying what students need (in addition to these intensive supports) to get them to a stable or regulated enough place that they can access their education. Similar to someone having a specific medical diagnosis wanting to go to a specialist (a cardiologist for a heart problem, for example), a student with a specific behavioral remediation need (such as intense anxiety or depression) needs someone who has specialized expertise in these areas in a school setting. Some students may face an immediate crisis (having experienced a recent traumatic event at home or attempted suicide) and need an immediate Tier 3 response. To relate this to a medical situation, when a patient enters an emergency room with a severe injury—such as one that involves profuse bleeding—the medical experts' first job is to stabilize the patient's vital functions—stop the bleeding! Once the situation is stable, then the medical team can shift its focus from ensuring the patient's basic survival to actually helping the patient thrive.

Intensive behaviors that are not stabilized and that lack sufficient, effective, and consistently implemented supports can have a significant impact at multiple levels—in the classroom, grade, department, and overall school culture and climate. The intensive behavior needs may escalate to a degree that the student cannot access basic educational needs with the proper supports in place. An example can be a student acting out, leaving, and entering the classroom repeatedly while a teacher is attempting to teach. With no structure or response to support these types of Tier 3 intensive needs, all involved feel overwhelmed and frustrated. In addition, resentment may build among staff if an intervention team does not provide support in a timely fashion.

Teachers may be afraid to ask for help in these cases. One teacher explained it this way:

> If I ask for help with Tier 3, I will only receive a drive-by observation from the school psychologist and a bunch of forms I do not have time to implement in my classroom when [the student] is running around, throwing chairs, and running in and out of my classroom. The last time Tier 3 supports were offered, I was told the student is very "attention seeking," so try ignoring the negative behaviors but not the student. (D. Foster, personal communication, September 20, 2019)

This teacher was visibly upset and almost in tears as she shared this story. Another teacher interjected:

> What she is trying to say is that our grade level no longer asks for help with intensive behavior cases because when you ask for help, the teacher is given *more* to try instead of receiving help to work together and develop a plan to help the child. (J. Jacks, personal communication, September 20, 2019)

Another challenge at this tier is that while students who are severely at risk often show the same kinds of behaviors, the causes, motivations, and functions behind the behaviors are not necessarily the same. For example, one student might demonstrate acting out to avoid a given task (commonly that happens with writing), while another may be attaining unplanned reinforcement—attention or escape—from escalating behavior. Likewise, one student with chronic absenteeism might miss school due to medical issues, while another might have an alcoholic parent incapable of consistently driving the student to school. Both students have the same symptoms—excessive absences—but require different supports.

For this reason, targeted information from the Tier 2 response, if applicable (student behavior data, stakeholder input, intervention data, and so on), can help guide Tier 3 behavior remediation, and then staff must consistently implement the remediation across the student's school day—from the bus ride to the classroom, playground, lunchroom, after school, break times, after-school programs, extracurricular activities, unstructured times, and transition times. Doing this requires a high level of collaboration and building on the school's behavior outcomes and supports at Tier 1 and Tier 2.

Another challenge arises when teachers are directed to develop a Tier 3 intervention and fully implement it in their classroom because, as mentioned, most teachers are not trained to develop intensive behavior interventions, nor are they equipped to implement these interventions on their own. For example, here is an unfortunately common scenario. A teacher asked experts in her building for help with a student who needed Tier 3 supports from the beginning of the school year. In response to the teacher's initial email pleading for behavior help, the experts said she needed to do what she could to support the student in her classroom because the student was very smart and did not qualify for special education.

The teacher immediately felt she was to blame for this student not responding to her attempts at supporting a Tier 3 behavior need, and she continuously tried her best to work with the student in her classroom, brainstorm ideas with her grade-level team, connect with the student's parents for support, and complete mental health documents to help provide a complete, whole-child profile of student needs. But the student's behaviors escalated both in and out of the classroom, and the teacher left work crying every day. To make matters worse, the teacher was reprimanded by the principal ("Why is this student wandering out of your classroom again?") whenever this particular student ran in and out of her room. Because this student's behavior continued to worsen inside and outside the classroom, one would think that the school would have gathered the right people in the room to put together a timely plan. This was not the case. Instead, the teacher received the following email.

> Dear Teacher,
>
> Your student was suspended again from school. We now need to hold a student support team meeting, and I need you to email me all previous interventions you have tried with him. I also would like you to meet with the vice principal to write a behavior support plan for him, so we have it ready for the meeting with the parent. I believe your class is too loud for him, so I am going to move him to another teacher's classroom to try another environment when he returns from his suspension.
>
> Sincerely,
> Principal

What went wrong? Why does this happen? What should have happened instead?

Sometimes, schools provide Tier 3 interventions at the special education level with a formal behavior plan protected by federal law, but even then, educators often do not feel equipped to prevent and respond to escalated behaviors. Ultimately, this all contributes to the systemic behavior gap identified in the beginning of this book (page 21) and often leads to union issues, lack of fidelity in implementation, a blame game, a poor school climate and culture, increased discipline rates, teacher burnout, resentment, and ultimately poor academic and behavior outcomes for students.

The PLC and RTI Processes for Behavior in Tier 3

Tier 3 behavioral supports provide frequent intensive remediation based on essential behaviors' functions and gives structures and supports for the identified essential academic or social behavior standards, including behaviors that students should have learned in prior years.

By the end of this chapter, you will learn how to complete the circled empty space in figure 5.1 as part of the culminating activity for Tier 3. Specifically, you will insert into the reproducible "RTI at Work Pyramid: Tier 3" (page 224) the Tier 3 behaviors, conditions, and intervention team responsibilities.

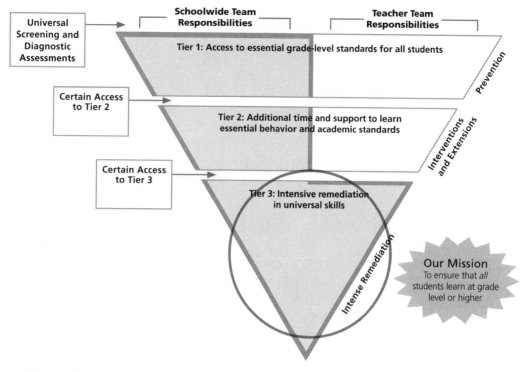

Source: Adapted from Buffum et al., 2018.

FIGURE 5.1: Culminating pyramid reference (Tier 3).

Similar to academics, there is a need for behavior remediation supports. The school leadership team and intervention team work collaboratively to implement Tier 3 interventions. The intervention team takes lead responsibility to diagnose, target, prioritize, and monitor Tier 3 remediation for each of the identified students. The leadership team is responsible for allocating the resources needed to support each student's remediation plan and to ensure that these supports are in addition to Tier 1 and Tier 2, not in place of them. Undoubtedly, teachers will have a role in implementing and monitoring Tier 3 remediation, but they do not take lead responsibility. Finally, all teams (leadership, intervention, and teacher) should work collaboratively to establish the behaviors and conditions for students who will receive Tier 3 remediation supports for essential academic and social behavior standards.

Keep in mind that each tier is value added and students do not move from tier to tier. For example, a student receiving Tier 3 behavior supports could also still benefit from the schoolwide behavior actions that all students get at Tier 1, and from targeted help in minor needs at Tier 2. But most importantly, do not delay Tier 3 support, if a student needs it, in an effort to have a student "prove" he or she tried Tiers 1 and 2 first.

At Tier 3, students need more intensified and frequent supports. Specifically, Tier 3 remediation provides individualized behavior supports as follows.

▶ Embedded in the student's daily education schedule

▶ Focused on specific essential academic or social behaviors and based on the behavior's function in a specific environment and structure

▶ Coordinated across multiple settings that a student might experience each day

▸ Not to the exclusion of the student's essential academic curriculum

▸ Inclusive of family needs, if necessary

This tier's supports require collaboration among the intervention team and all stakeholders who will be involved with the individual plan. The experts should design Tier 3 interventions in light of intervention team, stakeholder, and student feedback so they help the student learn and practice internalizing new skills. Tier 3 responses may look different for other types of Tier 3 behaviors being addressed.

The duration of a Tier 3 response depends on the individual student's response to the plan. The intervention team should meet at least weekly to monitor, adjust, revise, and continue Tier 3 plans based on student data and stakeholder input.

Tier 3 Remediation Cycle

This Tier 3 remediation cycle will help you understand what it means to leverage the PLC and RTI processes in order to target intensive behavior interventions based on individual student data and the *identified function* (*root cause*) *of behavior*.

Identify *one* standard or skill that requires remediation at a time, and help students build mastery. Keep in mind that teaching and progress monitoring for Tier 3 remediation should occur more frequently than for any other RTI supports at the school—at least weekly.

Remember that the school's behavior experts (on the intervention team) provide remedial services or teaching opportunities, but it remains important for the leadership team and teachers to contribute initial feedback, follow the Tier 3 remediation plan and implement its components in the classroom, monitor it, and provide ongoing feedback regarding effectiveness. Figure 5.2 shows the Tier 3 remediation cycle and where it exists in the RTI at Work pyramid.

The reproducible "Helpful Processes, Tools, and Forms" (page 58) is where you can record the tier and make notes about the processes, tools, and forms you find most helpful for each stage of the Plan–Do–Study–Act cycle. Also remember that we have provided best practice processes, tools, and forms from our collective experiences, but you can incorporate others that will help you.

The intervention team members tasked with the school's Tier 3 needs should utilize this cycle and current behavior data each time they meet (recommended at least weekly) to identify, design, and implement Tier 3 remediation supports and monitor their effectiveness and fidelity. The following sections highlight the Plan–Do–Study–Act stages (Deming, 1993) in greater depth, as well as commonly asked questions about the stages and processes, tools, and resources to help in each. Reference the purposes, roles, and responsibilities for Tier 3 identified in chapter 2 (page 43) as you apply this cycle in your PLC with your intervention team.

Plan: Identify students who are not responding to Tier 1 prevention or Tier 2 intervention based on schoolwide prevention data, Tier 2 intervention data, behavior or discipline data, and teacher input, and develop a Tier 3 remediation plan based on their individualized needs (that is, ten-day intensives, a behavior support plan, or a structured day plan) with entry and exit criteria (what constitutes a Tier 3 plan).

Who is responsible? The intervention team, based on Tier 1 and Tier 2 data, behavior and discipline data, and teacher input

Screen for prior skills and determine the function of behavior in order to match it with the appropriate remediation essential standard.

Tier 3 Remediation
Reteaching of the Essential Academic and Social Behaviors

Academic Behaviors		
Metacognition	Self-concept	Self-monitoring
Motivation	Strategy	Volition

Social Behaviors
Responsible verbal and physical interactions with peers and adults
Appropriate language
Respect for property and materials
Independently staying on a required task
Regular attendance

Act: Analyze Tier 3 remediation plans' summative results and other relevant data, and identify students who possibly need a different or additional layer to the individualized remediation plan (or who can exit Tier 3).

Who is responsible? The intervention team, based on current Tier 3 remediation plan data, behavior or discipline data, and teacher input

Continue to monitor students receiving or exiting Tier 3 remediation plans on a regular basis.

Do: Introduce students to the Tier 3 remediation learning targets, begin frequent remediation teaching, and design and structure the individualized plan that will teach and reinforce the identified academic and social behavior standards based on their identified function (including self-monitoring checks). At least daily remediation teaching for ten days at a time (at least three checkpoints a day) is recommended.

Who is responsible? The intervention team is the lead, the leadership team ensures the intervention team has all it needs to implement, and teachers may have an implementation role in the classroom setting, based on their identified role in the plan

Give frequent and formative skill-building checks for mastery and generalization of the learned behavior standards (such as SMART goal, self-monitoring, and stakeholder feedback check-ins).

Study: Analyze behavior data, stakeholder feedback, student feedback, SMART goals, and the fidelity of implementation results, and adjust or modify Tier 3 intervention based on the data.

Who is responsible? The leadership team and intervention team, based on schoolwide data and teacher input

Give a summative mastery assessment of the identified essential academic or social behavior standard at the end of remediation teaching.

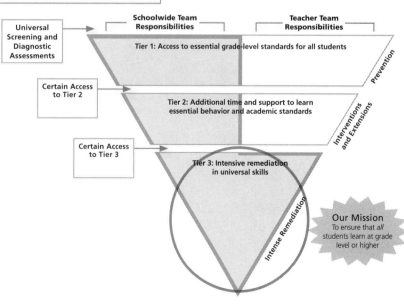

Source: Adapted from Buffum et al., 2018.

FIGURE 5.2: Tier 3 remediation cycle.

PLAN–Do–Study–Act

In the plan stage of the remediation cycle (highlighted in figure 5.3), the intervention team identifies individual student academic and social behavior needs, planning appropriate Tier 3 remediation opportunities, and implementing and monitoring them with ongoing stakeholder feedback.

Plan: Identify students who are not responding to Tier 1 prevention or Tier 2 intervention based on schoolwide prevention data, Tier 2 intervention data, behavior or discipline data, and teacher input, and develop a Tier 3 remediation plan based on their individualized needs (that is, ten-day intensives, a behavior support plan, or a structured day plan) with entry and exit criteria (what constitutes a Tier 3 plan).

Who is responsible? The intervention team, based on Tier 1 and Tier 2 data, behavior and discipline data, and teacher input

Screen for prior skills and determine the function of behavior in order to match it with the appropriate remediation essential standard.

Tier 3 Remediation
Reteaching of the Essential Academic and Social Behaviors

Academic Behaviors		
Metacognition	Self-concept	Self-monitoring
Motivation	Strategy	Volition

Social Behaviors
Responsible verbal and physical interactions with peers and adults
Appropriate language
Respect for property and materials
Independently staying on a required task
Regular attendance

Act: Analyze Tier 3 remediation plans' summative results and other relevant data, and identify students who possibly need a different or additional layer to the individualized remediation plan (or who can exit Tier 3).

Who is responsible? The intervention team, based on current Tier 3 remediation plan data, behavior or discipline data, and teacher input

Continue to monitor students receiving or exiting Tier 3 remediation plans on a regular basis.

Do: Introduce students to the Tier 3 remediation learning targets, begin frequent remediation teaching, and design and structure the individualized plan that will teach and reinforce the identified academic and social behavior standards based on their identified function (including self-monitoring checks). At least daily remediation teaching for ten days at a time (at least three checkpoints a day) is recommended.

Who is responsible? The intervention team is the lead, the leadership team ensures the intervention team has all it needs to implement, and teachers may have an implementation role in the classroom setting, based on their identified role in the plan

Give frequent and formative skill-building checks for mastery and generalization of the learned behavior standards (such as SMART goal, self-monitoring, and stakeholder feedback check-ins).

Study: Analyze behavior data, stakeholder feedback, student feedback, SMART goals, and the fidelity of implementation results, and adjust or modify Tier 3 intervention based on the data.

Who is responsible? The leadership team and intervention team, based on schoolwide data and teacher input

Give a summative mastery assessment of the identified essential academic or social behavior standard at the end of remediation teaching.

Source: Adapted from Buffum et al., 2018.

FIGURE 5.3: Tier 3 plan stage.

- ▶ **Why:** To identify students who are not responding to Tier 1 and Tier 2 based on schoolwide prevention data, Tier 2 data, behavior or discipline data, and teacher input, and to develop a Tier 3 remediation plan based on their individualized needs

- ▶ **Who:** The intervention team with teacher input

- ▶ **What:** Planning and coordinating Tier 3 remediation plans with entry and exit criteria

- ▶ **When:** Weekly and as needed based on crises

Commonly Asked Questions in the Plan Stage

Consider these questions.

▸ Who is responsible for planning, coordinating, and preparing Tier 3 remediation opportunities?

▸ How do we design a Tier 3 response with embedded remediation opportunities? Who teaches the remediation sessions, how often, and when?

▸ What happens during the remediation sessions?

▸ Who is responsible for identifying the function of behavior?

Tier 3 Plan Stage: Processes, Tools, and Forms

In this section, you will find processes, tools, and forms designed to help you begin the work in the plan stage.

Menu of Tier 3 Remediation Response Options

Remediation responses, shown in table 5.1, depend on the intervention team's recommendation. A student's behavior may require more than one response. As the intervention team works through the Tier 3 cycle, it should begin and refer back to the "Tier 3 Resource Inventory Check" reproducible (page 189) so it can make sure it keeps an inventory of the resources that all the chosen remediation options require.

TABLE 5.1: Menu of Tier 3 Remediation Response Options

Option	Description
Individualized counseling	One-on-one counseling with a behavior specialist designed to focus on and teach a student replacement behaviors that address the undesirable behavior's function
Transition plan	An individualized plan designed to transition a student with Tier 3 intensive needs back to the school, the classroom, the period, or another setting
Ten-day intensive plan	An intensive plan designed by all stakeholders to provide a student daily one-on-one remediation structures and supports for ten days
Structured recess plan	Structured activities designed to help a student generalize learned behavior skills in all settings
Structured day plan	A specific and individualized daily schedule for a student who needs the tightened structure and routine to master and generalize learned behavior skills
Wraparound service	A partnership among the home, the school, and community mental health services for a student who needs intensive supports in all settings

continued ➔

Option	Description
Individual academic and behavior instruction design (for those who need a different delivery)	A plan (such as online learning, project-based learning, or alternative settings for learning) in which a student receives a different design for learning but still has access to core instruction (This is an individualized specialized plan for general education students.)
Behavior support plan	An individualized support plan designed to identify the function of a general education or special education student's behavior, teach replacement behaviors, and monitor and reinforce the progress on the student's behavior goals
Mental health referral	Support that a behavior specialist provides to a student and his or her family with additional mental health resources
Individualized education program (IEP)	A special education plan designed to address a student's individual academic and social behavior needs
Functional behavioral assessment (FBA)	An extensive assessment, conducted by a behavior specialist with appropriate expertise and credentials, that uses applied behavioral analysis best practices to identify the function of behavior and provide recommendations for an individual plan (page 185)
Threat assessment	Designed to help keep students safe and violence free; process includes identifying a threat of violence, determining its seriousness (in the moment, no plan, or substantive plan), and intervening to help the person who made the initial threat and the threat victims stay safe and to resolve any conflict (See the "Threat Assessment Tool" reproducible, page 190.)
Student-focused treatment plan	All stakeholders supporting the student collaboratively develop an individualized student treatment plan. The student, with supports, leads and directs the plan.

Tier 3 Entry Criteria

Many criteria can qualify a student for Tier 3 support. The intervention team has to be aware of all types of Tier 3 needs, including the following, in order to respond adequately. The intervention team can use this menu of Tier 3 responses and criteria as a guide as members are discussing Tier 3 student data needs.

- ▶ Excessive discipline incidents and suspensions

- ▶ Student in a crisis situation (such as domestic violence, attempted suicide, or parental divorce)

- ▶ Failure in the majority of classes

- ▶ Chronic absenteeism and tardiness

- ▶ Exposure to adverse childhood experiences—trauma—at an early age, resulting in behaviors preventing the student access to learning

- ▶ Admittance to a behavioral health institution

▶ The need for special education services that provide a behavior plan with individualized behavior goals (such as for a student who has been professionally assessed as possibly having an emotional disturbance in the special education disability category)

▶ Untreated mental health disorders (including but not limited to anxiety, attention deficit, depressive, and bipolar disorders)

▶ No response to Tier 1 and Tier 2 supports and interventions

▶ Intervention team referrals based on teacher team input

▶ Positive result from a threat assessment

Function of Behavior Identification

Understanding a behavior's function is critical to the intervention team being able to adequately assign Tier 3 supports. Figure 5.4 is a function of behavior record taken prior for a first step in formal identification. Figure 5.5 (page 186) offers the intervention team a form to help identify the function of behavior and develop a Tier 3 plan that will ameliorate the behavior. In addition, the experts on the intervention team— school psychologist, school counselor, special education teacher—should have adequate training in identifying behavior functions.

Student name: Date:			
Describe the student's behavior:			
Which function seems to be most fitting to the identified behavior based on interview, observation, and environmental data? Common functions include (circle the primary perceived function):			
Tangible	Attention	Escape	Sensory
Based on the function identified, describe a replacement behavior that may be part of the Tier 3 remediation plan:			

FIGURE 5.4: Function of behavior record.

*Visit **go.SolutionTree.com/RTIatWork** for a free reproducible version of this figure.*

Student name:		Date:
What is the antecedent (behavior, common setting, and common time)?	**What does the student get from demonstrating the behavior (reward, extinction, correction, or safety)?**	**Is the behavior a *can't do* or a *won't do*? What remediation teaching is necessary?**
The escaping behavior is more common in the morning and in classes that require handwriting task.	*The student gets out of completing the handwriting task.*	*Won't do: Student has received lessons on handling being overwhelmed, but doesn't use the skill.*
Strategies **Environment or setting** **Antecedent** **Remediation** **Consequences**	**What is the perceived function of the behavior based on this information?**	**What is the intervention team's suggested plan and proposed starting date?**
Strategies: Learn how to ask for choice methods of showing mastery instead of leaving the room (such as text to writing).	*Based on this information and additional interview and observation information, the function appears to be escape.*	*Plan is to work with the student to develop a structured break schedule and choice options in the class during writing assignments. Plan to begin one day after all stakeholders are aware of their roles and responsibilities with the plan.*

FIGURE 5.5: Tier 3 behavior function identification guide.

*Visit **go.SolutionTree.com/RTIatWork** for a free reproducible version of this figure.*

Individualized Plan With Restrictions

Figure 5.6 is a sample individualized plan that has different restriction levels. There are generally four restriction levels applied to these types of plans. The idea is to begin with more restricted supports—more structure—and release the structure and supports to students who show evidence of learning how to self-monitor and apply learned behaviors.

1. **Restricted:** Student meets with designated staff identified by the intervention team to review replacement behavior. Environmental

structures are in place so the designated staff consistently reinforce and monitor replacement behavior.

2. **Less restricted:** The student meets with designated staff to review replacement behavior. Environmental structures are in place so the designated staff consistently reinforce and monitor replacement behavior; however, the monitoring checks decrease throughout the day.

3. **Restricted self-monitored:** The student receives the opportunity to generalize learned replacement behavior in multiple settings. Student check-in with designated staff is still required, but it occurs only once a day.

4. **Self-monitored:** The student is able to generalize learned, practiced, and reinforced replacement behavior without staff restrictions in an unstructured environment.

Figure 5.7 (page 188) is an example of a break system plan for the student indicated in figure 5.6. See where the student, Ron, goes to take the break during level one.

Daily plan for: *Ron*

Starting date: *February 1*

Focus replacement behavior: *Responsible verbal and physical interactions with peers and adults*

Focus replacement SMART goal: *Student will apply self-monitoring skills and use break system appropriately when he starts feeling like he wants to use inappropriate physical or verbal interactions with the teacher or other adult. Student will begin with level one restricted and move to level four self-monitored based on progress on SMART goal.* *Baseline prior to beginning the plan at level one restricted: Student is demonstrating verbal and physical interactions that are inappropriate with teacher. On average, it is taking three or four hours and three adults to help the student get regulated and go back to class. The plan will begin at level one.*

Restriction level (circle one):	
• *Level one: Restricted* (circled)	• *Level three: Restricted self-monitored*
• *Level two: Less restricted*	• *Level four: Self-monitored*

Level one: Restricted	*Student will begin with a special schedule designed with built-in check-in break times (every thirty minutes). In addition, student will meet with a check-in person in the morning to review how to ask for a break when needed and what to do during the break.*

FIGURE 5.6: Tier 3 restriction leveled individualized plan—example.

continued →

Designated Staff	Role
Administrator	*Morning check-in and review of the break system*
Counselor	*Twice weekly teaching of replacement behaviors (how to self-monitor when getting upset and regulating during break time)*
Break mentors (Teachers or other adult break designees)	*Allows student to come in between the designated time for check-in*
Intervention team	*Meets at the end of the week to see how student is doing with plan before moving and organizing the next level; ensures all stakeholders part of the plan understand their roles and responsibilities*

*Visit **go.SolutionTree.com/RTIatWork** for a free reproducible version of this figure.*

Directions: The student is directed to take these breaks during level one and will be escorted to breaks if necessary. The breaks are embedded within these time periods and locations.

Level One Break Times	Level One Break Locations and Adult Check-In Person
8:00–8:30 a.m.	Office: administrative designee
8:30–9:00 a.m.	Library: Mrs. Martinez
9:00–9:30 a.m.	Office: administrative designee
9:30–10:00 a.m.	Library: Mrs. Martinez
10:00–10:30 a.m.	Playground: Mr. Tyrell
10:30–11:00 a.m.	Counselor's office: Ms. Bills
11:00–11:30 a.m.	Office: administrative designee
11:30 a.m.–12:00 p.m.	Counselor's office: Ms. Bills
12:00–12:30 p.m.	Playground: Mr. Tyrell
12:30–1:00 p.m.	Lunchroom: administrative designee
1:00–2:00 p.m.	Counselor's office: Ms. Bills
2:00–2:30 p.m	Office: administrative designee

FIGURE 5.7: Tier 3 restriction leveled break system—example.

*Visit **go.SolutionTree.com/RTIatWork** for a free reproducible version of this figure.*

Tier 3 Resource Inventory Check

Date of Tier 3 resource inventory check: _____

Total students currently receiving or needing Tier 3: _____

Resources needed and who on the intervention team can help with each?

Resources	Student 1	Student 2	Student 3	Student 4	Student 5
Time					
Money					
Materials					
People					
Rooms					
Curriculum					
Expertise					
Other					

Threat Assessment Tool

The intervention team can use this tool to assess the seriousness of a student's threat—physical or verbal—to hurt him- or herself or other students. The student who made the threats will likely need Tier 3 supports. Specialists who have training in social-emotional supports are critical members of the intervention team on campus.

Meeting date:	Threat-assessment team-member names and roles:
Details:	Threat description: Who made threat: Possible threat victims:

Is the threat transient? (Quickly resolved with timely response) **Provide evidence for either yes or no answer.**	Is the threat substantive? (Serious intent and plan to harm self or others) **Provide evidence for either yes or no answer.**

Threat-assessment intervention plan:

Roles and responsibilities of all involved:

Starting date:

Progress-monitoring check-in dates:

Blurting-Out Self-Monitoring Sheet

Student directions: Please check in with your mentor or teacher at the beginning of class to go over this sheet, and then use it to monitor your progress throughout the class. Do this for each part of the day (under Time Period) as shown on the sheet.

- **Check in with your mentor or teacher at these times.**

    ▶ _____ a.m.

    ▶ _____ p.m.

    ▶ The end of the school day

- **Date:** Put today's date in the Date row.

- **Blurts:** Circle a 1 if you catch yourself blurting out. Circle a 1 each time.

- **Teacher Initials:** Ask your teacher to initial at the end of each period.

Date:			

Blurting out is when someone talks when someone else is speaking or when you have not been called on. The goal is to stay in the gray zone for every time period and to not have more than twenty-one blurts total per day.

Time Period	Blurts		Teacher Initials
	1 1 1	1 1 1 1 1 1 1 1 1 1 1 1 1 1	
	1 1 1	1 1 1 1 1 1 1 1 1 1 1 1 1 1	
	1 1 1	1 1 1 1 1 1 1 1 1 1 1 1 1 1	
	1 1 1	1 1 1 1 1 1 1 1 1 1 1 1 1 1	
	1 1 1	1 1 1 1 1 1 1 1 1 1 1 1 1 1	
	1 1 1	1 1 1 1 1 1 1 1 1 1 1 1 1 1	
	1 1 1	1 1 1 1 1 1 1 1 1 1 1 1 1 1	
Total blurts logged today:	Goal: <21		

Plan–DO–Study–Act

In the do stage of the remediation cycle (highlighted in figure 5.8), begin providing the planned Tier 3 remediation supports.

▸ **Why:** To provide the planned Tier 3 remediation opportunities for the identified essential academic and social behavior standards

▸ **Who:** The intervention team and teachers, based on their identified role in the plan

▸ **What:** Providing intensive, individualized structures and supports for students in need of Tier 3 remediation

▸ **When:** Daily (Remediation's duration depends on students' response.)

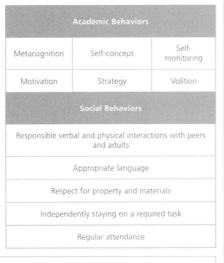

Plan: Identify students who are not responding to Tier 1 prevention or Tier 2 intervention based on schoolwide prevention data, Tier 2 intervention data, behavior or discipline data, and teacher input, and develop a Tier 3 remediation plan based on their individualized needs (that is, ten-day intensives, a behavior support plan, or a structured day plan) with entry and exit criteria (what constitutes a Tier 3 plan).

Who is responsible? The intervention team, based on Tier 1 and Tier 2 data, behavior and discipline data, and teacher input

Screen for prior skills and determine the function of behavior in order to match it with the appropriate remediation essential standard.

Tier 3 Remediation
Reteaching of the Essential Academic and Social Behaviors

Academic Behaviors		
Metacognition	Self-concept	Self-monitoring
Motivation	Strategy	Volition

Social Behaviors
Responsible verbal and physical interactions with peers and adults
Appropriate language
Respect for property and materials
Independently staying on a required task
Regular attendance

Act: Analyze Tier 3 remediation plans' summative results and other relevant data, and identify students who possibly need a different or additional layer to the individualized remediation plan (or who can exit Tier 3).

Who is responsible? The intervention team, based on current Tier 3 remediation plan data, behavior or discipline data, and teacher input

Continue to monitor students receiving or exiting Tier 3 remediation plans on a regular basis.

Do: Introduce students to the Tier 3 remediation learning targets, begin frequent remediation teaching, and design and structure the individualized plan that will teach and reinforce the identified academic and social behavior standards based on their identified function (including self-monitoring checks). At least daily remediation teaching for ten days at a time (at least three checkpoints a day) is recommended.

Who is responsible? The intervention team is the lead, the leadership team ensures the intervention team has all it needs to implement, and teachers may have an implementation role in the classroom setting, based on their identified role in the plan.

Give frequent and formative skill-building checks for mastery and generalization of the learned behavior standards (such as SMART goal, self-monitoring, and stakeholder feedback check-ins).

Study: Analyze behavior data, stakeholder feedback, student feedback, SMART goals, and the fidelity of implementation results, and adjust or modify Tier 3 remediation based on the data.

Who is responsible? The leadership team and intervention team, based on schoolwide data and teacher input, are responsible.

Give a summative mastery assessment of the identified essential academic or social behavior standard at the end of remediation teaching.

Source: Adapted from Buffum et al., 2018.

FIGURE 5.8: Tier 3 do stage.

Commonly Asked Questions in the Do Stage

Consider these questions.

▶ What does Tier 3 remediation look like?

▶ Is providing remediation supports the same for general education and special education students?

▶ How can we provide daily remediation teaching opportunities?

Tier 3 Do Stage: Processes, Tools, and Forms

In this section, you will find processes, tools, and forms designed to help you begin the work in the do stage.

Ten-Day Intensive Plan

A ten-day intensive plan is an alternate schedule designed to provide intensive remediation and environmental structures. For ten days, all Tier 3 resources are used to help stabilize, or *regulate*, the student and teach very specific essential behavior skills, and then the remediation is revisited at the end of the ten days to adjust the intensity of resources and supports as needed based on that student's data. In this case, student data are collected based on individual student goals. For one student, that may be the number of times blurting out (see the "Blurting-Out Self-Monitoring Sheet" reproducible, page 192). For another, it may be the time it takes to calm down after perceiving unfairness.

The work starts with everyone, the intervention team and other stakeholders (such as the administrator, support provider, and teachers), and then tapers off to some extra remedial supports and check-ins slightly after the student responds to the remediation.

This ten-day intensive plan requires a lot of resources up front but is worth the investment. The ten-day structure includes the following critical actions.

▶ **Target support:** Identify the behavior's function and target the daily remediation teaching and support opportunities based on the identified function. This requires that the daily remediation focus is on the essential behavior standard needed to replace the identified function with a newly learned skill (such as self-monitoring anger and using replacement behaviors to prevent emotions from escalating).

▶ **Tighten the environmental schedule and structure, and make them consistent:** This helps reinforce the taught, remediated essential behavior standard. Sharing responsibility across stakeholders ensures they follow the schedule and structure. (For example, stakeholders with roles in designing and implementing the ten-day intensive plan must know their responsibilities from the minute the student is on campus to the minute he or she leaves; the student follows a consistent schedule with embedded supports that multiple stakeholders monitor.)

▶ **Focus on stabilizing the behavior first:** Immediately attempt stabilization—getting student to regulate—by using all available Tier 3 resources, and then taper them off as the student begins accessing his or her education with supports. Establish *one* achievable, simple behavior goal at a time with input from the behavior experts and all the stakeholders, including the student. For example, a student with severe anxiety or unmanaged anger who leaves the classroom for hours to avoid written work may need a beginning goal as simple as Increase the time the student remains in the classroom with supports (for example, the supports may include a student-chosen alternative personalized assignment). After the student demonstrates seven out of ten successes, introduce a goal of working independently, applying learned remediation strategies to self-monitor anxiety or anger triggers, and using replacement behaviors instead of leaving the classroom.

For example, a student with severe anxiety or unmanaged anger who leaves the classroom for hours to avoid written work may need a beginning goal as simple as *Increase the time the student remains in the classroom with supports* (for example, the supports may include a student-chosen alternative personalized assignment). After the student demonstrates seven out of ten successes, introduce a goal of working independently, applying learned remediation strategies to self-monitor anxiety or anger triggers, and using replacement behaviors instead of leaving the classroom.

This takes time and dedication from all involved. *Do not discontinue this ten-day intensive structure after the first ten days.* The intervention team monitors this plan daily and revisits it every ten days to ensure effectiveness (student individual goals are being met with supports) and necessary changes. When implementing a ten-day plan, take the following into account.

▸ The ten-day intensive review meeting should occur on the eleventh day. However, the intervention team may revisit it sooner if student behavior continues escalating.

▸ The intervention team should log the number of designated staff and the time invested in supports and collect these data.

▸ The intervention team should continue working with families and stakeholders on additional mental health supports (wraparound services) the student needs during this time.

Figure 5.9 (page 196) helps teams plan a ten-day intensive intervention for those students in crisis. Notice the following required information. The key components necessary for success include the structured environment schedule, daily remediation opportunities, and stabilization (regulation) goal.

▸ **Structured environment schedule:** This schedule is designed to prevent escalation and to support success. It chunks critical times of the day (provides additional structure), such as the following, according to the behavior's function and the responsible stakeholder.

　　• Before-school and after-school free time

　　• Class, period, or block

　　• Morning recess or break

　　• Lunch recess or break

　　• Bus time

Student name: *Leo*   Start date: *October 7, 2020*

Ten-day intensive implementation plan team members: student, school psychologist, school counselor, special education aide, designated administrator

Description of the student's behavior:

Student is having difficulty regulating himself when he becomes anxious. When he is feeling this way, he does not know how to respond appropriately. He begins yelling, screaming, and throwing items when he is at this point. He often leaves the classroom and wanders throughout the school campus for hours without responding to an adult.

Perceived function of behavior:

Escape—he is escaping the environment that is triggering his anxiety.

Behavior skill focus:

Learn to apply essential social behavior skill to self-monitor when feeling anxious and use replacement behaviors learned in cognitive behavior therapy group.

Name and responsibility of members on the ten-day intensive implementation team:

School psychologist (Kelli Mondera): Works with the intervention team and student on the plan and helps monitor and collect data on the three components structured environment schedule, daily remediation opportunities, and stabilization (regulation) goal. Daily check-in with the student in the a.m. to reinforce skills learned in cognitive behavioral therapy group. Daily check-in can rotate with the counselor depending on days on campus if needed.

Designated administrator (Erika Lake): Ensures all specialists part of the plan are able to dedicate their time to the plan instead of being pulled for other scenarios.

Special education aide (Shané Gutierrez): Helps ensure the structured environment and schedule are being followed.

School counselor (Mary Bills): Teaches student strategies to practice when anxious (at least twice a week) and pushes into classroom to help him identify when he's feeling that way and remind him to use his learned skills.

Key Components	Structured Environment Schedule	Daily Remediation Opportunities	Stabilization (Regulation) Goal
	Provided to all members of the student's remediation plan	Daily with counselor or psychologist	Student self-monitors when beginning to feel anxious and uses skills instead of escape behavior described in detail in plan.

Fidelity Checks	How well did we follow this structured schedule? 1 = Not at all 2 = Somewhat 3 = Completely	To what extent did we provide daily remediation opportunities? 1 = Not at all 2 = Sometimes 3 = Completely	To what extent did the student meet the stabilization behavior goal? 1 = Not at all 2 = Somewhat 3 = Completely
Day 1 10-7-20	3	2 (missed two days in week one)	2 (started with mini goal of self-monitoring and verbalizing or showing an agreed-on signal with the teacher when feeling anxious)
Day 2 10-8-20	3	3	2
Day 3 10-9-20	2 (adult was out so missed that part of the schedule)	3	2
Day 4 10-12-20	3	3	2 (making progress but need to continue reminding student)
Day 5 10-13-20	2	2	2
Day 6 10-14-20	3	3	3
Day 7 10-15-20	2	1 (Counselor and psychologist were pulled to a workshop all week)	1
Day 8 10-16-20	3	3	3
Day 9 10-19-20	2	3	3
Day 10 10-20-20	2	2	2

FIGURE 5.9: Ten-day intensive plan form.   continued →

Day 11 *(10/22)* Ten-day intensive plan progress monitoring	*Revisit and modify the schedule to ensure happening with fidelity.*	*Have a backup plan for when the school psychologist or counselor is out. The morning precorrection and check-in are critical to reinforce the focus skill.*	*Set clear goals and add a reinforcement for student who is meeting goal to reinforce the behavior.*

In this section, log every time the ten-day intensive plan implementation team met on an as-needed basis for adjustments based on data. Conduct a daily check-in between the team members and a weekly data-based progress-monitoring discussion and data-based next steps.			

On what date did we hold the team meeting? *10/23*	Did we implement the plan with fidelity? (Yes or No) If no, why not? *Yes, we did for a majority of the days. But we did not have a back-up in place when key implementers were pulled out for a training, setting back both the implementation fidelity and student progress.*

What progress-monitoring data did we use? *Fidelity check ratings, student individual goals, and teacher input*

What are our next steps based on stakeholder feedback and progress-monitoring data? *We designated back-up implementers and a communication notification structure for all involved if a key member in the plan is out. We also discussed this with the student for his input.*

Visit **go.SolutionTree.com/RTIatWork** for a free reproducible version of this figure.

▶ **Daily remediation opportunities:** These opportunities are designed to ensure that the student receives daily precorrection, check-ins, replacement behaviors, and teaching opportunities. The intervention team bases these opportunities on behavior experts' recommendations. Examples follow.

• *Precorrection*—Prevention strategy at the initial and ongoing interactions with the student to interrupt the likelihood of an identified problem behavior from occurring; for example, in the morning students meet with designated staff for a precorrection opportunity

• *Replacement behaviors*—The behavior you want to take the place of an unwanted behavior; teacher may utilize a reminder or cue designed to trigger the replacement behavior

• *Teaching opportunities*—In the moment remedial teaching opportunities (that is, designated staff utilize an in the moment opportunity to teach and use calming down skills when student perceives a game or situation with another student to be unfair)

▶ **Stabilization (regulation) goal:** This goal is designed to focus on stability rather than mastery of all behavior standards and academic standards.

Figure 5.10, an abbreviated version of an individualized ten-day intensive plan, is another way all stakeholders can have a clear visual of the plan outlined in this chapter.

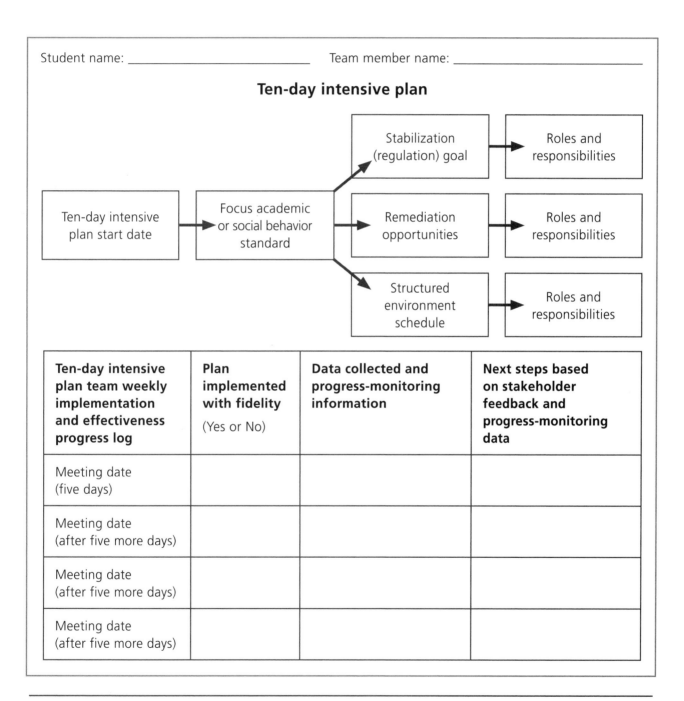

FIGURE 5.10: Abbreviated ten-day intensive plan form.

*Visit **go.SolutionTree.com/RTIatWork** for a free reproducible version of this figure.*

Student name: *Joe Beck*											

Start date: *February 1*   End date: *February 12*

Essential behavior standard being observed: *Using responsible verbal and physical interactions with peers and adults*

Yes = Student is using replacement behavior; No = Student is not using replacement behavior

Time Intervals Observed and by Whom	Day 1	Day 2	Day 3	Day 4	Day 5	Day 6	Day 7	Day 8	Day 9	Day 10	Day 11+ Ten-day intensive plan review date
8:00–9:00 a.m	Yes		Yes		Yes					Yes	Yes
9:00–10:00 a.m.		No		No				Yes			
10:00–11:00 a.m.									Yes		
11:00 a.m–12:00 p.m.	No			No	No	No		No			
12:00–1:00 p.m.							No				
1:00–2:00 p.m.	No							Yes		Yes	Yes
Total intervals observed	3	1									
Percentage of yes	33%	0%	100%	0%	50%	0%	0%	67%	100%	100%	100%

FIGURE 5.11: Ten-day intensive interval observation form.

*Visit **go.SolutionTree.com/RTIatWork** for a free reproducible version of this figure.*

The Ten-Day Intensive Interval Observation form in figure 5.11 (page 200) is for recording data collection about the identified essential behavior standard. The form lets team members gauge, at multiple times of day, whether a student is demonstrating appropriate replacement behaviors. You can use these data during the daily and weekly check-in dates. This is a snapshot—a tool for different times of the day, so you will notice blank spots in the form. At that time, the student was not actually observed. The goal is for no matter when the student is observed, the percentage the student is using appropriate behaviors is logged for progress monitoring.

Figure 5.12 shares a re-entry transition plan that the intervention team and designated teachers can use to decide how they will move a student, who is returning to school after mental health facility-level mental health needs, into a Tier 3 remediation

Goal: Help the student feel safe and provide the supports necessary for him to access his education, learn additional coping skills, and know who he can go to for help if he needs it. The intervention team may begin the re-entry into the school in smaller chunks or periods and add periods based on progress.

What are some criteria (entry access) for students to receive this level of Tier 3 support?

- A teacher referral, student referral, self-referral, or staff member referral
- An off-campus community referral identification as re-entering school following admittance to a behavioral health institution
- Identification as re-entering school following admittance to a behavioral health institution

How often do students receive this level of support?

- Daily and weekly
  - » Daily check-in with adult designee (mentor)
  - » Once weekly check-in with school counselor
- Students receive outside mental health services weekly. Information release is agreed on by the intervention team, mental health provider, and family. The nurse monitors the student—at least once weekly—regarding new (anti-depressant) medication.

What do students receive in this Tier 3 support level?

- What they may receive includes (but is not limited to) the following: relaxation, solution-focused therapy, cognitive behavioral therapy, or a narrative or life story change.
- They receive a medical care plan to manage medication (only students who have doctor recommendation and family approval to take medication) in partnership with the school and home.

How many students are currently in this Tier 3 intervention?

- Approximately ten as of April 10.

Do students at this support level have academic or social behavior goals?

They do. The idea is that students will be able to integrate back to a full day in all classrooms and use the school's resources and newly learned coping skills.

How is this intervention information shared with the school staff, and how often?

- Possible tips on awareness and signs for students and staff are shared in the newsletter.
- School counselors share tips and updates at staff or department meetings at least quarterly.

How is the structure of the day adjusted for students receiving this Tier 3 response?

These students have an alternative schedule on returning. For example, they may begin with a regular schedule starting with one or two periods, and then progress to a full day as all supports are put into place collaboratively by the intervention team members.

What are the exit criteria for this level of response?

This will be adjusted case by case. But ultimately, the goal is for the student to re-enter fully in all courses all day long and for the student to know how to use new skills when feeling down.

FIGURE 5.12: Re-entry transition plan form—example.

*Visit **go.SolutionTree.com/RTIatWork** for a free reproducible version of this figure.*

and then transition the student back into the normal school day when the student is ready. Monitoring a student who is re-entering a regular class schedule may include the following criteria.

▶ The student's intervention attendance

▶ The time it takes to support this student daily

▶ The student's academic and behavior goals

▶ The student's number of behavior incidents daily

CICO Plus Structured Scheduled Option

Figure 5.13 is an example of a student who continues to receive Tier 2 CICO support but has additional Tier 3 intensive structures in place with more intensity.

Figure 5.14 (page 204) and the "Individual Behavior Student Check-In" reproducible (page 207) are other elementary-level examples of focusing on one behavior.

The intervention team lead uses the "Red Zone Monitoring" reproducible (page 208) to track and log the number of times in each day students go to the red zone. This form is an alternative option for calming down, applying skills, and completing preferred tasks. If a student does escalate to this level, he or she can at least have a safe location to go and have a prepared set of academic items to engage in. Obviously, it requires intense monitoring and skills practice to avoid having to use often. However, during the time a student is just beginning to learn how to use and apply new social behaviors, having this ready-to-go spot is better than the student not doing any academic tasks all day.

Tier 3 Frequent Remediation and Reinforcement

Follow these five steps for Tier 3 frequent remediation and reinforcement.

1. Develop a chart like the one in figure 5.15 (page 205) and place it in an area where the student can easily see and access it. Explain to the student that earning eleven happy faces throughout the day will result in a reward. For secondary students, you can do tally marks or check marks to indicate meeting target behavior benchmarks.

2. Review the graphic reminder in figure 5.16 (page 205) every morning and before each time period. Mention the target behaviors.

   » Keeping one's hands and feet to oneself

   » Following directions

3. After the time period has ended, walk the student to his or her chart, or take the chart to the student. There, rate the behavior. For secondary students, you can remind them to complete the chart with your support.

   » Circle or highlight the happy face if the student displayed the target behavior.

Date range: November 16–December 14

Intervention: CICO plus a structured schedule layer

Before school

- The student checks into the office to pick up his CICO folder and CICO form; the administrator touches base with the student.
- The student gets escorted to class by the home volunteer or designated school personnel (who will ensure that he turns in his homework or any classwork he did not complete the day before and that he understands the given task).
- The classroom teacher teaches class as usual and documents any minor misbehaviors the student engages in on the student's CICO form
- Suggestion: The teacher should complete the CICO rating form at the end of the day so the student will not be thrown off throughout the day if he receives a rating he does not like but the student's parent will still know of the rating as well as the behavior that led to it.

After morning recess

The student goes to the office and is escorted to class by the home volunteer or designated school personnel (who will ensure he understands the task he has to complete in class).

After lunch recess

The student goes to the office and is escorted to class by the home volunteer or designated school personnel (who will ensure he understands the task he has to complete in class).

At the end of the day and after school

- The designated school personnel or home volunteer will ensure the student has his folder of incomplete work and homework ready to take home and complete.
- A parent will pick up the student after school daily (the student will not be walking home per the plan). Student will have the responsibility to share CICO score with parent or guardian.

Notes

Throughout the day: red zone

- If the teacher notices the student is disrupting teaching or is about to engage in attention-seeking behavior with the teacher (a power struggle), the teacher sends the student to the office with a red folder or calls the office with the selected code for someone to come help with the situation.
- If the student has to be removed, he will complete one of the following examples of structured assignments (other options may apply): read an Accelerated Reader book (take notes and pass a quiz), do JiJi (online mathematics program) for forty minutes, do Lexia (online literacy program) for forty minutes, review mathematics facts, write an essay on appropriate behavior, or finish any incomplete work the teacher wants completed.

FIGURE 5.13: CICO plus structured scheduled option, individualized scheduling—example.

*Visit **go.SolutionTree.com/RTIatWork** for a free reproducible version of this figure.*

RJ's Schedule

Carpet Time	Bathroom Break	Centers	RTI	Recess
1	2	3	4	5
Lunch	Bathroom Break	Carpet Time	Centers	Time to Pack Up
6	7	8	9	10

FIGURE 5.14: Individual student schedule graphic reminder.

Visit go.SolutionTree.com/RTIatWork for a free reproducible version of this figure.

Date: *Tuesday, March 8*		
Hands and Feet to Self		
8:00–8:30 a.m.	☺	☹
8:30–9:00 a.m.	☺	☹
9:00–9:30 a.m.	☺	☹
9:30–10:00 a.m.	☺	☹
10:00–10:30 a.m. (recess)	☺	☹
10:30–11:00 a.m.	☺	☹
11:00–11:20 a.m.	☺	☹
11:20 a.m.–12:15 p.m. (lunch)	☺	☹
12:15–1:00 p.m.	☺	☹
1:00–1:30 p.m.	☺	☹
1:30–1:50 p.m.	☺	☹

Comments

Collin kept his hands and feet to himself during a really challenging time today.

FIGURE 5.15: Frequent remediation and reinforcement chart for keeping one's hands and feet to oneself—example.

*Visit **go.SolutionTree.com/RTIatWork** for a free reproducible version of this figure.*

| Hands and feet to self | No kicking | No pushing or shoving |

FIGURE 5.16: Graphic reminder to keep one's hands and feet to oneself.

*Visit **go.SolutionTree.com/RTIatWork** for a free reproducible version of this figure.*

» Circle or highlight the sad face if the student didn't display the target behavior. Briefly explain what he or she needs to work on. For example, if a student receives a happy face for keeping hands to herself for that period of time and then pushes another student, the teacher could remind the student of her replacement behavior (such as clasping hands, taking a deep breath, putting hands in pockets, or walking away).

4. Praise the student if he or she earned a happy face for each time period. Be sure to use *process praise*, which connects the "*work a student did to a learning outcome*, no matter how small" (Haimovitz & Dweck, 2017; McNeece, 2020, p. 33). An example is "Well done! You worked hard to keep your hands to yourself. You earned happy faces" (Haimovitz & Dweck, 2017).

5. Repeat these steps for the remainder of the day.

Ultimately, the point of Tier 3 supports is providing students with the skills and environmental supports to access their education and learn how to independently monitor their behaviors as well. The "Individual Daily Self-Monitoring" reproducible (page 209) helps students learn how to self-monitor their learned behaviors. The "*My New Narrative* Individual Contract" (page 210) and "*My New Narrative* Commitment Check-In Schedule" reproducibles (page 211) help students understand that they can envision and make a plan for improved behavior or applying a new academic or social behavior that will allow them to access their education.

Individual Behavior Student Check-In

Directions: Please complete this form with one behavior in mind. In Tier 3, it is important to begin focusing on one behavior at a time and then add to expand on that behavior application. This form is for students with one taught behavior skill.

Student:					
Focus behavior:					
Goal:					
	Monday	**Tuesday**	**Wednesday**	**Thursday**	**Friday**
Beginning of day to recess					
Recess to lunch					
Lunch and lunch recess					
After lunch recess to the end of the day					
_____ ☺ = Daily reward			_____ ☺ = Friday reward		
Parent or guardian signature and date:					

Red Zone Monitoring

Directions: Indicate how many times a day a student decided to go to the structured red zone location. This location may be in or out of a classroom. This information will be used at least weekly by the intervention team to progress monitor and adjust Tier 3 response. This form can be completed by the teacher or by a designee who is part of monitoring the student while he or she is in the red zone.

Date Range	How many times did the student get in the red zone today, and why?	Did we follow the plan with fidelity today? S = Student T = Teacher P = Parent A = Administrator			
Week 1		S	T	P	A
Monday					
Tuesday					
Wednesday					
Thursday					
Friday					
Week 2		S	T	P	A
Monday					
Tuesday					
Wednesday					
Thursday					
Friday					
Week 3		S	T	P	A
Monday					
Tuesday					
Wednesday					
Thursday					
Friday					
Week 4		S	T	P	A
Monday					
Tuesday					
Wednesday					
Thursday					
Friday					

Individual Daily Self-Monitoring

Student name:	Week of:				
Goal					

	How well did I use my replacement skills? (Circle one rating per class period: W = well, F = fairly, and P = poorly)				
	Monday	**Tuesday**	**Wednesday**	**Thursday**	**Friday**
Period one	W F P	W F P	W F P	W F P	W F P
Period two	W F P	W F P	W F P	W F P	W F P
Period three	W F P	W F P	W F P	W F P	W F P
Period four	W F P	W F P	W F P	W F P	W F P
Period five	W F P	W F P	W F P	W F P	W F P
Period six	W F P	W F P	W F P	W F P	W F P
Period seven	W F P	W F P	W F P	W F P	W F P
Period eight	W F P	W F P	W F P	W F P	W F P
Period nine	W F P	W F P	W F P	W F P	W F P
Total Ws					

What worked for me?

What didn't work for me?

Contract and goal for this week:

I, _____, will work on _____ this week to meet my behavior goal.

Student signature _____ Mentor or advisor signature _____

My New Narrative Individual Contract

Complete each prompt to the best of your ability.

Who I am:
Some poor choices I have made at school in the past (my old narrative):
What I want to see for myself when it comes to behavior and academics in school (my new narrative):
How I plan on making this new narrative come true:
What help I need to make this new narrative come true:
The person I will reach out to who can help me make this new narrative come true, how I can reach that person, and how often I will reach out to that person:
My short-term goals toward this new narrative:
What actions I commit to so I can meet these short-term goals:
My long-term goals toward this new narrative:
The date on which my work toward my new narrative will begin:
My signature, showing my commitment to my new narrative

My New Narrative Commitment Check-In Schedule

Date: _____ Check in with: _____

Commitments: _____

_____

_____

_____

_____ Initials: _____

Date: _____ Check in with: _____

Commitments: _____

_____

_____

_____

_____ Initials: _____

Date: _____ Check in with: _____

Commitments: _____

_____

_____

_____

_____ Initials: _____

Date: _____ Check in with: _____

Commitments: _____

_____

_____

_____

_____ Initials: _____

Date: _____ Check in with: _____

Commitments: _____

_____

_____

_____

_____ Initials: _____

Plan–Do–STUDY–Act

In the study stage of the remediation cycle (highlighted in figure 5.17), the intervention team reviews the Tier 3 implementation data (for both general education and special education), receiving Tier 3 supports with teacher team input, and develops collective Tier 3 SMART goals.

- ▶ **Why:** To analyze Tier 3 behavior implementation data and interpret Tier 3 SMART goals

- ▶ **Who:** The intervention team with teacher team input; the leadership team also has to ensure the intervention team has the time and resources to provide this level of timely support.

- ▶ **What:** Developing precise problem statements based on data and identifying next steps and Tier 3 intervention solutions

- ▶ **When:** At least weekly

Plan: Identify students who are not responding to Tier 1 prevention or Tier 2 intervention based on schoolwide prevention data, Tier 2 intervention data, behavior or discipline data, and teacher input, and develop a Tier 3 remediation plan based on their individualized needs (that is, ten-day intensives, a behavior support plan, or a structured day plan) with entry and exit criteria (what constitutes a Tier 3 plan).

Who is responsible? The intervention team, based on Tier 1 and Tier 2 data, behavior and discipline data, and teacher input

Screen for prior skills and determine the function of behavior in order to match it with the appropriate remediation essential standard.

Tier 3 Remediation
Reteaching of the Essential Academic and Social Behaviors

Academic Behaviors		
Metacognition	Self-concept	Self-monitoring
Motivation	Strategy	Volition

Social Behaviors
Responsible verbal and physical interactions with peers and adults
Appropriate language
Respect for property and materials
Independently staying on a required task
Regular attendance

Act: Analyze Tier 3 remediation plans' summative results and other relevant data, and identify students who possibly need a different or additional layer to the individualized remediation plan (or who can exit Tier 3).

Who is responsible? The intervention team, based on current Tier 3 remediation plan data, behavior or discipline data, and teacher input

Continue to monitor students receiving or exiting Tier 3 remediation plans on a regular basis.

Do: Introduce students to the Tier 3 remediation learning targets, begin frequent remediation teaching, and design and structure the individualized plan that will teach and reinforce the identified academic and social behavior standards based on their identified function (including self-monitoring checks). At least daily remediation teaching for ten days at a time (at least three checkpoints a day) is recommended.

Who is responsible? The intervention team is the lead, the leadership team ensures the intervention team has all it needs to implement, and teachers may have an implementation role in the classroom setting, based on their identified role in the plan.

Give frequent and formative skill-building checks for mastery and generalization of the learned behavior standards (such as SMART goal, self-monitoring, and stakeholder feedback check-ins).

Study: Analyze behavior data, stakeholder feedback, student feedback, SMART goals, and the fidelity of implementation results, and adjust or modify Tier 3 intervention based on the data.

Who is responsible? The leadership team and intervention team, based on schoolwide data and teacher input

Give a summative mastery assessment of the identified essential academic or social behavior standard at the end of remediation teaching.

Source: Adapted from Buffum et al., 2018.

FIGURE 5.17: Tier 3 study stage.

Commonly Asked Questions in the Study Stage

Consider these questions.

- How do we function as a PLC with a focus on Tier 3 behavior data? What steps do we take?

- How do we get the data, and what type of data will we use to decide if our students are responding?

- What Tier 3 data do we use to identify problem statements?

- What does implementing Tier 3 behavior supports look like in action, and what processes or tools can we utilize to help?

- How can we access input from the teacher teams?

- Do we connect with the leadership team designee who pushes in monthly and gathers data, or do we wait until the teacher teams provide input using the "Behavior Support Form" (page 98)?

Tier 3 Study Stage: Processes, Tools, and Forms

In this section, you will find processes, tools, and forms designed to help you begin the work in the study stage.

Tier 3 Teacher Input Collection

To get to the study stage in this Tier 3 cycle, teams must have a method of collecting data. The leadership team collects teacher team input at the following frequencies as part of this cycle. The representative from the leadership team who collects this information for all tiers provides the Tier 3 teacher input to the intervention team.

- **At least monthly:** The leadership team representative who pushes into every teacher team meeting monthly to gather Tiers 1, 2, and 3 input shares the information regarding Tier 3 with the designated representative from the intervention team.

- **When requested:** A designated representative from the intervention team pushes into a teacher team meeting based on receipt of a "Behavior Support Form" (page 98) that requires Tier 3 remediation.

- **Ongoing:** The leadership team, intervention team, and teacher teams have a shared Google data document; it might include meeting minutes with space for teachers' Tier 3 behavior input and student identification gathered at every teacher team meeting (see figure 3.16, page 93). For example, the data collected here could be more perception based, such as a request for supporting a student who is escalating with disruptive behaviors, a request for supporting a student who has recently begun looking incredibly down and disengaged from all peers and the teachers, or a request for help with a student who has a behavior plan but no longer appears to be demonstrating positive results.

SMART Goals Monitoring

The following two figures offer examples of a Tier 3 remediation: SMART goals monitoring forms. (You may also refer back to figure 4.16, page 163, for a Tier 2 version of this form.) It is essential that the intervention team have a set of SMART goals so they can measure overall positive impact of the Tier 3 supports provided at the school for both general education and special education students. In figure 5.18, the students happen to all be receiving special education services. In figure 5.19, the students receive a mixture of special education and general education.

Date: *October 30*

Tier 3 Remediation: *Individualized behavior support plan attached to an IEP*

Total Students Receiving Tier 3 Remediation: *Six students*

Tier 3 Remediation: Weekly Behavior SMART Goal Check			
Date: *November 6*	**Date:** *November 13*	**Date:** *November 20*	**Date:** *November 27*
1 of 6 met goal	*2 of 6 met goal*	*4 of 6 met goal*	*3 of 6 met goal*

Behavior SMART goal: *By the end of the school year, suspensions assigned for students receiving a Tier 3 intervention will decrease overall by at least 50 percent from the previous school year, when 100 percent of students receiving a Tier 3 intervention were suspended at least once during the school year.*

Note: Of the six students currently receiving a Tier 3 intervention, one has already been suspended in the school year.

Tier 3 Remediation: Weekly Academic SMART Goal Check			
Date: *November 6*	**Date:** *November 13*	**Date:** *November 20*	**Date:** *November 27*
1 of 6 met goal	*1 of 6 met goal*	*3 of 6 met goal*	*3 of 6 met goal*

Academic SMART goal: *By the end of the school year, there will be a 50 percent overall increase in IEP academic goal progress for special education students receiving a Tier 3 intervention, as compared with the previous school year, when such students made no increase in IEP academic goal progress.*

Note: Of the six students currently receiving a Tier 3 intervention, zero are meeting IEP goal progress markers.

FIGURE 5.18: Tier 3 SMART goals monitoring form for teachers—example with special education goals only.

*Visit **go.SolutionTree.com/RTIatWork** for a free reproducible version of this figure.*

Date: *October 30*

Tier 3 Remediation: *Ten-day intensive plan*

Total Students Receiving Tier 3 Remediation: *Eight students*

Tier 3 Remediation: Weekly Behavior SMART Goal Check			
Date: *November 6*	**Date:** *November 13*	**Date:** *November 20*	**Date:** *November 27*
2 of 8 met goal	*3 of 8 met goal*	*3 of 8 met goal*	*4 of 8 met goal*

Behavior SMART goal: *By the end of the school year, the total number of suspensions for students receiving Tier 3 supports will decrease by at least 50 percent from the previous school year (twenty-six suspensions).*

Note: Of the eight students currently receiving Tier 3 supports, three have already been suspended in the school year. One of the three has been suspended multiple times (six times).

Tier 3 Remediation: Weekly Academic SMART Goal Check			
Date: *November 6*	**Date:** *November 13*	**Date:** *November 20*	**Date:** *November 27*
1 of 8 met goal	*2 of 8 met goal*	*2 of 8 met goal*	*3 of 8 met goal*

Academic SMART goal: *By the end of the school year, 80 percent of students receiving Tier 3 supports will make a minimum of five points' growth on their third trimester reading goal as compared with their first trimester reading goal.*

Note: Of the eight students currently receiving Tier 3 supports, zero are meeting reading goals at their grade level.

FIGURE 5.19: Tier 3 SMART goals monitoring form—example with special and general education goals.

*Visit **go.SolutionTree.com/RTIatWork** for a free reproducible version of this figure.*

Tier 3 Precise Problem Statements

Every time the intervention team meets, members should be able to develop a precise problem statement based on their data. Doing so, in turn, helps them use data to make decisions and responses for Tier 3 needs of the school. Remember that precise problem statements give details about behaviors, including when and where they occur and what the antecedents may be, and that their solutions are based on data. You can refer back to the section Problem Statements (page 88) in chapter 3 for more information. See figure 5.20 (page 216) for an example.

Tier 3 Precise Problem Statement
A seventh-grade student has been receiving Tier 3 support since the beginning of the school year, but his individualized behavior data and seventh-grade teacher team input indicate that his behavior has escalated to the point that it takes multiple adults multiple hours to calm him down when he perceives a situation with a teacher or peer to be unfair. He has been suspended multiple times (four separate incidents; six days total) in the first two weeks of November.
Current State
Not all stakeholders are consistently following the Tier 3 plan, the structure and schedule designed to prevent the student's behavior from escalating. Specifically, they do not schedule opportunities and checks throughout the day for the student to express his feelings and practice his remediation skills when he perceives unfair situations.
Solution Action: Tier 3 Response
Tighten up the Tier 3 plan by designing a ten-day intensive plan with the commitment from all stakeholders to follow through.
Retrain the student on the plan.
Follow up with the student's parent on the student's mental health check with his doctor regarding his difficulty self-regulating emotions.

FIGURE 5.20: Tier 3 problem statement matched to a Tier 3 response—example.

*Visit **go.SolutionTree.com/RTIatWork** for a free reproducible version of this figure.*

Plan–Do–Study–ACT

In the act stage of the remediation cycle (highlighted in figure 5.21), the intervention team brings together the actions it identified during the plan stage based on data and adjusts as needed to meet set goals.

- **Why:** To implement the modifications and adjustments based on the study stage to get the desired results of Tier 3 remediation

- **Who:** The intervention team

- **What:** Implementing modified actions and timelines and restarting the cycle on an ongoing basis

- **When:** At least weekly

Commonly Asked Questions in the Act Stage

Consider these questions.

- Who is in charge of implementing the actions?

- What do we do if the plan does not work?

- How do we communicate and receive input from stakeholders about our actions?

Plan: Identify students who are not responding to Tier 1 prevention or Tier 2 intervention based on schoolwide prevention data, Tier 2 intervention data, behavior or discipline data, and teacher input, and develop a Tier 3 remediation plan based on their individualized needs (that is, ten-day intensives, a behavior support plan, or a structured day plan) with entry and exit criteria (what constitutes a Tier 3 plan).

Who is responsible? The intervention team, based on Tier 1 and Tier 2 data, behavior and discipline data, and teacher input

Screen for prior skills and determine the function of behavior in order to match it with the appropriate remediation essential standard.

Tier 3 Remediation
Reteaching of the Essential Academic and Social Behaviors

Academic Behaviors		
Metacognition	Self-concept	Self-monitoring
Motivation	Strategy	Volition

Social Behaviors		
Responsible verbal and physical interactions with peers and adults		
Appropriate language		
Respect for property and materials		
Independently staying on a required task		
Regular attendance		

Act: Analyze Tier 3 remediation plans' summative results and other relevant data, and identify students who possibly need a different or additional layer to the individualized remediation plan (or who can exit Tier 3).

Who is responsible? The intervention team, based on current Tier 3 remediation plan data, behavior or discipline data, and teacher input

Continue to monitor students receiving or exiting Tier 3 remediation plans on a regular basis.

Do: Introduce students to the Tier 3 remediation learning targets, begin frequent remediation teaching, and design and structure the individualized plan that will teach and reinforce the identified academic and social behavior standards based on their identified function (including self-monitoring checks). At least daily remediation teaching for ten days at a time (at least three checkpoints a day) is recommended.

Who is responsible? The intervention team is the lead, the leadership team ensures the intervention team has all it needs to implement, and teachers may have an implementation role in the classroom setting, based on their identified role in the plan

Give frequent and formative skill-building checks for mastery and generalization of the learned behavior standards (such as SMART goal, self-monitoring, and stakeholder feedback check-ins).

Study: Analyze behavior data, stakeholder feedback, student feedback, SMART goals, and the fidelity of implementation results, and adjust or modify Tier 3 intervention based on the data.

Who is responsible? The leadership team and intervention team, based on schoolwide data and teacher input

Give a summative mastery assessment of the identified essential academic or social behavior standard at the end of remediation teaching.

Source: Adapted from Buffum et al., 2018.

FIGURE 5.21: Tier 3 act stage.

Tier 3 Act Stage: Processes, Tools, and Forms

In this section, you will find processes, tools, and forms designed to help you begin the work in the act stage.

Tier 3 Behavior Data Wall

As mentioned in chapter 4 (page 164), the behavior data wall is a process designed to help teams monitor progress for students receiving Tier 2 and Tier 3 supports. While the leadership team's Tier 2 subset monitors progress for students receiving Tier 2 supports, it is the *intervention team's role* to update the behavior data wall and shared log for students receiving Tier 3 supports.

Refer back to figure 4.18 (page 165) for a visual example of a behavior data wall, and to figure 4.19 (page 167) for the sample interventions at-a-glance form as reference. In this section, you will find the Tier 3 remediations at-a-glance—form. The intervention team should also have a log of the Tier 3 remediation plans being implemented and a log of that progress. Figure 4.20 (page 167) is an example of the shared log that the intervention team should update electronically (for shared, timely, updated information). This data-based process ensures that all students who need additional support receive it with fidelity, and that the intervention team continuously adjusts that support if students do not respond to what they are currently receiving.

Figure 5.22 is a example student's individual plan results for both goals met and team implementation fidelity. The intervention team can provide information about two criteria after reviewing the individual data charts.

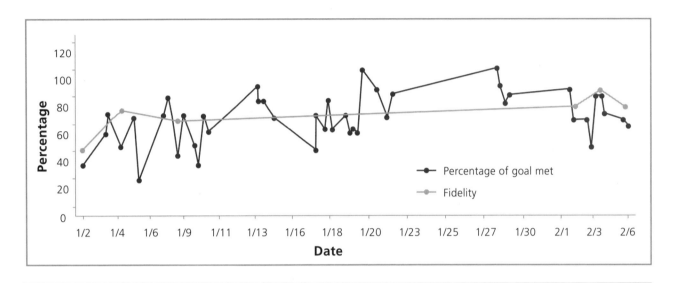

FIGURE 5.22: Tier 3 plan graph results sample.

In this case, the team explains two things: (1) that the lower fidelity of Tier 3 plan implementation impacts the student's progress, making the reason for inconsistency clear, and (2) that members want to revisit the plan and all involved stakeholders' roles and responsibilities February 12 to make any necessary adjustments.

Figure 5.23 is an example Tier 3 remediations at-a-glance form that the intervention team uses to identify how the Tier 3 supports are working.

Intervention	Total Students	Total Students Meeting Goal	Percentage of Students Meeting Goal
Individual counseling	15	8	53 percent
Re-entry transition plans	4	3	75 percent
Ten-day intensive plans	5	3	60 percent
Behavior support plans (attached to an IEP)	7	3	42 percent

FIGURE 5.23: Remediations at a glance—example.

PLC and Tier 3 RTI Integration Criteria Guide

Figure 5.24 (page 220) outlines four priority criteria in Tier 3 and sample evidence indicators for each. Build on the four Tier 1 criteria (figure 3.27, page 113) and the four Tier 2 criteria (figure 4.21, page 169) to help your school function as a PLC, and use the essential academic and social behavior standards and your school's behavior data when assigning Tier 3 remediation.

Behavior Integration Assessment: Tier 3

How do you measure the implementation of the integration criteria? With the BIA. The comprehensive assessment tool is for all three tiers of integration criteria designed to address and prevent the systemic behavior gap. This assessment is designed for the leadership team to utilize as a guide to ensuring the criteria is in place to avoid the systemic behavior gap.

Keep in mind that the evidence indicators from each of the four criteria provides your team with tangible evidence to justify your score. We've seen teams score themselves high on rubrics or say "We're doing all those things" when criteria are broadly written or lacking specificity. For this reason, we created the evidence indicators that allow teams to hold themselves accountable with artifacts and other evidence to justify a score of 2 (in place). It also gives teams a target toward mastery to put in place so they can achieve a score of 2 on the BIA.

Complete the following reproducibles as a schoolwide team (led by the intervention team).

- ▶ "Behavior Integration Assessment: Tier 3" (page 223)

- ▶ "RTI at Work Pyramid: Tier 3" (page 224)

- ▶ "Reflection Three" (page 225)

PLC and Tier 3 RTI Integration Criteria	Tier 3 Evidence Indicators	Reflect on These Evidence Indicators and the Systemic Behavior Gap They Will Address
Establish and operate an effective intervention team to address Tier 3 remediation needs.	Team purposes, roles, and responsibilities are clear. The principal is an active member of the team. The intervention team has weekly meetings and completed agendas or minutes. The intervention team has a data-based process for identifying students for Tier 3. The intervention team utilizes the Tier 3 remediation cycle stages and up-to-date data at meetings. The intervention team considers multiple data points when identifying precise problem statements and developing and implementing Tier 3 plans. An identified leadership team member conducts monthly teacher team push-ins to gather teacher input on RTI. An identified team lead helps ensure the fidelity of team meetings and Tier 3 implementation. The intervention team establishes SMART goals for Tier 3 implementation based on student needs. The intervention team coordinates, designs, and provides resources that teacher teams need to support implementation of Tier 3 remediation in their classrooms. The intervention team ensures Tier 3 plans are in place with fidelity. Behavior specialist and expert time is protected to ensure Tier 3 supports. The intervention team conducts a Tier 3 resource inventory.	

Identify students who need Tier 3 interventions (remediation), identify the function of the behaviors, and match replacement needs to essential behavior standards.	Students and staff can identify and articulate the *why* of designing and implementing Tier 3 supports. The intervention team uses processes, resources, and tools to gather Tier 3 implementation data. Teachers clearly understand how to ask for help with students they identify who may benefit from Tier 3 supports. Students receive Tier 3 remediation in a timely fashion. There is evidence of Tier 3 remediation opportunities.	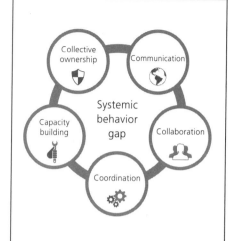
Establish teacher teams' roles and responsibilities in ensuring Tier 3 supports are in place and invest in building their capacity and maintaining their commitment to their role and responsibilities.	Clear responsibilities and roles for Tier 3 remediation are established for teacher teams. Teachers understand and feel equipped to meet their role in Tier 3 remediation (that is, following the plan and monitoring it to provide input). Each teacher team meeting includes an opportunity for teachers to assist each other with RTI needs and use the teacher team minutes or agenda to communicate Tier 3 needs to the leadership team and relayed to the intervention team. The intervention team establishes a culture of high expectations for supporting all students. The intervention team provides Tier 3 teacher training materials based on need. Staff receive communication on Tier 3 successes and challenges. Staff feedback and input on Tier 3 implementation is regularly gathered (every all-staff meeting). The intervention team establishes a Tier 3 incentive program based on individual students' motivation and behavior goal mastery.	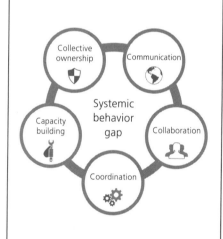

FIGURE 5.24: PLC and Tier 3 RTI integration guide.

continued →

Establish effective procedures for collecting multiple adequate levels of Tier 3 remediation data and provide ongoing training and support on how to use those data for decision making.	The intervention team establishes and maintains staff commitments to Tier 3 remediation implementation. The intervention team maintains an up-to-date data-based Tier 3 intervention process (that is, a behavior data wall and progress-monitoring log). The intervention team has a Tier 3 data-entry procedure and review plan in place; at least once a week, it intentionally reviews the progress of individual students receiving Tier 3 remediation. The intervention team has a process for checking the fidelity of Tier 3 implementation. Tier 3 progress is collectively monitored with SMART goals. Staff understand the difference between Tier 1 prevention, Tier 2 intervention, and Tier 3 remediation in regard to behavior. Staff receive ongoing training on how to ask for support and how to monitor progress using Tier 3 forms, plans, and so on. The school has an established system for monitoring the Tier 3 plan and communicating it to all stakeholders. A designated leadership team member ensures he or she collects data from the teacher teams regarding Tier 3 behavior needs and provides them to the intervention team at least monthly. A process is in place so more urgent Tier 3 support requests are provided directly to the intervention team. The intervention team ensures it has a timely response plan for Tier 3 needs.	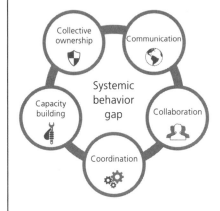

*Visit **go.SolutionTree.com/RTIatWork** for a free reproducible version of this figure.*

Behavior Integration Assessment: Tier 3

With your schoolwide team, indicate what best describes your school's behavior tiered system RTI and PLC integration. Be honest. This assessment is designed to help you monitor your integration and reveal what tier and construct you need to focus on to improve.

Criteria	Score	Next Steps and Evidence
PLC at Work and Tier 3 RTI at Work	Circle one. 0 = Not in place 1 = In progress 2 = In place	For any item scored 0 or 1, list next-step processes, tools, or forms that will help your school meet this criterion. For any item scored 2, list evidence (processes, tools, and forms) it is in place.
Establish and operate an effective intervention team to address Tier 3 remediation needs.	0　1　2	
Identify students who need Tier 3 interventions (remediation), identify the function of the behaviors, and match replacement needs to essential behavior standards.	0　1　2	
Establish teacher teams' roles and responsibilities in ensuring Tier 3 supports are in place and invest in building their capacity and maintaining their commitment to their roles and responsibilities.	0　1　2	
Establish effective procedures for collecting multiple adequate levels of Tier 3 remediation data and provide ongoing training and support on how to use those data for decision making.	0　1　2	

RTI at Work Pyramid: Tier 3

Use information from chapters 2 and 5 to complete the two indicated sections on the RTI at Work pyramid. Use the Plan–Do–Study–Act cycle (figure 5.2, page 181) as a visual guide to all the processes, tools, and forms shared in each of the stages of Tier 3.

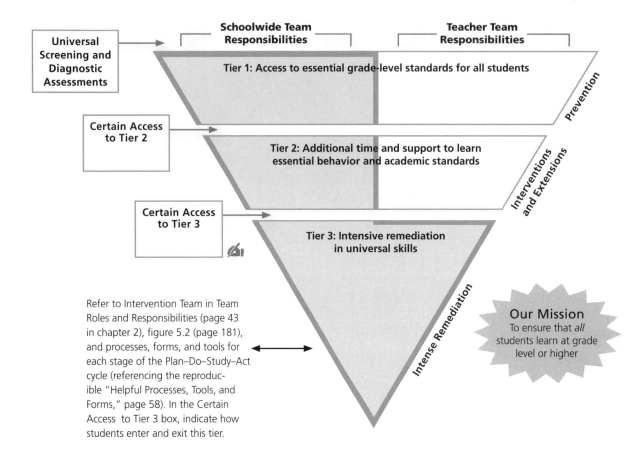

Refer to Intervention Team in Team Roles and Responsibilities (page 43 in chapter 2), figure 5.2 (page 181), and processes, forms, and tools for each stage of the Plan–Do–Study–Act cycle (referencing the reproducible "Helpful Processes, Tools, and Forms," page 58). In the Certain Access to Tier 3 box, indicate how students enter and exit this tier.

Source: Adapted from Buffum, A., Mattos, M., & Malone, J. (2018). Taking action: A handbook for RTI at Work. *Bloomington, IN: Solution Tree Press.*

Reflection Three

We know this is hard work. Take a minute to reflect and celebrate your learning with your team.

_____

_____

_____

Ask yourselves the following questions.

- "How are we feeling about Tier 3 implementation?"

- "What can we commit to as a team at this point in our journey?"

Record your responses here and date them so you log your RTI at Work journey with the focus on behavior.

Date: _____

_____

_____

_____

_____

_____

_____

_____

_____

_____

_____

_____

_____

_____

_____

_____

_____

_____

EPILOGUE

You now have the collaborative structures and specific tools that you need to select, teach, prevent, reteach, remediate, monitor, and ensure all students' mastery of the essential academic and social behaviors needed for success. You know that schools must function as professional learning communities within the PLC at Work process and offer tiered response to intervention within the RTI at Work process. And you know that, at every tier of support, you must use the research-based protocols we have provided in this book to assess your students' current behavior needs, target specific interventions, allocate resources, and evaluate your effectiveness.

You started this book by taking an audit of your school's current state using the systemic behavior gap as a frame (page 21). Now you have read this book and completed the RTI at Work pyramid for each tier, pulling from your learning of roles, responsibilities, and actions from each tier. You have utilized the behavior integration assessment (BIA) with evidence criteria to avoid the systemic behavior gap and the issues that stall implementation.

Whether you're just beginning to create behavior supports in your school or you're improving existing behavior programs, you must remember that becoming a PLC and successfully implementing RTI are ongoing processes. To increase student achievement, all educators study best practices, apply what they have learned, and continue to learn and act until they remove every barrier to student learning (DuFour & Eaker, 1998). This continuous process is necessary to create a highly effective system of behavior supports.

As your school embarks on this journey, let us close with this advice: *why* your faculty is committing to this work is just as important as *how* effectively you do it.

Know that effective behavior interventions are not about disciplining students, punishing them, or holding them accountable. If the adults on campus use their advantages of experience, positional power, and classroom authority to collaborate and then act punitively to demand compliance, they can expect to break their students' wills, destroy their love of learning, and deny them opportunities to develop the behaviors they will need for academic and social health. However, if your staff view behavior interventions through the lens of education, understanding, and compassion, your actions will result in learning and change.

You create a cohesion between compassion and accountability when you use this lens for those you lead. View the information and resources we have provided as actions to take *for* students, not actions to do *to* them. Such a mindset, applied through the proven best practices, can positively transform a school—for both the students and the adults!

APPENDIX A

ESTABLISHING AND SUSTAINING AN RTI SYSTEM FOR SUCCESS

A well-designed plan keeps a district aligned, puts systems in place, improves a process, and most importantly promotes sustainability. A comprehensive strategic plan to implement the RTI at Work process in a PLC will help a district define itself, create purpose, and move everyone in the same direction. Each year, school-improvement plans should reflect a consistent mission. The result will be improved instruction, enhanced student achievement, and a district with high expectations that students and educators meet.

Successfully establishing and sustaining an RTI system evolves as five phases.

1. Complying

2. Identifying the need

3. Identifying roles and responsibilities for all

4. Analyzing and adopting the essential behaviors that students must learn

5. Collective ownership of the Plan–Do–Study–Act process

The following reproducibles help teams plan, establish, and sustain RTI at their school.

▶ "Five Stages of Functioning as a PLC for RTI" (page 230)

▶ "Tiers 1, 2, and 3 Integration Planning Guide" (page 232)

▶ "Three-Year RTI Implementation Plan" (page 235)

Five Stages of Functioning as a PLC for RTI

Questions That Define the Stage	Tier 1 (Prevention): Stage Description	Tier 2 (Intervention): Stage Description	Tier 3 (Remediation): Stage Description
Stage 1: Complying			
What is the purpose of this meeting? What do we do in this meeting? Why do we have to meet?	The schoolwide team is established but does not understand the purpose or outcomes for meeting. The team members do not know what they are supposed to do in the meeting. Administrators are not clear on where to begin. Members typically believe this meeting is a waste of their time because nothing gets done. Meetings become a venting session about student behavior. There is a meeting structure.	The schoolwide Tier 2 subset team is established but does not understand the purpose or outcomes for meeting. The team members do not know what they are supposed to do in the meeting and how often they are supposed to meet. Administrators are not clear on where to begin. Members typically believe this meeting is a waste of their time because nothing gets done. Meetings become a venting session about limited resources and student behavior.	The intervention team is established but does not understand the purpose or outcomes for meeting. The team members do not know what they are supposed to do in the meeting. Specifically, the general education and special education members are confused as to why they have to meet together. Administrators are not clear on where to begin. Members typically believe this meeting is a waste of their time because nothing gets done. Meetings become a venting session about student behavior.
Stage 2: Identifying the need			
What are we doing to address our students' behavior needs? What do we currently have in place for data collection?	The team meets regularly but does not utilize data to identify the school's needs. The team has not established shared commitments. The team understands there is a need for RTI but does not follow the PLC process to identify the need.	The schoolwide Tier 2 subset team meets regularly but does not utilize data to identify and establish entry and exit criteria for Tier 2 interventions. The team has not established shared commitments. The team understands there is a need for RTI but does not follow the PLC process to identify the need.	The intervention team meets regularly but does not utilize data to identify and establish the school's Tier 3 needs. Although there are general education and special education members on the team, they revert to working in silos after identifying individual students' needs. The team has not established shared commitments. The team understands there is a need for RTI but does not follow the PLC process to identify the need.
Stage 3: Identifying roles and responsibilities for all			

What should we focus on when it comes to essential behavior standards for our students? What should we teach, and what does intervening look like for our school? What data do we use if students are not responding?	The team begins to understand its role and responsibilities, but the PLC process is not consistently in place. Data are used at some, but not all, meetings to make decisions. Not all stakeholder input is considered. Tier 1 prevention decisions are not based on schoolwide behavior data. No schoolwide SMART goals are established.	The schoolwide tier 2 subset team begins to understand its role and responsibilities, but the PLC process is not consistently in place. Tier 2 data are used at some, but not all, meetings to make decisions. Not all stakeholder input is considered. Tier 2 decisions are not based on schoolwide behavior data. No Tier 2 SMART goals are established.	The intervention team begins to understand its role and responsibilities, but the PLC process is not consistently in place. Tier 3 data are used at some, but not all, meetings to make decisions. Not all stakeholder input is considered. Tier 3 decisions are not based on individual student behavior data or fidelity of the implementation of the behavior plan. No Tier 3 SMART goals are established.

Stage 4: Analyzing and adopting the essential behaviors that students must learn

What does mastery of essential behavior standards look like? How will we know if students have learned and generalized them? How can we help each other improve the culture in our school and in every classroom?	Meetings center on students demonstrating essential behavior standards. Tier 1 interventions are designed and implemented based on schoolwide data and stakeholder input. SMART goals are developed around schoolwide teaching and prevention needs. In-depth conversations about data and stakeholder input lead to next steps. Criteria for proficiency are established as a team and shared with all stakeholders.	Meetings center on students who need Tier 2 reteaching opportunities for essential behavior standards. Tier 2 interventions are designed and implemented based on schoolwide data and stakeholder input. SMART goals for Tier 2 interventions are developed and revisited at every meeting. In-depth conversations about data and stakeholder input lead to next steps. Criteria for mastery are established as a team and shared with all stakeholders.	Meetings center on students who need Tier 3 remediation opportunities for essential behavior standards.

Stage 5: Collective ownership of the Plan–Do–Study–Act process

How do we use a continuous improvement model (such as Plan–Do–Study–Act) to make sure teams are implementing best practices for behavior? How do we function as a PLC to assign RTI? How do we know if our response is working for students?	The team understands that schoolwide practices need to be adjusted based on schoolwide data and needs. The team revisits its schoolwide SMART goals, schoolwide data-based problem statements, implemented actions, roles, responsibilities, timelines, and decision rules for success (meeting goals) at every meeting. Extension opportunities are established for students mastering essential behavior standards.	The schoolwide Tier 2 subset team understands that Tier 2 practices need to be adjusted based on schoolwide data and needs. The team revisits its Tier 2 SMART goals, Tier 2 data-based problem statements, implemented actions, roles, responsibilities, timelines, and decision rules for success (meeting goals) at every meeting. Additional opportunities for mastering retaught essential standards are offered to students.	The intervention team understands that Tier 3 practices need to be adjusted based on schoolwide data and needs. The team revisits its Tier 3 SMART goals, Tier 3 data-based problem statements, implemented actions, roles, responsibilities, timelines, and decision rules for success (meeting goals) at every meeting. Data-based collaboration between general education and special education guides decision rules and additional intensive supports.

Tiers 1, 2, and 3 Integration Planning Guide

Each tier of implementation has four priority actions (pages 113, 169, and 220). Use what you have learned from each tier's Plan–Do–Study–Act cycle to identify each stakeholder team's corresponding tasks as you plan implementation for each tier.

Tier 1 Criteria			
	Leadership Team	**Intervention Team**	**Teacher Teams**
Establish and operate an effective leadership team to address schoolwide prevention for behavior.			
Identify and teach schoolwide essential academic and social behavior standards.			
Establish teacher teams' role and responsibilities in ensuring Tier 1 prevention is in place in every classroom, invest in building their capacity, and maintain their commitment to their role and responsibilities.			
Establish effective procedures for collecting multiple adequate levels of Tier 1 schoolwide data and provide ongoing training and support for how to use those data for decision making.			

Behavior Solutions © 2021 Solution Tree Press • SolutionTree.com

Visit **go.SolutionTree.com/RTIatWork** to download this free reproducible.

page 1 of 3

Tier 2 Criteria			
	Leadership Team	**Intervention Team**	**Teacher Teams**
Establish and operate an effective Tier 2 subset of the leadership team to address Tier 2 intervention needs.			
Identify students who need Tier 2 interventions (reteaching) for the essential academic and social behavior standards.			
Establish teacher teams' role and responsibilities in ensuring Tier 2 implementation, and invest in building their capacity and maintaining their commitment to their role and responsibilities.			
Establish effective procedures for collecting multiple adequate levels of Tier 2 intervention data and provide ongoing training and support on how to use those data for decision making.			

Tier 3 Criteria			
	Leadership Team	**Intervention Team**	**Teacher Teams**
Establish and operate an effective intervention team to address Tier 3 remediation needs.			
Identify students who need Tier 3 interventions (remediation), identify the function of the behaviors, and match replacement needs to essential behavior standards.			
Establish teacher teams' role and responsibilities in ensuring Tier 3 supports are in place and invest in building their capacity and maintaining their commitment to their role and responsibilities.			
Establish effective procedures for collecting multiple adequate levels of Tier 3 remediation data and provide ongoing training and support on how to use those data for decision making.			

Three-Year RTI Implementation Plan

Year	How to Function as a PLC at Tier 1 (Prevention)	How to Function as a PLC at Tier 2 (Intervention)	How to Function as a PLC at Tier 3 (Remediation)
Year 1:			
Year 2:			
Year 3:			

APPENDIX B

BEHAVIOR REHEARSAL LESSON CARDS

Follow these steps when using Tier 2 behavior rehearsal cards. Visit **go.SolutionTree .com/RTIatWork** for a free downloadable version of these instructions. These are the suggested steps for all the Tier 2 behavior rehearsal cards provided.

1. Ask students to check in. They should rate how well they met their behavior goals for the week (or another determined amount of time) between 1 and 5 and explain their self-rating.

    » 1 = I need to continue working on skills.

    » 2 = I am making improvements but need to continue working on skills.

    » 3 = I need to continue working on consistently using my learned skills.

    » 4 = I almost met all my goals for the week with a few minor hiccups.

    » 5 = I met all my goals for the week.

2. Identify and define the focus behaviors and skills that the students will need to learn to demonstrate mastery as part of the behavior academy and determine the students' current knowledge of those skills and behaviors.

3. Explain to the students the key behavior skills necessary to master the behavior academy. Ask them to define the skills in their own words by writing or drawing them. Tell the students that they can look up the skills if they are unable to identify and define them.

4. As a small group or whole class, practice one of the behavior skill scenarios on the behavior rehearsal cards together by role playing. This helps students process the meaning of the behavior and practice the wrong way and right way to respond to the given scenario.

5. Pair or put students in trios and ask them to practice the next skill together. After practicing, ask every student to come up with an example related to that card.

6. Ask students to write a journal entry in which they reflect and commit to how they will practice the newly learned skill or skills throughout the week (provide sentence strips if necessary)—have the students initial them.

7. For academy culmination, you can give the students behavior rehearsal cards as a mastery exam at the end of the academy. You can ask them to provide written or oral responses based on each scenario or to do a culminating project related to their newly learned behaviors and skills, such as filming a video, solving a real-life problem, or completing a service learning project.

8. Repeat the process until the students have mastered all the skills.

The following reproducibles are for students to use as they practice their behavior skills.

CICO Skills Behavior Rehearsal Lesson Cards

Why: To provide reteaching opportunities for students on CICO

What: CICO behavior rehearsal lesson cards (role-playing and practice opportunities)

How: Print the cards on card stock and cut them out. Distribute the cards to students so they can role-play one-on-one with you or in pairs or triads with other students.

Additional suggestions: After students rehearse with the card or cards, have them complete their CICO self-monitoring sheet. Then have students complete a journal entry explaining what they rehearsed and commit to further practicing the skills. Assign homework to practice the skills on the card or cards, and have students share how they practiced at the next session.

Follow Instructions Your teacher has given you instructions, but you do not feel like doing what she or he asked you to do. You would prefer doing what you want to do instead. What is the right way? What is the wrong way?	**Show Self-Control** You are having a difficult time staying in your seat and following the class rules. What is the right way? What is the wrong way?
Stay on Task Your teacher has had to remind you repeatedly to get back on task because all you want to do is walk around and avoid doing the assignment. What is the right way? What is the wrong way?	**Hold Yourself Accountable** Your teacher has told you that you did not earn full points on a section of your CICO form because you were not demonstrating appropriate behaviors. You argue with the teacher about your CICO ratings and do not accept responsibility for your behavior. What is the right way? What is the wrong way?
Stay Organized You are not prepared for class. You do not know where your homework is, and you cannot find the worksheet your teacher wants you to work on in class. It takes you several minutes of looking in your desk and backpack to find a pencil. In addition, you often lose your CICO sheet and forget to check in. What is the right way? What is the wrong way?	**Be Motivated** You do not feel like the current task or assignment is anything you want to do. You are having a difficult time getting started and have no desire to do so. You would rather receive zero points. What is the right way? What is the wrong way?
Listen and Ask for Help You have missed the teacher's instructions because you were engaged in another activity when she or he was speaking. You blurt out, "I do not know what to do," instead of properly asking the teacher for help. What is the right way? What is the wrong way?	**Seek Appropriate Attention** You want to get the attention of students in your class, so you decide to find ways to get them to look at you and laugh. You make noises, make faces, distract them, and dance around instead of doing your work. What is the right way? What is the wrong way?
Accept Feedback and Reflect You perceive your teacher to be unfairly rating your CICO behavior in class. You decide that, since you did not gain full points in the morning segment of your CICO form, you will not change your behavior for the rest of the day. What is the right way? What is the wrong way?	**Self-Monitor and Self-Correct** You notice you are not demonstrating the behaviors identified on your CICO form that would earn you full points. You decide to continue with your behavior instead of replacing it with the appropriate behaviors. What is the right way? What is the wrong way?

Civility Skills Behavior Rehearsal Lesson Cards

Why: To provide reteaching opportunities for students on civility skills

What: Civility skills behavior rehearsal lesson cards (role-playing and practice opportunities)

How: Print the cards on card stock, and cut them out. Distribute the cards to students so they can role-play one-on-one with you or in pairs or triads with other students.

Additional suggestions: After students rehearse with the card or cards, have them complete their civility skills self-monitoring sheet. Then have students complete a journal entry explaining what they rehearsed and commit to further practicing the skills. Assign homework to practice the skills on the card or cards, and have students share how they practiced at the next session.

Be Respectful You do not agree with a classmate's opinion on a discussion topic, so you tell the classmate to stop talking, and you say nobody cares about his opinion. What is the right way? What is the wrong way?	**Be Patient** You perceive a decision to be unfair, so you decide to take matters into your own hands. You often get your way, so it is difficult for you to get past the anger you feel about the decision. What is the right way? What is the wrong way?
Peacefully Coexist You really do not like a few students at your school and decide to make it known by making rude comments about them in person and online. What is the right way? What is the wrong way?	**Problem Solve** You hear that someone is talking bad about you and your group of friends, so you decide to verbally confront the student during lunch instead of asking for help. What is the right way? What is the wrong way?
Self-Regulate You notice you are getting more and more upset about a disagreement that arises while working with a group of students on a collaborative project. Instead of expressing how you feel in a calm manner, you decide to scream at them all and quit the group. What is the right way? What is the wrong way?	**Be Empathic** You decide you do not like someone because your best friend told you not to. You think the person is nice, but you decide to be mean to her anyway to appease your best friend. You know it is hurting her feelings, but you do it anyway. What is the right way? What is the wrong way?
Be Considerate You know a student struggling to make friends is continually being picked on and talked about. Instead of being considerate of his feelings, you continue to be a bystander. What is the right way? What is the wrong way?	**Show Good Character** You treat people you do not like differently when no one is watching. What is the right way? What is the wrong way?
Be an Empathic Listener You constantly interrupt when people are trying to give their side of a story. You tend to ignore what they are saying. What is the right way? What is the wrong way?	**Be Tolerant and Open-Minded** You are not open to learning about others' perspectives on difficult topics. What is the right way? What is the wrong way?

Organizational Skills Behavior Rehearsal Lesson Cards

Why: To provide reteaching opportunities for students on organizational skills

What: Organizational skills behavior rehearsal lesson cards (role-playing and practice opportunities)

How: Print the cards on card stock, and cut them out. Distribute the cards to students so they can role-play one-on-one with you or in pairs or triads with other students.

Additional suggestions: After students rehearse with the card or cards, have them complete their organizational skills self-monitoring sheet. Then have students complete a journal entry explaining what they rehearsed and commit to further practicing the skills. Assign homework to practice the skills on the card or cards, and have students share how they practiced at the next session.

Be on Time You are constantly late to class from breaks and transitions, and you turn in work late. What is the right way? What is the wrong way?	**Be Prepared** You often come to school without any work completed and have not studied for upcoming exams. What is the right way? What is the wrong way?
Hold Yourself Accountable You make up excuses for not being organized for class. You get defensive when you are held accountable for your missing work. What is the right way? What is the wrong way?	**Ask Questions** You often do not understand the purpose or relevance of the assignments in class, but instead of asking for clarity, you decide it is not worth it. What is the right way? What is the wrong way?
Be Resourceful You do not understand your assignment, so you decide to not complete it. What is the right way? What is the wrong way?	**Be Motivated** You continue to get behind, and you see no value in the work that is being assigned in class. What is the right way? What is the wrong way?
Monitor Yourself You are getting behind with classwork and homework, and you do not see a reason to pay attention to it until it is the end of the grading period. What is the right way? What is the wrong way?	**Set Goals** You do not set short-term or long-term goals for yourself. You feel like going to class is a waste of time. What is the right way? What is the wrong way?
Manage Time You do not set aside enough time for yourself to complete tasks. You always wait until the last minute and end up running out of time. What is the right way? What is the wrong way?	**Prioritize** You get overwhelmed with the amount of work you have to complete, and you do not know where to start. What is the right way? What is the wrong way?

Social Skills Behavior Rehearsal Lesson Cards

Why: To provide reteaching opportunities for students on social skills

What: Social skills behavior rehearsal lesson cards (role-playing and practice opportunities)

How: Print the cards on card stock, and cut them out. Distribute the cards to students so they can role-play one-on-one with you or in pairs or triads with other students.

Additional suggestions: After students rehearse with the card or cards, have them complete their social skills self-monitoring sheet. Then have students complete a journal entry explaining what they rehearsed and commit to further practicing the skills. Assign homework to practice the skills on the card or cards, and have students share how they practiced at the next session.

Allow Personal Space You do not understand why students and adults are always telling you to get out of their personal space. You are just trying to speak to them and do not understand why they do not want to speak to you. What is the right way? What is the wrong way?	**Show Self-Control** You are having a difficult time listening to others when they speak and waiting for your turn. You are so determined to say what comes into your head that you often interrupt. What is the right way? What is the wrong way?
Show Courage You are told to do something you know is not right, but you want to be friends with the group of students who are telling you to do it. What is the right way? What is the wrong way?	**Take Turns** You have been told you have to wait for your turn to speak or begin an activity. You do not understand why you have to wait. What is the right way? What is the wrong way?
Empathize You do not understand why you are upsetting others around you. You continue to make comments to others that hurt their feelings, and you do not know how to stop yourself. What is the right way? What is the wrong way?	**Be Aware** You continue to make inappropriate noises in the classroom and outside settings. You feel like you always have to be making noise to interact with others. What is the right way? What is the wrong way?
Ask for Help You do not know what to do in a social situation with some of the students in your class. You feel confused, so you end up acting out and getting into trouble. What is the right way? What is the wrong way?	**Seek Appropriate Attention** You are often making inappropriate comments to make others laugh. What is the right way? What is the wrong way?
Accept Feedback You are constantly being told to stop "acting that way," and you do not understand what that means and feel mad and defensive. What is the right way? What is the wrong way?	**Self-Monitor and Self-Correct** You notice you are not demonstrating the appropriate social skills during free time or breaks. You are constantly getting in trouble and losing privileges, but you continue to demonstrate the same behaviors. What is the right way? What is the wrong way?

Upstander Skills Behavior Rehearsal Lesson Cards

Why: To provide reteaching opportunities for students on upstander skills

What: Upstander skills behavior rehearsal lesson cards (role-playing and practice opportunities)

How: Print the cards on card stock, and cut them out. Distribute the cards to students so they can role-play one-on-one with you or in pairs or triads with other students.

Additional suggestions: After students rehearse with the card or cards, have them complete their upstander skills self-monitoring sheet. Then have students complete a journal entry explaining what they rehearsed and commit to further practicing the skills. Assign homework to practice the skills on the card or cards, and have students share how they practiced at the next session.

Be Aware You see the same person keep getting teased by a group of students at lunch, but you don't say anything because no one else seems to mind. What is the right way? What is the wrong way?	**Be Supportive** You witness someone being picked on about something that happened over the weekend. No one in the room except the teacher is acknowledging this person because of the incident over the weekend. What is the right way? What is the wrong way?
Be Action Oriented You know there is a way to anonymously report bullying at your school, but you decide someone else should do it, not you. What is the right way? What is the wrong way?	**Speak Up** You are close friends with the person who is bullying a younger student, but you do not tell him to stop. You laugh at his comments because you do not want him to stop being your friend. What is the right way? What is the wrong way?
Stand Up You know the bullying behavior you are seeing from some students toward others at school is not OK, but you do not want to say anything so you are not the next victim. What is the right way? What is the wrong way?	**Be Courageous** You decide to stay quiet about a bullying situation you have witnessed from a group of girls toward another girl over a boy. You want to say something, but you are afraid, so you don't. What is the right way? What is the wrong way?
Be a Responsible Digital Citizen You know of two or three students who are constantly the center of every online joke. Instead of stopping the behavior, you comment and like the mean posts online. What is the right way? What is the wrong way?	**Lead** You are asked to get involved in a classroom discussion about bullying behaviors at the school. You choose to not be honest about the bullying behaviors you have witnessed. What is the right way? What is the wrong way?
Be Inclusive You notice the new student at the school is always left out and has no one to speak to or hang out with during break times. You feel bad, but you do not want to risk missing anything going on with your group, so you continue as usual without inviting the student to join your group. What is the right way? What is the wrong way?	**Be Resourceful** You do not know how to get help for students who are being bullied, and you make no effort to find out. You figure someone else will do it and it is not your business. What is the right way? What is the wrong way?

APPENDIX C

RTI AT WORK—CULMINATING EXERCISE EXAMPLE

Figure C.1 is an example of a completed RTI at Work pyramid. Yours will look different, of course, because your school will have a different combination of needs. This is simply for reference.

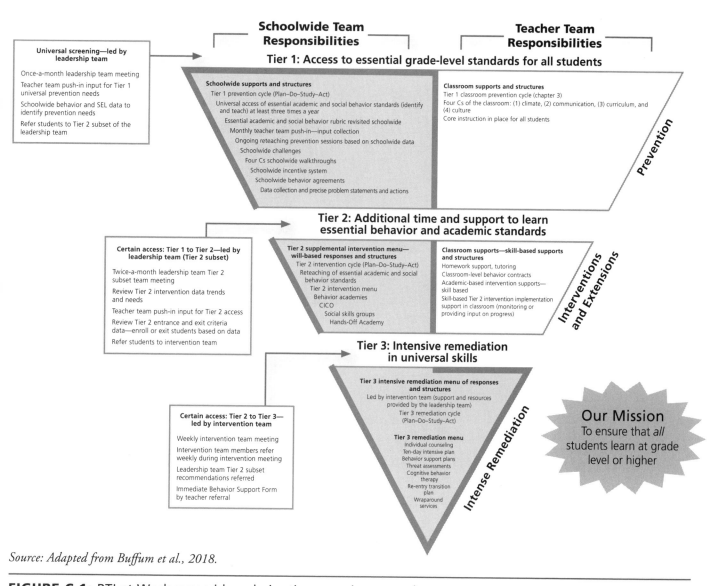

Source: Adapted from Buffum et al., 2018.

FIGURE C.1: RTI at Work pyramid—culminating exercise example.

RTI at Work—Culminating Exercise

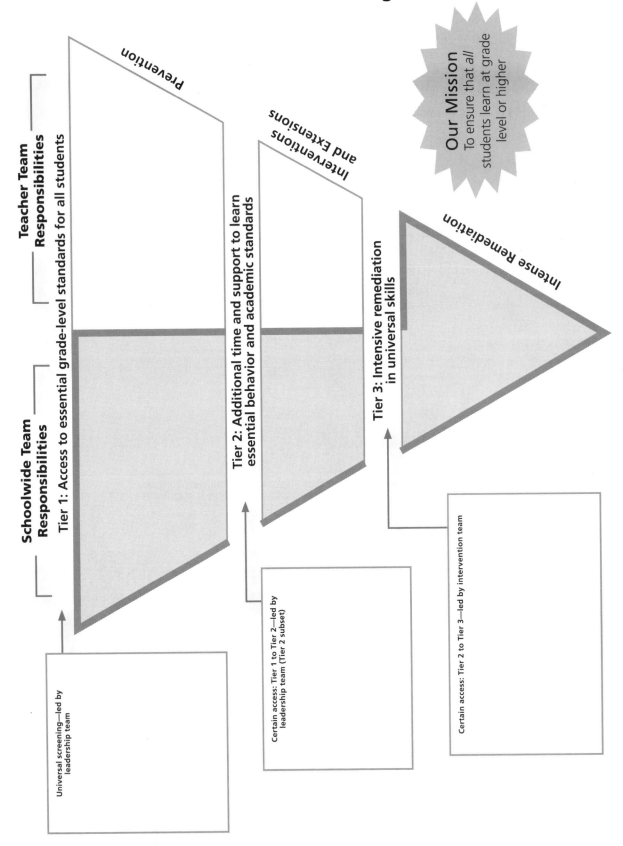

Teacher Team Responsibilities

Schoolwide Team Responsibilities

Prevention

Tier 1: Access to essential grade-level standards for all students

Interventions and Extensions

Tier 2: Additional time and support to learn essential behavior and academic standards

Intense Remediation

Tier 3: Intensive remediation in universal skills

Our Mission
To ensure that *all* students learn at grade level or higher

Universal screening—led by leadership team

Certain access: Tier 1 to Tier 2—led by leadership team (Tier 2 subset)

Certain access: Tier 2 to Tier 3—led by intervention team

Source: Adapted from Buffum, A., Mattos, M., & Malone, J. (2018). Taking action: A handbook for RTI at Work. *Bloomington, IN: Solution Tree Press*

Behavior Solutions © 2021 Solution Tree Press • SolutionTree.com
Visit **go.SolutionTree.com/RTIatWork** to download this free reproducible.

REFERENCES AND RESOURCES

Ainsworth, L. (2014). *Power standards: Identifying the standards that matter the most.* Boston: Houghton Mifflin Harcourt.

Balfanz, R., & Boccanfuso, C. (2007). *Falling off the path to graduation: Middle grade indicators in [an unidentified northeastern city].* Baltimore: Center for Social Organization of Schools.

Barber, M., & Mourshed, M. (2007). *How the world's best-performing school systems come out on top.* New York: McKinsey.

Borrero, K. K. (2019). *Every student, every day: A No-Nonsense Nurturer approach to reaching all learners.* Bloomington, IN: Solution Tree Press.

Buffum, A., Mattos, M., & Malone, J. (2018). *Taking action: A handbook for RTI at Work.* Bloomington, IN: Solution Tree Press.

Buffum, A., Mattos, M., & Weber, C. (2009). *Pyramid response to intervention: RTI, professional learning communities, and how to respond when kids don't learn.* Bloomington, IN: Solution Tree Press.

Buffum, A., Mattos, M., & Weber, C. (2012). *Simplifying response to intervention: Four essential guiding principles.* Bloomington, IN: Solution Tree Press.

Buffum, A., Mattos, M., Weber, C., & Hierck, T. (2015). *Uniting academic and behavior interventions: Solving the skill or will dilemma.* Bloomington, IN: Solution Tree Press.

California Department of Education. (n.d.). *Definition of MTSS.* Accessed at https ://cde.ca.gov/ci/cr/ri/mtsscomprti2.asp on September 13, 2019.

CAST. (n.d.). *Provide multiple means of action and expression.* Accessed at http ://udlguidelines.cast.org/action-expression on August 31, 2020.

Centers for Disease Control and Prevention. (2019). *About adverse childhood experiences.* Accessed at www.cdc.gov/violenceprevention/childabuseandneglect /acestudy/aboutace.html on November 1, 2019.

Centers for Disease Control and Prevention. (2020). *Social and emotional climate.* Accessed at www.cdc.gov/healthyschools/sec.htm on July 1, 2020.

Centers for Disease Control and Prevention, & Kaiser Permanente. (2016). *The ACE study survey data* [Unpublished data]. Accessed at www.cdc.gov /violenceprevention/childabuseandneglect/acestudy/ace-graphics.html on October 24, 2019.

Character Counts! (n.d.). *The six pillars of character*. Accessed at https:// charactercounts.org/program-overview/six-pillars/#:~:text= on February 27, 2020.

Chard, D., Smith, S., & Sugai, G. (1992). Packaged discipline programs: A consumer's guide. In J. Marr & G. Tindal (Eds.), *1992 Oregon conference monograph* (pp. 19–27). Eugene: University of Oregon.

Collaborative for Academic, Social, and Emotional Learning. (2017). *Social and emotional learning (SEL) competencies*. Accessed at https://casel.org/wp-content /uploads/2019/12/CASEL-Competencies.pdf on February 27, 2020.

Collie, R. J., Shapka, J. D., & Perry, N. E. (2012). School climate and social-emotional learning: Predicting teacher stress, job satisfaction, and teaching efficacy. *Journal of Educational Psychology, 104*(4), 1189–1204.

Conzemius, A. E., & O'Neill, J. (2014). *The handbook for SMART school teams: Revitalizing best practices for collaboration* (2nd ed.). Bloomington, IN: Solution Tree Press.

Deming, W. E. (1993). *The new economics for industry, government, education*. Cambridge, MA: MIT Press.

Duckworth, A. (2016). *Grit: The power of passion and perseverance*. New York: Scribner.

DuFour, R., DuFour, R., Eaker, R., Many, T. W., & Mattos, M. (2016). *Learning by doing: A handbook for Professional Learning Communities at Work* (3rd ed.). Bloomington, IN: Solution Tree Press.

DuFour, R., & Eaker, R. (1998). *Professional Learning Communities at Work: Best practices for enhancing student achievement*. Bloomington, IN: Solution Tree Press.

Felitti, V. J., Anda, R. F., Nordenberg, D., Williamson, D. F., Spitz, A. M., Edwards, V., et al. (1998). Relationship of childhood abuse and household dysfunction to many of the leading causes of death in adults: The Adverse Childhood Experiences (ACE) study. *American Journal of Preventive Medicine, 14*(4), 245–258.

Haimovitz, K., & Dweck, C. S. (2017). The origins of children's growth and fixed mindsets: New research and a new proposal. *Child Development, 88*(6), 1849–1859.

Hanna, D. P. (1988). *Designing organizations for high performance*. Reading, MA: Addison-Wesley.

Hannigan, J. D., & Hannigan, J. E. (2018a). *The PBIS tier three handbook: A practical guide to implementing individualized interventions*. Thousand Oaks, CA: Corwin Press.

Hannigan, J. D., & Hannigan, J. E. (2018b). *The PBIS tier two handbook: A practical approach to implementing targeted interventions*. Thousand Oaks, CA: Corwin Press.

Hannigan, J. D., & Hauser, L. (2015). *The PBIS tier one handbook: A practical approach to implementing the champion model.* Thousand Oaks, CA: Corwin Press.

Hattie, J. (2009). *Visible learning: A synthesis of over 800 meta-analyses relating to achievement.* New York: Routledge.

Hattie, J. (2017). *Visible learning: 250+ influences on student achievement.* Accessed at https://us.corwin.com/sites/default/files/250_influences_chart_june_2019.pdf on March 19, 2020.

Horner, R., Sugai, G., Vincent, C. (2005). School-wide positive behavior support: Investing in student success. *Impact, 18*(2), 4–5. Accessed at https://ici.umn.edu/products/impact/182/182.pdf on August 26, 2020.

Irvin, L. K., Tobin, T. J., Sprague, J. R., Sugai, G., & Vincent, C. G. (2004). Validity of office discipline referral measures as indices of school-wide behavioral status and effects of school-wide behavioral interventions. *Journal of Positive Behavior Interventions, 6*(3), 131–147.

Klassen, R. M., & Chiu, M. M. (2010). Effects on teachers' self-efficacy and job satisfaction: Teacher gender, years of experience, and job stress. *Journal of Educational Psychology, 102*(3), 741–756.

Kõlves, K., & De Leo, D. (2014). Suicide rates in children aged 10–14 years worldwide: Changes in the past two decades. *British Journal of Psychiatry, 205*(4), 283–285.

Lane, K. L., Kalberg, J. R., Menzies, H., Bruhn, A., Eisner, S., & Crnobori, M. (2010). Using systematic screening data to assess risk and identify students for targeted supports: Illustrations across the K–12 continuum. *Remedial and Special Education, 32*(1), 39–54.

Leone, P. E., Christle, C. A., Nelson, C. M., Skiba, R., Frey, A., & Jolivette, K. (2003). *School failure, race, and disability: Promoting positive outcomes, decreasing vulnerability for involvement with the juvenile delinquency system.* College Park, MD: National Center on Education, Disability, and Juvenile Justice.

Lezotte, L. W., & Snyder, K. M. (2011). *What effective schools do: Re-envisioning the correlates.* Bloomington, IN: Solution Tree Press.

Losen, D. J. (2011, October). *Discipline policies, successful schools, and racial justice.* Boulder, CO: National Education Policy Center. Accessed at https://nepc.colorado.edu/publication/discipline-policies on September 13, 2019.

Marzano, R. J., Heflebower, T., Hoegh, J. K., Warrick, P., & Grift, G. (2016). *Collaborative teams that transform schools: The next step in PLCs.* Bloomington, IN: Marzano Resources.

Mattos, M., & Buffum, A. (Eds.). (2015). *It's about time: Planning interventions and extensions in secondary school.* Bloomington, IN: Solution Tree Press.

Mayer, G. R. (1995). Preventing antisocial behavior in the schools. *Journal of Applied Behavior Analysis, 28*(4), 467–478.

McNeece, A. (2020). *Loving what they learn: Research-based strategies to increase student engagement.* Bloomington, IN: Solution Tree Press.

Mojtabai, R., Olfson, M., & Han, B. (2016). National trends in the prevalence and treatment of depression in adolescents and young adults. *Pediatrics, 138*(6), 1–10.

Mourshed, M., Chijioke, C., & Barber, M. (2010). *How the world's most improved school systems keep getting better.* New York: McKinsey.

National Institutes of Mental Health. (2018). *Statistics.* Accessed at www.nimh.nih .gov/health/statistics/index.shtml on July 1, 2020.

Office for Civil Rights. (2014, March). *Civil rights data collection: Data snapshot— Teacher equity* (Issue Brief No. 4). Washington, DC: Author. Accessed at www2.ed.gov/about/offices/list/ocr/docs/crdc-teacher-equity-snapshot.pdf on September 13, 2019.

O'Neill, J., & Conzemius, A. (2006). *The power of SMART goals: Using goals to improve student learning.* Bloomington, IN: Solution Tree Press.

Partnership for 21st Century Skills. (2006). *A state leader's action guide to 21st century skills: A new vision for education.* Tucson, AZ: Author.

Polanczyk, G. V., Salum, G. A., Sugaya, L. S., Caye, A., & Rohde, L. A. (2015). Annual research review: A meta-analysis of the worldwide prevalence of mental disorders in children and adolescents. *Journal of Child Psychology and Psychiatry, 56*(3), 345–365.

Prothero, A. (2020). *Schools struggle to meet students' mounting mental-health needs.* Accessed at www.edweek.org/ew/articles/2020/05/01/schools-struggle-to-meet- students-mounting-mental-health.html on August 31, 2020.

Rumberger, R. W., & Losen, D. J. (2016). *The high cost of harsh discipline and its disparate impact.* Los Angeles: Center for Civil Rights Remedies.

Saeki, El., Jimerson, S. R., Earhart, J., Hart, S. R., Renshaw, T., Singh, R. D., et al. (2011). *Response to Intervention (RtI) in the social, emotional, and behavioral domains: Current challenges and emerging possibilities.* Accessed at https://files. eric.ed.gov/fulltext/EJ934705.pdf on August 27, 2020.

Skiba, R., & Peterson, R. (1999). The dark side of zero tolerance: Can punishment lead to safe schools? *Phi Delta Kappan, 80*(5), 372–376, 381–382.

Skiba, R., & Rausch, M. K. (2006). School disciplinary systems: Alternatives to suspension and expulsion. In G. G. Bear & K. M. Minke (Eds.), *Children's needs III: Development, prevention, and intervention* (pp. 87–102). Washington, DC: National Association of School Psychologists.

Stuart, T. S., Heckmann, S., Mattos, M., & Buffum, A. (2018). *Personalized learning in a PLC at Work: Student agency through the four critical questions*. Bloomington, IN: Solution Tree Press.

Substance Abuse and Mental Health Services Administration. (2014). *SAMHSA's concept of trauma and guidance for a trauma-informed approach*. Accessed at https://store.samhsa.gov/system/files/sma14-4884.pdf on February 27, 2020.

U.S. Department of Education. (2014). *Guiding principles: A resource guide for improving school climate and discipline*. Washington, DC: Author. Accessed at www2.ed.gov/policy/gen/guid/school-discipline/guiding-principles.pdf on September 13, 2019.

U.S. Department of Justice, & U.S. Department of Education. (2014). *Notice of language assistance: Dear colleague letter on the nondiscriminatory administration of school discipline*. Washington, DC: Authors. Accessed at www2.ed.gov/about /offices/list/ocr/letters/colleague-residential-facilities-201412.pdf on March 20, 2020.

Visser, S. N., Danielson, M. L., Bitsko, R. H., Holbrook, J. R., Kogan, M. D., Ghandour, R. M., et al. (2014). Trends in the parent-report of health care provider-diagnosed and medicated attention-deficit/hyperactivity disorder: United States, 2003–2011. *Journal of the American Academy of Child and Adolescent Psychiatry, 53*(1), 34–46.

Wald, J., & Losen, D. J. (2003). Defining and redirecting a school-to-prison pipeline. *New Directions for Youth Development, 99*, 9–15.

Webb, N. L. (1997). *Criteria for alignment of expectations and assessments in mathematics and science education* (Research Monograph No. 6). Madison: University of Wisconsin–Madison.

Webb, N. L. (1999). *Alignment of science and mathematics standards and assessments in four states* (Research Monograph No. 18). Madison: University of Wisconsin–Madison.

World Health Organization. (n.d.). *Mental health*. Accessed at www.who.int/ mental_health/maternal-child/child_adolescent/en/#:~:text=Worldwide%20 10%2D20%25%20of%20children,young%20people%20in%20all%20regions. On August 31, 2020.

INDEX